Michael Vatikiotis has worked as a writer and journalist in Southeast Asia for the past twenty years, first as a student living in Thailand, then as a journalist in Indonesia, Malaysia, and Thailand. He currently lives in Hong Kong, where he is editor of the *Far Eastern Economic Review*. *The Spice Garden* is his first novel.

In his stories and his reports, Vatikiotis dwells on social and political change, charting the region's awkward embrace of modernity and democracy. *Debatable Land*, a collection of short stories published in 2001, was widely praised in Asia. In his writing, the *Straits Times* of Singapore noted: "The refreshing absence of a didactic, hectoring, morally superior tone that one comes to expect from Westerners when they write about the East. Instead, one detects gentler tones – sympathy, empathy and restraint, with a patina of melancholy." *Time* magazine said of his short stories that, like the region, they are "diverse, offering glimpses into the lives of a wide array of everyday characters," Vatikiotis was born in the US of Greek and Italian parents with a Middle Eastern background. He was educated at London and Oxford University, with short stints at Chiang Mai University in Thailand and the American University of Cairo. As a correspondent, he was posted in Jakarta for five years and continues to write and comment on contemporary Indonesian affairs for a wide variety of journals and periodicals.

MICHAEL VATIKIOTIS

THE SPICE GARDEN

EQUINOX
PUBLISHING
JAKARTA SINGAPORE

EQUINOX PUBLISHING (ASIA) PTE. LTD.
PO Box 6179 JKSGN
Jakarta 12062
Indonesia

www.EquinoxPublishing.com

ISBN 979-97964-2-3

First Equinox Edition 2004

1 3 5 7 9 10 8 6 4 2

AUTHOR'S NOTE

My primary debt is to the people of Indonesia, my many friends, teachers, and countless ordinary people whose struggle to build a nation free of tyranny and prejudice goes on and on. In writing this novel, I have delved deeply into a real and painful conflict between two great religions, which in Maluku has killed several thousand people since 1999. The events and locations portrayed in this book bear some resemblance to reality, but all the characters are fictitious.

The story told here would never have been completed without the generous advice and counsel of some close colleagues. David Plott and Jane Camens in Hong Kong provided constant encouragement and kindly read drafts of the manuscript more than once. Father Joe Maier in Bangkok, Felia Salim and John McGlynn in Jakarta also read a draft of the manuscript and their comments were invaluable. Countless others helped in big and small ways to give me the space and time to finish the book whilst managing a full-time job — none more than my wife Janick and two children, Chloe and Stefan. This book is dedicated to the memory of my beloved Uncle Yanni (1925-2002), who opened my eyes and ears to art and instilled a passion for life. Finally, without the faith and persistence of Mark Hanusz, the story of Noli and its people would never have been told.

THE SPICE GARDEN

PART ONE

From where he sat in the coffee shop of Hotel Merdeka, Father Xavier Lunas could make out the bronzed arms of the fishermen glistening with sweat as they sorted out the day's catch. He caught the sound of their laughter as they tossed the slippery fish flashing in the bright sunlight into blue plastic buckets made out of bisected machine oil canisters. The crashing surf drowned the flow of mirth momentarily as though captured in a film without sound. Then he watched as the fishermen hauled the laden buckets, their arms taut and straining, up the beach and onto the landing. There, under the shade of a flimsy thatched awning, Ghani the fish merchant eyed the catch as two boys in his employ worked the scales.

A good day for the fishermen of the little island of Noli, considered Father Xavier; and a set of new roof-tiles for the corpulent Ghani. Strict seminary training never quite erased a resentful streak that ran like a dark vein through the otherwise flawless marble of Father Xavier's character, and Ghani's commercial prowess aroused ill feeling in the priest. The best of the tuna was plucked from the gullible fishermen for a good deal less than the prevailing market price and tossed in the back of a freezer Ghani had built on the back of an old truck. The fish were frozen for up to a month and sold – at what the priest presumed was an inflated price – to the crew of the ferry that dropped anchor offshore every month to take on mail and passengers. How maddening it was that Ghani, a man who had probably never actually caught a fish in his life, profited from this deal. It pained Father Xavier as a priest, and somebody who ought to know better, that his resentment had roots in their religious differences. For Ghani was a Muslim, and it was widely perceived in these parts – without the slightest grounds, mind you – that Christians were more honest in business matters than Muslims.

Father Xavier sighed, allowing the glorious scenery before him to wash away the bitterness and assume full control of his senses. The late afternoon sun turned the incoming waves into liquid gold. Farther out, beyond the reef, the sea shimmered like a sequin-studded golden cloth. The priest in him moved mechanically to match the beauty of the moment to a divine reference, laying the foundation of some future sermon. At the same time, a residual impulse from his carefree and passionate youth released a surge of untrammelled earthly pleasure.

Before signing up in his mid-twenties to serve Christ, the young Xavier had been zealous in his pursuit of physical stimulation. His entry to the priesthood was more of a hastily-planned escape than fulfilled ambition. After his mother died, a striking island woman with a hint of European ancestry that bequeathed him green eyes and a square jaw, the young Xavier was left to shoulder family responsibilities. His father found solace in a jar of palm toddy, so he and two younger brothers were left to man the small fishing boat from which the family earned its living. He often recalled with clarity the day he left Noli for the seminary on Java, how he felt he was running away from everything, which left him weeping in the stern of the ferry, lying on a coil of ropes with the rough jute chafing his skin. It was one of the last truly physical sensations he remembered. Such moments as these were therefore fraught with ambiguity for the priest, and often left him trembling with a form or pleasure unbecoming of his calling. To help dissipate the awkward emotion, and stave off the pangs of guilt that always followed, he reached for a plastic comb in his front shirt pocket and passed it roughly through his thick black hair, tugging at the roots and inflicting a mild jolt of therapeutic pain. The moment passed.

Above him, an old ceiling fan beat the air and circulated the smell of musty old walls and stale onions. Its rotor creaked and moaned; Noli's year-round humidity was unfriendly to most kinds of modern machinery. It wasn't much kinder to humans. The heat drove the hotel staff into dark corners of the building where they lurked, like beetles sensitive to light, unless summoned. This particular table by the verandah in the coffee shop of the island's only hotel was Father Xavier's favourite spot, a regular resting-place on the way from his humble tin-roofed house close by the shore to the whitewashed Catholic church on Sutan Sjahrir Street. If time allowed – and mostly it did – he would stop for half an hour or so at the end of the day to watch the fishermen sort their catch, sip an iced tea, and consider the few challenges in his life. Who would pay for a new altar cloth? Would there be any youngsters taking first communion this month? Which route would the Feast of the Virgin parade take this year? Then there was the wedding to think about.

The fishermen came in around five, landing the fish and then loitering on the beach to smoke and relax under the bow-shaped coconut trees that fringed the shore. The sun steadily sunk, tipping bright red ink onto a blotting paper sky, and the surf subsided to a rhythmic murmur, leaving the beach placid and the soft yellow sand close to the shore as smooth as a woman's powdered skin. Just after six o'clock, as moths and mosquitoes started frantically buzzing around the naked strip lights strung out on the verandah, Father Xavier let out a contented sigh and ambled outside, heading for the church, which lay diagonally across a rudimentary square that everyone called "Medan Merdeka," or Freedom Square.

Outside, a noisy chorus of insects welcomed the night's cool embrace. This was the hour when the island's perspective changed as the ceaseless expanse of the sea turned black and, on moonless nights, there was no horizon. It was a time when you had to navigate the environment using sounds – yelping dogs, whimpering babies, and the sizzle of hot oil – all indicating that the community was safe and sound. In the square, people strolled or sat dangling bare, mosquito-bitten legs and flip-flopped feet over crude wooden benches set around a small concrete obelisk erected to commemorate the revolution of 1945. Merdeka Square could be described as the focal point of the island. The dusty little public space, no bigger than half a football field, was filled with the bright glare of kerosene pressure lamps and the odours of outdoor cooking – garlic, lamb, and chilli over char-coal, a trilogy of flavours that teased Father Xavier, for he would have to hear confession before taking his dinner. Another nagging reminder for him that duty, and his calling in general, threw up huge obstacles to the smaller pleasures of life. Such were the challenges and minor ambiguities that filled most days for Father Xavier Lunas. Even here on gentle Noli, far from the wider world of human chaos and insuf-ficiency, God's work was never really done.

"Good evening, Father. Good fishing?"

Father Xavier smiled awkwardly on hearing Ghani's jovial greeting. As much as he liked Ghani, he was a little peeved about the fish. He'd already passed through the hotel's always open and dilapi-dated wrought iron gate when Ghani himself rounded the corner, on his way back from the fish landing. The comment about fishing re-ferred to the church's everlasting quest for new souls. In addition to the lucrative fish franchise, Ghani owned Hotel Merdeka and he was on his way home for dinner.

"Not, I'm sure, as good as your haul today, my friend," came Father Xavier's jovial, if similarly barbed, reply. "The tuna are a lot easier to hook in these parts than new souls," the priest added with a wry smile.

The rich coral reef ringing Noli like an incandescent halo drew the muscular tuna in teeming numbers near the island's crystal-clear waters. Beyond the reef, the sea thrashed and heaved with gigantic schools of yellowfin tuna and barracuda. Man-sized garoupa lurked in the deeper reaches. Blue marlin streaked through these waters feasting on shoals of jack, wrasse, and snapper. Rarely a boat plied the sea around Noli without an escort of shimmering leaping dolphins; hardly a net or line cast that wasn't hauled out the sea quivering with a blazing spectrum of tropical fish. Like a giant colander, the reef itself held a bewildering variety of smaller fish, whose innocent languor made easy catches even for the youngest of foragers in the shallows along the beach. For as long as people could remember, the fishermen of Noli were well-fed and life was easy. A family with a small plot of land could get by with just a few days work in a month, and most of those were spent beating stringy sago to provide an insipid yet nutritional base to food. On Noli, a dozen eggs cost more than a kilo of tuna, chicken meat is considered a delicacy, and the finest crabmeat is turned into ordinary fish bait.

Ghani's sweat-streaked face broke into a broad grin: "Oh, not so big, Father. Not as big as I've seen." He clasped his fleshy hands submissively over his stomach – a feat that required some dexterity, given his prodigious girth. Ghani was already well into his fifties with patches of grey lapping at his temples. His jowls flapped like great sails in the wind. A ship's doctor had warned him recently of a worrying cholesterol level. By contrast, Father Xavier was slim, dark-haired, and chisel-faced. Like many priests who assumed the emotional burdens of others but were protected by their vows from the wearing effects of personal crisis, he possessed the preserved complexion of a man much younger than his fifty-one years.

Father Xavier moved to pass the portly fish merchant, nodding goodbye.

"What's this? Going so soon? Father, I insist. You must stay for another iced tea. Ah, perhaps you'd like some, ah, real tea? Come, it's a glorious evening, is it not?" Ghani advanced on the priest awkwardly with arms open, like a crab courting a much smaller mate. "Shouldn't we discuss plans for the feast? What about the wedding? Surely you've not forgotten. There's much to arrange and so little time when…"

"As you always say, Ghani, time flies in paradise," the priest sighed, continuing to advance past Ghani in the direction of the church. Father Xavier well knew that Ghani liked to drink beer or whiskey with him to shield his own conscience about taking liquor. Ghani called it "real tea" in case anyone was listening. The priest wasn't sure which religion to admire: one that exhorted followers to abjure liquor – or one that turned a blind eye to occasional drunkenness. All the same, he wasn't about to become a proxy-drinking partner this particular evening, as he had other things on his mind, and he lowered his head so that he could evade Ghani's gaze.

"Sorry, Ghani, I've really got to rush. Someone burned the altar cloth with a candle and it needs repairing. Lord only knows where I'll find the funds for a new one."

Father Xavier regretted divulging this piece of news, with its implicit plea. Ghani was generous, and would willingly make a donation in accordance with island tradition. For between these two religions, the deep doctrinal and historical divide was bridged by common communal needs. As Noli was a small island with no more than six thousand inhabitants, there was little scope for segregation. Nor was there the manpower available to allow for a division of labour along religious lines. Hence, the island's principal purveyor of poultry, a Christian by faith, was skilled in the art of ritual *halal* slaughter. It was customary for Muslims and Christians to help each other build their places of worship. If a church needed repair, neighbouring Muslims sent donations. The same could be said about mosque building:

Father Xavier himself had helped raise an onion-shaped dome hammered out of aluminium biscuit tins on the mosque near his battered old church on Sutan Sjahrir Street. Still, it was the begging that bothered him.

Ghani stared after the priest as he shuffled across the square, his shoulders slightly hunched as though he carried a great burden. Ghani liked the man for the way that he carried the island on his shoulders. He knew little about the priest's former family, except that they were islanders with a history of recent tragedy, and that the young Xavier had run away to become a priest shortly after his mother died. He'd returned to Noli shortly after being ordained and assumed leadership of the parish a year or so after the death of the old Dutch-speaking half-caste pastor, Father Aloysius. Father Xavier was the island's first native-born priest and this endeared him greatly to the people of Noli. Whenever there was a dispute of some sort, Father Xavier was on hand to mediate, like the time he helped divide up the beached whale found on the North Shore a month or so back. Ghani was amazed at the sight, which stimulated his own acquisitive instincts. There the priest had stood, barebreasted in a pair of bloodstained khaki shorts, directing dissection of the carcass, piece by blubbery piece – and not giving in to any arguments about communal rights. "There's enough for everyone," Father Xavier kept shouting above the cackle of querulous islanders blinded by blubber. Kerosene and cooking oil were expensive imported commodities on the island, so the chance to tap into nature's oil supplies was very welcome.

Ghani sighed before turning his great jib of a nose upon heading into the hotel. It was empty as usual and the only sound was that of a large fly buzzing furiously at a dusty windowpane. Father Xavier's bill, which had been running for some years, was conveniently mislaid each time the priest dutifully asked to settle. For Ghani, who wasn't convinced that paradise had clearly marked boundaries, this small act of charity served as a useful down payment on life in the hereafter – a sort of indulgence, if you will. Soon the monthly ferry would come and take his truckload of frozen fish. Hopefully the cash would tide him over for another month or so. Then again, perhaps the ferry would deposit a travelling sales representative or government official on a rare mission from Ambon. These fleeting visits were rare and unprofitable. Government officials demanded huge discounts in the name of the Republic and the salesmen made extravagant promises about supplies of soap or toilet paper that never materialised; island-hopping freeloaders, he called them. Tourists armed with cold cash came once in a very blue moon. With luck, he might soon be able to replace the rotting planks on the terrace, or the cracked and storm-abused roof tiles. Such were the matters that preoccupied a small island entrepreneur who depended entirely on the sea around him for sustenance and profit.

For all that, Ghani could be called the island's big man. He owned the biggest building, ran the biggest business, and as gossip had it, also possessed the biggest libido. He certainly carried himself around as if he were the island's chieftain. The size of the stones and the quantity of gold it took to encase them in rings around his pudgy little fingers lent substance to perceptions of great wealth. Needless to say, Noli's real chieftain, the rather grandly titled Sultan Tarmizi Shah bin-Shah, wasn't happy about Ghani's pretensions, though he lacked the financial means and the strength of character to match Ghani's swagger. The down-at-heel Sultan Tarmizi brooded alone in a mildewed old wooden palace jutting out on rickety stilts from a hillside on the edge of the town; his powers had dwindled to the periodic interpretation of long-forgotten island tradition. The ebullient Ghani, on the other hand, was welcome in any of the six communities dotted around the island, where he was greeted with broad smiles and treated as an honoured guest. Everyone seemed to owe Ghani something, one way or another.

His full name was Abdulghani Hadrami, though everyone called him Ghani. Descended, he liked to boast, from a Yemeni Arab trader from the desolate Hadramut region, who in turn claimed descent from the prophet Muhammad. They were *sayids*, or holy men, in the Islamic world. Ghani's family had lived on Noli for as long as anyone kept records. A large protuberant nose, pale skin, and fleshy Semitic lips testified to genetic origins in far-off Arabia, perhaps by way of the Malabar Coast. Literacy and a modicum of status were acquired in the colonial period when Ghani's grandfather Ali, who was leader of the Arab community, or "*kapiten* arab," appointed by the Dutch, was fortunate enough to marry off a sister to a red-faced Dutch colonial officer called Anders. He was stationed on Noli to plant and harvest camphor for a Dutch company. Ghani vaguely remembered the fellow; large red nose, thin yellow hair that was always damp and a pungent body odour about him that made Ghani feel as if he would become sick.

Still, like many Dutchmen of the age, Anders was liberal and benevolent, and as a result of European patronage, Ghani's father Abdullah was sent to school in Amsterdam. On his return, Abdullah told tiresomely repetitive stories about Europe's pre-war grandeur and insisted on dressing up in white flannel and using good silverware whenever guests came to the house. "This is how we do things in Europe," he would say. Ghani was raised a member of the island's rather limited and seedy elite and ate rough bread made of expensively imported wheat instead of sago biscuits. They used Dutch words for everyday items like "bread" and "cake" and always greeted each other using the familiar Dutch "*dag.*" The patina of European identity, complete with a straw boater for Ghani and frilly white dresses for the girls on Sunday outings, inevitably affected religious obligations. Despite being one of the first islanders to make the Muslim pilgrimage to Mecca, Abdullah was partial to a Jenever and lime at sundown. Besides, life on Noli was too carefree and abundant to make much of a fuss over the finer points of religious dogma. "You can pray at any time of day, son," his father would say; "Allah watches Noli all day long for the sheer pleasure of it."

Ghani was proud of being a Nolian. As a child, he'd search the school atlas for Noli, a tiny speck of an island situated south of the bigger islands in the Moluccan chain that bounds Indonesia's eastern sea. He searched in vain. The cartographer had used the spot where Noli should have been to place the name of the Moluccan island chain. Noli was a long-forgotten speck not considered important enough to get in the way of a name. Things weren't always this way. When Ghani reflected on his family, he had the little island of Noli to thank for its fortunes. For Ghani's forefathers were people who came from far away, sprung from the lonely loins of commerce, on account of the island's close association with what was once an unusually valuable spice. The pungent noli kernel comes from a nondescript tree that grows only on Noli's dusky volcanic soil. Almost forgotten today, the robust little nut, which took the name of the island from where it hails, once brought fabulous riches and unceasing violence to the vicinity of Noli. Men fought and killed one another over noli, a hairy nut the size of a plum that stubbornly refused to grow anywhere else.

Noli was famous for its preservative properties, and more than five hundred years ago, many everyday items, especially food, required preservation. So for a century or more, Noli and the other Spice Islands became important strategic assets in the medieval world. Ghani invariably trotted out the story of Noli to his hotel guests, when he had them. Thanks to his father's Dutch education, Ghani knew quite a bit of the history and boasted a set of mildewed books on the subject published in far-off Leiden and Utrecht. "You know at one time in the 1500s, noli was worth its weight in silver," he would begin, fingering a burnished nut he kept at hand for these occasions. "It was said the

Ottoman Sultans of Istanbul rewarded their favourite eunuchs with leather pouches filled with dried noli, going to great lengths to keep where it came from a secret. Venetian merchants told stories of spice gardens clinging to dangerous volcanic slopes and guarded by fire-breathing lizards." Guests were usually unaware that this desolate spot, so far from anywhere, was once so famous, and the story held their attention. "At one time, the European trading city of Bruges was as famous for its bootleg noli as for its wool." When he wasn't worrying about his fishing business or repairs to the hotel, Ghani trawled for scraps of noli trivia and had a lively correspondence with a retired Dutch professor who even sent him an ode to noli, recently uncovered in Oxford University, which was briefly attributed to Shakespeare.

Noli's fortunes fell with the arrival of more hygienic methods of food preservation and preparation. Yet, for a short time in the mid-seventeenth century, London was swept by rumours that noli cured impotency, generating a sharp spike in its price. At this point in his presentation, Ghani offered his guests something he called the "Noli cocktail." It was made with sago syrup and coconut frothed in a blender and served in old coconut shells with a sprinkling of powdered noli, a dash of stale palm toddy, and crowned with little paper parasols he'd picked up in Bali at a tourist convention some years back. Whilst the wide-eyed guests imbibed the sticky brew with difficulty through paper straws, Ghani ploughed on with the story of noli. "Gradually, the little nut was reduced to the status of a mere condiment, and for much of the eighteenth century was used to relieve the symptoms of gout. By the nineteenth century, smaller and smaller quantities were imported to Europe, where it remained in use only as flavouring for cakes and jams. Oh, by the way, you can purchase freshly-made noli jam or cordial from the hotel desk – just ask."

With the decline of the spice trade over the last two centuries, the island of Noli sank into gentle obscurity, left to its own devices and social chemistry. Tranquillity brought decay. The spice merchants built grand mansions with tall thatched roofs, marble floors and pillared shaded verandahs that were once adorned with a profusion of flowers and orchids. Neglected or left empty, they crumbled. Their stucco turned green with mould, their gardens became a tangle of weeds. An old European fort on a rocky outcrop above the town, its great basalt walls once impregnable, was home to ferocious snakes and lizards. A few of the aged granite blocks brought to the island as ship's ballast centuries ago still poked through tufts of tough sea grass on the outskirts of the little town. Ghani was proud of the centuries-old bronze cannon that he'd salvaged and hauled onto the terrace overlooking the sea. "They once guarded the most prized real estate in the civilised world," he boasted to guests, who were drawn to them as objects to pose against as the sun set in the background.

The key to Noli's present, and to Ghani's own immediate antecedents, was the diversity of its peopling in the past. Muslims came first, traders from the coast of Gujarat. Then the Jesuits, stumbling up the beach sweating in heavy wool and close to death after months at sea. With most of their teeth missing and skin fetid and sallow from the effects of scurvy, they must have been a grotesque sight. The jagged reef churned their worm-infested vessels to matchwood, so they were often forced to stay. Both groups of intruders were happy to take the plump island women with their flat noses and thick curly hair, procreating in the name of their God.

At first, there was a race to convert the locals, but the languor of the place was ill-suited for the competition for souls. And so the two communities learned to live side-by-side, bound together first by the spice trade, and later by the need to marry. This had the effect of relaxing the demonstrative display of faith; Muslims went mostly bareheaded and danced to Christian music at their weddings. Their habits and rituals blended. Muslims outnumbered Christians, but not by very much any longer. Regardless of religion, intermarriage was common. Life for most people was happy, tranquil, and unusually long.

Being of the island's burgher stock, Ghani had married up – a pretty girl from a rich Ambon family of Buginese extraction who bore him two children. Tragically, Amina died before reaching the age of fifty. Moreover, she died before Ghani was ready to live a life of fidelity, adding guilt to the burden of his grief. In fact, Ghani's private life might have offered plenty of scope for scandal if not for his standing on the island. Nobody questioned what went on behind the crumbling ochre façade of Hotel Merdeka – or why a succession of housekeepers fled, sometimes screaming into the night, after Ghani had drunk too many beers. Ghani knew his faults, and was aware that Father Xavier thought of him as a portly repository of sin.

"Your God requires me to recite my sins; mine is content with a ritual cleansing – one prayer covers everything. It's a great deal, don't you think?" Ghani quipped one day.

"Come now, Ghani. Your religion expressly forbids drinking, adultery and usury. Everything you seem to enjoy," the priest playfully shot back.

"Ah, but you must be found guilty first. Innocent until proven guilty. And you know what? The rules make it very hard to prove. Look, for adultery, you must have more than one eyewitness – and they should be blood relatives of the aggrieved party. Imagine how easy that is to arrange."

"Perhaps not here in this place," the priest laughed, gesturing at the walls which, in his mind, by their grimy hue took on the pallor of the fish merchant's sins.

"That's not the point," Ghani countered. "You Christians ask people to confess."

"God is merciful to those who know their sins and atone for them."

"God is all-knowing – and, thankfully, forgiving."

"Our God be praised," the priest said, raising his glass and winking at his friend.

"Amen to that."

Anyone who visited Noli stayed at Hotel Merdeka. For it was the island's only hotel, only bar serving alcohol, and sole purveyor of what the menu misleadingly called "international cuisine." Within the crumbling walls, long overdue for a whitewash, they would also invariably encounter the slim, slightly stooping figure of Father Xavier Lunas and the portly Ghani enjoying a libation or two. Such was the island's torpor that these sessions could last hours and invariably result in a degree of intoxication. The two friends dissected island tittle-tattle, and endlessly argued over matters of faith. Faith divided them, yet it was a divide that somehow lubricated their friendship. The godless Ghani and God-fearing Father Xavier – each, in his own way, a study in contradiction. For it was Ghani who feared God, and the complex and sensitive Father Xavier who sometimes questioned His primacy in the face of the awesome simple beauty of Noli with all the passion it so evoked.

Deprived this particular evening of the good priest's company, Ghani wondered how to fritter away the yawning chasm in time before the next meal, after which, his breath laden with garlic, he would attempt to lay a pudgy finger or two on one of the chambermaids. He glanced up at the large grandfather clock on his way through the lobby. It had not been wound in years and an ancient cobweb gathered dust between the big hand and the little hand. Someday he should wind the clock and set a pace for his life, he thought. Days began and ended without marking the hours and minutes of their passage. Shuffling over to the far end of the small coffee shop that occupied the lower floor, Ghani switched on a dusty old valve radio. The old machine hummed and whined, then spat static, almost drowning the urgent tones of a distant announcer. Reception was never good at this distance from the provincial capital of Ambon. Even so, Ghani could hear that the news from outside wasn't good. Far away in the capital, trouble was brewing. The people were restless and demonstrating in the streets. Change was in the air.

Felix Ling desperately yearned for change. Profitable as it was, his ambitiously named "Noli Superstore" was a pale shadow of the Chinese entrepreneur's lofty retail aspirations. He had grand visions of a chain of stores stretching across the Moluccan islands; he dreamt of tie-ups with major Japanese companies. He'd even conceived his own brand name: Spice Trader. But Noli's tiny consumer market, coupled with his wife Sonia's extravagant tastes, dissolved such dreams as fast as they evolved.

This particular afternoon, Felix was confronted by a fisherman with a rough-hewn face wanting to return a new outboard motor he claimed was faulty. The man hauled the heavy machine onto the counter and now huffed and puffed in front of him. Being a small man with frail limbs – even after frantic morning sessions with a chrome-plated chest expander – Felix Ling was never happy about engaging with angry customers and shrank from these trying and tedious experiences. Felix stared at the man through thick wire-rimmed spectacles, taking in the situation before pointing out that he did not, as a rule, sell new motors with bent and twisted propellers like the one this man had brought back.

"Perhaps you hit the reef, my friend."

"No, No, the machine is faulty, I tell you." The dissatisfied customer stood his ground with all the stubborn resilience Felix Ling knew to be typical of Nolians. These people were generally not acquisitive or fussy about appearances. Brand names meant very little to a community more or less cut off from trendsetting centres of consumption – a fact that allowed Felix Ling to palm off a whole range of substandard consumer goods of dubious origin on his customers without fearing complaints. However, when it came to fishing gear, or any kind of machinery associated with boats, Felix was on weaker ground; the hardy fishermen of Noli knew what they were talking about and insisted on durability. This kind of altercation being so common, Felix Ling deployed patience as a stealth weapon. He wore a blank expression and fixed his gaze somewhere near the angry fisherman's brow, avoiding his flashing eyes.

"I haven't had other complaints about this model," Felix said in flat tone.

"So? It's faulty and I want my money back," the man insisted angrily.

"I could see if it's still under warranty," Felix replied at last, disarming him immediately with this technicality.

Felix was born on Noli, one of the island's very few "native" Chinese. His father had come from the distant Fujian province in China, arriving in Ambon when it was still under Dutch rule to teach the local Chinese their mother tongue. He married the bow-legged and pale-skinned daughter of a local Hakka trader who had acquired property on Noli, probably the result of some long forgotten gambling debt. Together the newlyweds moved to the island to escape suffocation at the hands of querulous and demanding in-laws. His father's family proudly claimed descent from the Mandarin class. Family legend had it that a distant ancestor travelled with the great Admiral Cheng Ho on his conquering journeys across the China Sea. Felix was proud of his family's ancestry and not ashamed to be Chinese. Yet Felix had also read lately of the trouble Chinese faced in other parts of the country, the prejudice, and even violence. Just the other week, he read of a businessman in Bandung who was lynched after beating up a maid. The case made him wince; Sonia was always screaming at the two maids that they employed to clean the house. Oh well, at least here on Noli, life is peaceful, he reflected; the profits are small but tidy.

Over the years, the parsimonious shopkeeper managed to salt a little money away into a bank account he had opened in Singapore. There was even some money wisely invested in the stock market. His plan, such as it was, envisioned saving enough to buy a small apartment, either there or in neighbouring Malaysia, perhaps Malacca. He dreamt of living out the last of his years surrounded by modern amenities – especially hospitals. There was a family history of diabetes, and then there was his hectoring harridan of a wife; life could be cut short by the stress of pleasing Sonia. The grumbling fisherman left bearing a flimsy receipt for his damaged engine. Felix agreed to repair the machine for free because it was still under warranty. Nonetheless, he planned to charge the fisherman for the spare part under the guise of "freight costs." Over the years, Felix had learned how to reconcile the peculiarities of doing business on Noli: It was one thing to preserve the dignity of his customers, quite another to incur a pecuniary loss.

Felix reached up to a shelf behind the counter and switched on the radio to hear the early evening news bulletin. Outside, a bat chattered and a pair of moths chased each other around the flickering neon lamp that illuminated the misnomer of a store sign. To save electricity, Felix turned all the lights off, save for the ones directly over the counter. The newsreader sounded nervous; the news was serious. Unlike Ghani, who lived off the ubiquitous and uncomplaining tuna, Felix worried about events in Java. His business depended on a network of human cooperation stretching across the archipelago. Profit margins were calculated against the vagaries of commercial shipping, tariffs, and the weather. A missing shipment or damaged cargo meant lost business and cost him a slice of his savings. Hopes for a bright new era after the old dictator was ousted dissolved when it became clear that workers and students would continue their protests. Reports were confusing, some pinned the blame on economic recession; others pointed accusing fingers at members of the old regime out to destabilise and discredit the new government ahead of scheduled free elections. Politics! It all seemed so pointless at this distance.

"Trouble. I sense trouble," Felix said in the vague direction of his wife Sonia, whose face was buried in a glossy fashion magazine, snug in the little cubicle they used to house the shop's aged cast-iron safe.

"Eh?" Sonia pretended that she had not heard her husband. Then, after a while, she sighed and surrendered. "Yes, so you always say."

"So what happens if the trouble reaches Noli? You know what happens to Chinese like us when trouble breaks out? You've read about the riots in Medan last year. It was a bloodbath for the Chinese. Ah, what a shame, it's always that way; you help these people, give them service and extend credit, often with no hope of any repayment. What do they do? They slit your throat. Don't you think we should at least make arrangements, you know, just in case?"

"In case of what? Eh? Nothing will happen here. Nothing ever does," Sonia said impatiently. She resented her husband's worrying nature. Like everything else about him, it was a sign of weakness.

"Nothing ever reaches Noli, not even a winning lottery number," Sonia called out nastily from her corner. Felix winced.

Sonia Ling believed in a different world, one so distant from their little island that not even modern comforts like silent air-conditioners and a new model Toyota sedan could create the illusion of modern opulence Sonia dreamed of between the glossy pages of her lifestyle magazines. Sonia dreamed of tone ups, face-lifts, and gambling trips to Macau. She kept her hair long, plucked her eyebrows, and wore heavy mascara to highlight the alluring slant of her eyes. She had the splayed hips and bowlegs characteristic of her genes, but kept a slender figure and had a wasp's waist. Set against the broad-hipped island matrons that waddled into the store with splayed toes and cracked feet, she considered herself something of a beauty. Although in her early forties, Sonia was unwilling to abandon her youth for the security of encroaching middle age; she fantasised about illicit trysts with dark strangers that involved sudden fortune as well as sexual fulfilment. They were the same dreams she had as a teenager minding her parents' store; although here on Noli, they assumed an intensity that often left her blushing in the dark corner by the iron safe. Noli wasn't really home for Sonia; it was a way station to opulence, long-delayed opulence. And whose fault was that? She would quietly curse her parents for pushing her on the pale-skinned boy with thick spectacles and a concave chest who had nothing of a chin, but whose face was round and was therefore considered propitious. Felix sensed his wife's deep loathing and bore it like a cross. Still, life wasn't so unbearable when you owned the island's only general store and your customers were for the most part gullible islanders who didn't ask too many questions. Yet, listening to the news, something stirred deep inside Felix Ling; it was a kind of instinctive fear that tripped an alarm.

The telephone jangled. Father Xavier was calling about the Feast of Mary.

"Of course, you can count on me, Father," Felix loudly exclaimed. He leaned across the counter to see if Sonia was still hiding from him in the alcove. "I've already set aside the cash and alerted Gus for the catering," he said in a hushed tone. Felix patronised a Manadonese noodle seller with a penchant for hot Sichuan spicing. "Yes, I promise you; this year, no pork – not even in marked dishes." The feast was a yearly obligation that Felix never missed and his selfish, godless wife sorely resented. Felix Ling was never one to neglect communal responsibilities. On Noli, all shared religious holidays. They were social obligations that helped bind the community. And quite apart from the merriment and mingling, every holiday was a chance to curry favour with customers and make a little more money.

Putting down the phone, Felix allowed his fears to subside: "You're right, my dear, how could there be any trouble on Noli?" Sonia didn't respond, but Felix went on, seeking to fill the chasm of boredom that attended their loveless marriage. "We're so isolated here, a speck of insignificance." A speck from which, with any luck, they might escape from with a little money to live out their old age, Felix earnestly hoped. "Besides, everyone knows each other – everyone is practically from the same family. Isn't that so?" Felix winced at the thought, which reminded him of his own burden: the absence of children. From her corner of the shop, he sensed Sonia's unremitting bitterness and thought better of going on with his soliloquy of self-reassurance. The radio announcer droned on about rioting in the capital. There was the sound of raucous students demanding an end to corruption. "Reform or die!" they screamed. There were Islamic activists calling for holy war against corrupt oppressors and thunderous chants of "God is great" that clattered over the radio's static sounding like a great thunderclap. "What about the communists everyone was told to fear all these years by the government? What happened to the communist threat?" Felix asked, still hoping for a response. "When did religion come into the picture? It's all those preachers on the radio – you've heard them, haven't you dear? They want everyone to fast and pray all the time. All the same, this religious fanaticism seems very far off. I don't see too much of that thing going on here. That's a comfort, at least. Besides, whoever had heard of a Christian feast with catering arranged by a Chinese Buddhist, with donations from a Muslim trader? Eh, dear?"

⤳ ⤶

Father Xavier gently replaced the receiver in its elderly Bakelite cradle and pondered the gaping hole in his altar cloth. Another cost to consider, which, truthfully, was the real motive behind the call to Felix Ling.

"These Chinese – so insecure. They take no chances. Milk them for everything," had been the advice offered by a spiritual mentor in the seminary – a wise old Jesuit from Java called Father Sudiono.

"Religion is a refuge, son," he'd say. "It offers shelter from prejudice, it cleanses and legitimises. It's the next best thing to citizenship in divided states like ours." That was why so many Chinese patronised the church in Java. They came with their babies and asked for baptism, then later enrolled them in Catholic schools. It was a way of integrating in a state that was suspicious of their wealth and exclusivity.

Felix Ling's charity notwithstanding, the ritual paraphernalia of the church were a constant and costly headache. There were candles to be made, silverware to be polished, and incessant problems with mildewed prayer books. How he hated all the begging. Father Xavier dreamt of holding Bohemian services on the beach instead, with a rough altar made of driftwood, shaded and decorated with palm fronds, coconuts for chalices, and a crucifix made of shiny bright cowry shells. "Being closer to nature, you find yourself closer to God," he argued in a favourite and recurring sermon. "Look at the astonishing beauty the Lord has endowed our island with – surely, the appreciation of this beauty must be a pillar of our faith." He was all for liberation from the conventional trappings of faith that needed to be paid for out of the pockets of his constituents. But senior members of his congregation frowned whenever the idea was raised.

"You want to degrade the religion, reduce it to a level of savagery associated with our pre-civilised traditions," railed a portly elder of the church. "Animism, even cannibalism; that's what the beach is for."

"How will our Muslim neighbours take it?" asked another. "Really, Father, we must preserve the dignity of the church."

Father Xavier was saddened and a little worried when he heard parishioners talk this way. Sometimes when the choir sang in church, the Muslim muezzin was calling the midday prayer, and he sensed a contest as both sides belted out their devotion. The delicate semi-tones of the muezzin clashed discordantly with the crudely composed chords of the hymns. The truth is, for all the show of communal harmony, all Christians inwardly looked down on Muslims, with their prophet who had taken more than one wife. Father Xavier also knew, of course, that native spiritual beliefs lingered on the island and were still actively practiced. There were the flowers that his parishioners wore on Sundays, a pink hibiscus that was said to represent a potent island deity. And when the moon was full, hanging like a great yellow pie in the sky, he knew that people said special prayers to ward off evil and young children were kept indoors.

The church, like the mosque, offered a refuge from the profusion of spirits that stalked the island. The beach was a profane place where the lost souls of Noli roamed, their footsteps revealed by the shifting sand in the wind. That's not to say the people of Noli neglected their modern faiths. The mosques were full on Friday and the roughly-hewn pews creaked and bulged in Father Xavier's little church on Sutan Sjahrir Street each and every Sunday. Young and old they came, broad-shouldered family matrons with their shuffling long-suffering husbands; pretty girls batting their eyelashes at testosterone-charged boys with pimples. They wore crisp clean shirts and plain taffeta dresses. Nolians wore religion like jewellery, as a mark of status as well as identity. And there was always death to consider. Nolians enjoyed life so much that when it came to dying, they liked to assume that their faith in religion and devotion to the church or mosque ensured an extension, if you like, of their time in paradise.

"You're still here, Father." Yaakob, an elderly boatman who helped look after the church now that his fishing days were over, stood respectfully in the doorway of the grubby little room that served as Father Xavier's vestry. Wispy grey hair and a pockmarked, bearded face gave the man a fierce demeanour, rather like some recently rescued castaway. In reality, the old boatman was a gentle soul. He was something of an island legend as well. For it was Yaakob who helped save a dozen lives when a fishing boat got stranded on the reef in a howling storm some twenty years ago.

"Too much work, Father? You must be hungry." Yaakob ventured, pawing his beard and licking his dry, weather-beaten lips. Father Xavier knew he was angling for an invitation. Dinner, perhaps – or at the very least some tea or coffee out on the square. Father Xavier suppressed a mild feeling of irritation. Yaakob's strength of character and record of bravery, two qualities Father Xavier admired and craved, made him a stout pillar of the community. Yet the old man's cloying dependence on the church oddly struck him as a sign of weakness, for it ran counter to everything he'd been taught.

"Yaakob, it's late. Did you notice anyone waiting for confession out there?"

"No, Father. Not a soul." His voice had a rasping quality that reminded Father Xavier of the sound a line makes over the gunwale of a boat.

"Then I'll be going shortly."

"Oh, but what about me? It's been about a week since I last confessed. Please, Father, please. Hear my confession." Quite apart from the obligation of his calling, there was a pleading in his tone that the priest could not resist.

"Yaakob, gentle Yaakob. But of course, come."

Father Xavier laid aside the burned cloth and rose wearily to his feet. Beside him, Yaakob the eager believer had already brought over the faded purple vestment that hung behind the door. There was a gleam in his eyes. Even if it was just saying confession through a crude wooden screen, this poor man would have company for the next few minutes, and he could seek refuge from loneliness in his faith.

His face shaded by the confessional screen, Father Xavier lost himself in other thoughts – making sure he issued a string of pious "ums" and "ahs" to signal that he was following the old man's confession. His assumption: Yaakob was such an innocent soul, what sins could he possibly have committed? Besides, the priest was distracted. A wedding was in the offing. When he wasn't worrying about upcoming feasts and festivals, Father Xavier fretted about how to justify before his superiors in far-off Java (although ultimately in Rome) the loss of a good Catholic soul to another faith. Such was the finely-tuned balance of religious power on the island that in the matter of the joining in holy matrimony of young Adam Junaidi to the beautiful Alicia Gordon, it was the Catholic Alicia who agreed to enter her prospective husband's Islamic faith. The community assented and the arrangement was compensated by two of Adam's cousins who had already converted to Christianity by marriage. Thus, the island's communal ledger was balanced. Ironically, Father Xavier reflected, he would still be required for the ceremony seeing that he was related to the Gordon family – a not-too-distant cousin. The priest smiled as he savoured this intersection of faith and kinship and wondered what his Jesuit mentor Father Sudiono would say. Doubtless he'd approve, in the cause of the sustaining of faith without conflict.

"One last thing Father, if I may," old Yaakob whispered from behind the screen.

"Of course, go ahead," mumbled Father Xavier. But he wasn't really listening.

The plan was for Ghani to host the wedding ceremony seeing as Adam Junaidi was *his* nephew. The wedding would be held at Hotel Merdeka and was expected to be quite an elaborate affair, the event of the year.

"Father, I think I saw an evil thing happen on the beach just now." There was a note of urgency in Yaakob's voice that the priest all but missed.

"What's that?" Father Xavier asked after a short pause. There were times when he wished he could pay more attention to the mundane duties of priesthood instead of dreaming of its rich rewards. Outside, it was getting late and the familiar sounds of communal life were fading. A dog barked in the distance.

"Nothing, Father. I'll go now."

～ ～

At the age of twenty-two, Adam Junaidi thought he had seen the world. He'd left Noli on account of the island's deficient schooling system, which required him to attend secondary school in Ambon. There, he'd met people from the main islands, like Java and Sumatra. Strange people, who spoke the Malay language with a stiff and clipped accent, lacking the singsong quality of the eastern islands; they looked down on the curly-haired Ambonese with contempt because they had joined the Republic late in the day. Adam was low on the pecking order, bullied and beaten for being a hick from Noli. He made up for it by winning all the swimming awards and being a hero on the football pitch. He might have held his own and emerged as a leader but had to leave before graduating in order to earn money for the family. Adam's father wasn't a poor man by island standards, but the truth was that with one brother already away and working, he was loath to see his only other son leave as well. So, putting away his books and dreams of a job in the wider world, Adam came home to Noli and worked on a fishing boat owned by several members of his North Shore community. There, old Yaakob would often come across him staring out to sea with a far away dreamy look in his eyes.

"There's a whole world inside this reef," old Yaakob would say when he stopped by to watch them beach the boat and land the catch – always willing to lend a hand. The old man sensed Adam's restless thoughts, torn away from the wider world to fulfil a family responsibility. "People travel, they wander far from home in search of something unique. Why, I'll tell you what's unique: try finding two kinds of the same starfish. Have you ever seen that?"

Tall and long-limbed with a thick mop of undisciplined hair, Adam spent his days casting lines while riding the deep blue swell lying just off the reef where the waters plunged almost a thousand metres and the tuna teemed in multistorey schools. On good days, the tuna was hooked so easily they scarcely needed any bait. By nightfall he'd showered, put on a fresh shirt, squirted on some cheap cologne and was ready for courtship. For Adam was in love with Alicia Gordon, an attractive Christian girl from the same village.

Adam had met Alicia when they were just scrawny children playing the noisy games children play in the dusty village spaces between houses. While Adam went away to study in Ambon, Alicia blossomed in the island schoolhouse, with its bare wooden benches and warped blackboards, which made teacher's chalk fly off. Her long limbs and fine posture marked her as an island beauty as early as her twelfth year, the last of her formal schooling. Island girls were rarely sent away for secondary schooling and married as early as sixteen. But Alicia was a strong-willed girl; quick to take offence and unhappy when she was denied her way. Her mother sensed in her daughter a temper and decisive inclination that a future husband would find hard to tame or tolerate and it worried her. Nolian men like their women to be as calm and predictable as the crystal-clear waters inside the reef; those married to more tempestuous characters were teased for being caught in the choppy waters beyond the reef. So it was with some relief that Alicia's parents saw the Adam's relationship with Alicia blossom on his return from Ambon. When Adam returned, stuffed with knowledge and tales about the larger island,

Alicia would sit and listen to his stories with more than childlike interest in her eyes. In her eyes, Adam had the right combination of physical strength and mental agility; he was the perfect man on an island scarce for choice. They started seeing more of each other, beginning with furtive early evening walks along the shoreline. Inevitably, the elders noticed and that's when their courting was confined to the village headman's well-lit porch.

"After we're married, let's move to the town," Adam proposed to his sweetheart, dawdling over a soft drink shared on the porch. Propriety governed that courtship occurred in public; and since everyone watched who came and went from the headman's house, the spacious well-lit porch, ringed by fragrant jasmine bushes was, by tradition, the preferred spot. Alicia, already mesmerised by the prospect of marriage to the man she truly loved, readily agreed to a move into the small main town of Noli.

"Of course. I can work with your Uncle Ghani at the hotel."

"Doing what?" Adam asked. He wasn't sure it was a good idea, knowing his uncle.

"I can help him fix the place up. He's always dreaming of adding a touch of class," Alicia said softly, fingering the straw that extended from her bottle of green soda in an absentminded but nevertheless sensual manner. Her eyes locked on Adam's in the dim light cast by the porch lamp and Adam felt a stirring in his loins. Only a few weeks now, he thought.

Alicia possessed the pale complexion and angular features that, like Father Xavier, suggested distant European ancestry. The Gordon family traced its roots back centuries to the apex of the spice trade. The name apparently came from an English seaman with the East India Company who, fearing death on the long journey home, decided to abandon his rotting and scurvy-ridden ship for the tropical luxury of Noli. Dutch records show that the hapless Gordon nevertheless perished of fever within months – but presumably not before siring a son. At the age of seventeen, Alicia was strikingly beautiful, a beauty that was more delicate than robust, from the thin brown hair that fell straight and bounced off her sloping shoulders to the fragile tenderness that marked her expression. Her hands were small, her fingers long, and there was a lightness about her skin that suggested she spent a lot of time indoors. Balanced against these delicate physical attributes were the strength of her character and a robust sense of humour. Alicia was always smiling and her laugh sounded like a peal of bells. When she fixed her eyes on someone, it was hard not to be drawn into her orbit. Everyone agreed that Adam was marrying up in the little world of Noli. They made a pretty couple, a marriage of beauty and strength – not to mention island pedigree. The wedding was set for late August, shortly after the Feast of Mary.

CHAPTER TWO

Now it was about this time, with the Feast of Mary some eight weeks off, that the awful news from Ambon started to reach the gently sloping shores of Noli. Reports were sketchy – news travels poorly across the sea and arrives in tangled bits that need sorting by self-appointed island sages like Ghani.

"There was a fight, you see," Ghani said. He and Father Xavier sat around their usual table in the hotel coffee shop, lingering over a late afternoon libation. For effect, Ghani brought his face close to the priest's and fixed him with a watery gaze.

"It was something rather petty, nothing really."

"What happened?" asked Father Xavier, leaning back in his chair to avoid the paralyzing stench of the fish merchant's neglected gums. In addition to the merchant's avarice, Father Xavier recoiled from his poor personal hygiene.

"Apparently, an argument over a bus fare."

"So? It happens all the time."

"No. Not like this. Somebody was killed; a Muslim boy, I hear."

"Oh God in heaven…how?" Father Xavier clasped a pale sinewy hand to his mouth and inhaled. Ghani raised a hand and brought down the side of his palm on the table with a thud.

"Chopped," he said in a matter-of-fact way.

Father Xavier anticipated what must have happened next. The church teaches self-sacrifice, as symbolised by the holy cross, not retribution: "the tree of man's defeat became his tree of victory," as the liturgy puts it. Yet he struggled to overcome his own comfortable understanding of revenge, the basest of human instincts. Ghani took a sip of beer before ploughing on with the story. He was sweating. He perspired a lot when he was excited; the beads of sweat gathered on his nose and dripped into his beer.

"Then it began. Christians were randomly attacked. The Muslims swept through the market. It was sudden and spontaneous." Ghani used the tablecloth to wipe the moisture from his brow, almost tipping over the bottle of beer.

"Oh, the horror!" said Father Xavier, reaching for his comb and tugging at some wayward roots.

"Yes. Shops were burned and their owners dragged out into the streets and senselessly slaughtered. That's what I heard."

"And the police? The army? What did they do?"

"Agh, useless idiots," Ghani waved a hand contemptuously. "Nothing. What do you think?"

Father Xavier didn't know what to think; he was trained to trust authority and not to question those above him. "Respect the law of the land, and honour those who govern;" those were the bishop's instructions when he was given his ministry on Noli. There was no provision for dealing with anarchy. As a priest, he mostly encountered passive states of supplication. In church, when he asked people to stand and pray, they did so obediently. At the start of the Eucharist,

he would say: "The Lord be with you," and the congregation dutifully replied: "And also with you." It was the order of things that he'd
come to expect from the people among whom he lived and worked;
chaos and disorder were not anticipated. "Go in the peace of Christ,"
he would say when mass concluded; and the people went in peace
saying, "Thanks be to God."

"How could this happen?" he asked Ghani. It troubled him
that a Christian was responsible for initiating the carnage. It troubled
him even more that he could only imagine Muslims doing the massa-
cring. The church always had a problem dealing with the history of
its own perfidy. Theirs was a history of persecuted martyrs who died
with compassion in their eyes, not the foul-smelling trader soldiers
who overran these islands centuries ago and justified greed and brutality in the name of Christ.

"Well," Ghani continued. "I hear that some outsiders were
making trouble in town all week. A gang of Christian thugs, originally Moluccans: they used to roam the streets in Jakarta working as
pimps and hired toughs, mostly. The army sent 'em back. I've no idea
why – maybe to get reformed. Heh, heh."

Father Xavier ignored the dig and there was an awkward silence. Both men stared at their hands. The soft light of the afternoon
filled the coffee shop with a golden glow that masked the true shab-
biness of the place, like a new coat of paint. It was the best time of the
day on Noli, usually a time for feeling good about the oncoming
evening with the promise of soft breezes that awakened the senses.

"Let's have another beer," Ghani said, finally.

Father Xavier looked up, wearing a frown, and said: "God save
us from ourselves."

The beers came and they drank for a while in silence. Father
Xavier wanted to know more.

"You know, there's something very odd about this story. Why
did these street thugs return from Jakarta? I can understand how the

incident on the bus might have created a fracas, but why wasn't order restored promptly? Who allowed the killing to spread? It just doesn't make sense. The army doesn't usually let these things get out of hand."

"I'm as suspicious as you are, my friend, but I'm afraid there isn't much more to go on. The ferry is two weeks off. The damn radio doesn't tell us much because everything is reported from Jakarta, from their point of view. What are we to them? A mere speck in a dreary backwater."

Father Xavier shook his head in disbelief.

"It all seems rather petty, little more than a market brawl that got out of hand, a trifling little local difficulty. Nothing the army couldn't handle, thugs that they are. So what on earth went wrong? It scares the hell out of me, I can tell you."

The trouble in Ambon dragged on and grew worse. Rumours, washed ashore like fragments of a shipwreck, pieced together a more alarming calamity. There were raids on villages, rapes, and murders – an all-out religious war, according to some reports. Fact mingled easily with fiction. It was said that severed heads were used as footballs and that infants were impaled and hoisted on bamboo spears. A newspaper that came by way of a passing Buginese fishing boat carried a picture of Ambon's smouldering marketplace. People who saw the picture, which Father Xavier did his best to hide, gasped with disbelief. Father Xavier was concerned, for nothing so calamitous had ever come so close to the peaceful shores of Noli. The last world war, for instance, had passed the island by with only the rumble of the odd patrol boat or warplane buzzing overhead. Afterwards, the retreating Dutch thought Ambon, with its loyal soldiery, was worth keeping for the House of Orange, but they forgot all about Noli. Even when the Ambonese tried to break away from the Republic in the 1950s, the rebels bypassed the little island. Independence from where? island wags quipped; we already govern ourselves. No one bothered much about sleepy Noli.

Gradually, though, the trouble on Ambon became harder to ignore. People gave each other suspicious sidelong looks and mild precautions were taken. Doors and windows were locked at night amid much public muttering about a recent rash of burglary. Young men slept with the long knives they used to slash sago palm. Fewer people strolled on the beach stargazing after dark. Fear loomed in the back of people's minds, a dull nagging fear. Fear, which stayed indoors and out of sight, treated like a contagious affliction.

～ ～

The fearful news from Ambon brought on a tingling sensation to the back of Cornelius Lahatula's rather fleshy neck. All local authority on Noli, such as it was, rested on the sloping, dandruff-flecked shoulders of Cornelius Lahatula. Cornelius was Noli's District Officer, the sole representative of the Republic and possibly its most disgruntled servant. As District Officer, Cornelius was responsible for everything remotely official on the island. His shabby tin-roofed office, close to the crumbling main jetty and a stone's throw from Hotel Merdeka, was all but obscured by a forest of weather-beaten signage indicating the functions that he and he alone was appointed to fulfil. By his count, Cornelius Lahatula was the island's chief health and hygiene officer, information officer, education director, forestry department representative, fisheries department inspector, delegated cadre of the youth and sports ministry, and inspector of taxes. This last position was never clear to him, since no one that he could remember ever presented any form of taxation for inspection. He also held the exalted position as local chairman of the ruling political party, which boasted the biggest sign of all. It was truly a heavy yoke of responsibility for one man to bear. At least when it came to law and order, there was somebody he could turn to.

"Where are the instructions?"

Cornelius's question was aimed at Captain Widodo, the island's only policeman who inhabited a grimy wooden office across the street from his. Next to Cornelius Lahatula, Captain Widodo was the only other official representative of the Republic on Noli. A government of two people like the two founders of the nation, Sukarno and Hatta, went the joke: "they can never agree on anything except when to eat and sleep." Nonetheless, on hearing the bad news from Ambon, Cornelius summoned Widodo for an urgent consultation. It seemed like the right thing to do in the circumstances.

"What's up?" Widodo asked sleepily. A policeman's life is prone to sloth on an island as small as Noli, and Widodo was forever on the edge of slumber, his eyelids perched precariously midway down the eyeballs, ready to crash shut at any time.

"The situation demands some guidance. Surely there's a stipulation. Perhaps a cable from Jakarta?" Cornelius muttered nervously. He had a small protuberant mouth and beady eyes. Sideways, he looked like a certain kind of butterfly fish common in the shallow reef pools around Noli. Captain Widodo sat slumped in a grey steel office chair that squeaked with every heaving breath the corpulent policeman took. He pulled hard on the last half of a kretek cigarette, allowing the sweet clove-scented smoke to escape through the two hairy chimneys of his great flat nose. Cornelius loathed him.

"What situation?"

"The trouble in Ambon – the violence. Haven't you heard? It's out of control."

Uh…I ain't seen anything," the portly policeman said cagily, extending a stubby paw to scratch for something in his ear. Everything about Captain Widodo was blunt and fleshy, like a species of sea elephant periodically seen in the waters of Noli.

"Check for yourself, Pak Nels," he added with a wave of the hand not mining for earwax.

Captain Widodo was in exile, which explained a lot of the man's failings. Javanese with some distant aristocratic ancestry, Widodo was marooned and Noli was his prison. His crime: a bribe accidentally misrouted. One of the myriad links in the heavy chain of patronage was broken and resulted in a loss of dignity for some higher-up. Poof! All that investment in a lucrative career had gone up in smoke. "Son, you're going to disappear one way or another for a very long time," the offended commanding officer had told him. And disappear he did, first to Ambon, and then beyond to Noli, where Widodo drowned his immense sorrow and lost esteem in the ample bosom of Martha, a local woman. Martha bore him a son, learnt to cook a spicy curry using the Javanese fermented soybean cakes he loved, and tended the little trading business they built on the side to supplement the meagre policeman's salary. As for actual policing, most of the job was done by committees composed of village elders and run by headmen with official standing under Cornelius Lahatula's tiny little empire. The amiable and always smiling Widodo mostly presided over rare minor disputes or outbreaks of crime that, for the most part, were resolved or contained by the village committees. Widodo was a policeman for show, not much more use than the life-size concrete replica of a policeman that he was ordered to install on the main road out of town to mark an official "traffic accident awareness" week a few years back.

"Nah." Captain Widodo examined the wax deposit hauled out of his ear by the curved fingernail left long for that purpose.

"Can't see what the fuss is about, myself. I mean, what could possibly happen here? This is Noli, for God's sake."

Irritated by his lack of concern, Cornelius stared past the policeman and out of the window. Outside, a knot of fishermen walked by, their peals of relaxed laughter suggesting they had eaten and were heading home to their community. It was early evening, the conclusion of another peaceful day in the course of which only fish were murdered. Nearby, waves gently lapped the shore offering a rhythmic lullaby. Happy Noli, happy Noli, the waves seemed to sing.

⋘ ⋙

Adam Junaidi was happily on his way home with his friends. The day's catch was good, as was the case on most days. The only real headache was a broken line or two and the usual haggling over fish prices with Ghani on the landing. Ahead lay the ten-minute drive to their village, swaying and rubbing their exhausted, sweat-stained shoulders on a wheezing local bus. Once there, waiting for Adam as usual on the headman's porch, would be the lovely Alicia Gordon. As they went, they joked as men do about Adam's impending captivity.

"It's the end for you," said one.

"Not even the fish will look at you anymore," said another.

"You're cooked, my friend. Cooked in chilli sauce."

"Grilled fish with fried banana! Ha!"

Everyone thought this was very funny. The island was noted for its raw and raucous humour. Not that the friendly ribbing troubled Adam, who looked forward to a simple life of fishing for sustenance and sowing his seed.

A little further on, their laughter died down and talk turned to the news from Ambon. Adam played the cognoscenti because of his schooling on the larger island.

"They had it coming, actually. The Christians, you know. They're loud and think they own the place. The way they sing in those churches of theirs. They're always trying to drown out the Muslim call to prayer." The others fell silent. Someone coughed nervously. One of them, a Christian, hunched his shoulders defensively. Adam was prone to thoughtless outbursts, but somehow his fine looks and infectious laugh always got him through awkward situations. As children, they all grew up making jokes about each other's religion. The Christian boys at school were all ragged for their foreskins. Sea anemones, they called them, for obvious reasons.

"No offence, my friend," said Adam, turning to the Christian and patting him lightly on the shoulder. "We're all different here on Noli."

"It's nothing, really," mumbled the cowed Christian. Adam actually liked the boy, whose name was Thomas, because of his easy smile and gentle ways. His parents had him circumcised at a young age so that he would fit in at school.

The friends fell silent as they drew farther from the shore with its rhythmic surf lullaby. Fear dogged their thoughts as they walked towards the spot where the bus picked them up. No one had ever experienced the sort of communal conflict the news from Ambon conveyed. It seemed inconceivable that the people of Noli, despite their religious differences, circumcised or otherwise, could fall savagely upon each other, driven by hatred – even if the Christians were a little on the loud side. Away from the phosphorous glow of the beach and the yellow lamps of the food hawkers, the night closed in around them. They waited for the bus in darkness and Adam regretted his remarks.

Reaching home, Adam found a group of men drinking tea with his father, which was unusual. Most village gatherings were held at the headman's house – he was a Christian elder. The men huddled on the floor around his father mostly wore sarongs and some had prayer rugs thrown over their shoulders. Back from the mosque, Adam realised, thinking nothing more of it.

"Adam, son. Come over here," his father ordered sternly.

"I must shower and eat, father. Alicia's waiting," Adam replied.

"No. Not tonight, son, please. There's something we must discuss." His father wore a serious look and the other men nodded in assent, some pulling on little goatees that sprouted from their chins. This was serious. Adam blinked, unable to fathom this interruption to his simple daily routine.

"Has somebody we know died?" Adam asked, idly removing the plastic netting from the dining room table to peek at his dinner. The aroma from a freshly cooked fish curry, swimming in a light yellow coconut sauce, bathed his senses momentarily. He was hungry and eager to see his fiancée. The village men exchanged glances, which Adam took to mean that something really was up. One of them muttered nearby: "God help us if this ever reaches Noli. Our children are innocent and know nothing of prejudice."

CHAPTER THREE

First came the refugees. Although a mere spot on the map, Noli's location in relation to other Moluccan islands made it a certain refuge for small boats sailing into the wind, and there was no dry land further south until you hit Nusa Tenggara, the Timor chain, or Sulawesi further to the west. Once in sight of the island, the trick was to navigate through the reef. The strong surf that foamed over the ancient coral could cut a man to shreds, and sharks lurked nearby, ready to respond to the slightest whiff of blood. Many a human skeleton buttressed these calcified ramparts. It was nature's way of maintaining the island's defences. Once inside the reef, safety was assured. The ocean's fury was held at bay by a living wall of coral. Lulled by the beauty of warm-coloured reef fish that darted in the turquoise shallows, the people of Noli grew accustomed to assuming that whatever made it through the reef was benign and friendly.

Father Xavier was doing his simple accounts in the small office behind the church when he received the call. He wore a wrinkled batik shirt and an old pair of jeans, an outfit that kindled memories of lost youth. A young mop-haired choirboy popped his head around the door and cried:

"Father, Father. Hurry, please. The North Shore. People need you there."

Without saying a word, Father Xavier dropped everything, grabbed his battered crash helmet and jumped on the ageing Honda motorcycle that carried him around the island with a squeaking of exhausted shock absorbers and a throaty four-stroke gurgle.

"People need you. Hurry." The words stirred the priest. Such calls put him above Ghani's profane and materialistic world – even if he got the same feeling of power. There was little he could normally do in serious medical cases, for he had no training in first aid. But these calls were mostly about communal disputes, a neglected obligation, or some perceived slight, and he always rushed in to mediate to make sure that religion did not enter the equation.

On reaching the North Shore with its gently sloping white sand beach, Father Xavier found a knot of people sitting in the shade of a wind-blown tamarind tree. The mottled shade offered scant respite from the heat. A breeze blew in hot off the white sand, rustling the sea grass. The sea shone a brilliant azure blue. Down on the beach, some men inspected a tattered boat they'd pulled from the surf. Sitting at the base of the tree on a threadbare rush mat, a group of five women and two men, their faces streaked with sand and tears, were telling their story to about a dozen villagers.

They spoke in turn. When one grew tired or was overcome by emotion, another took up the story, and so their tragedy unfolded in relay. Those not speaking set up a low-pitched moaning accompaniment like the chorus in a Greek tragedy – although even the most talented dramatist would have difficulty concocting what followed. It began like this: For whatever reason, no one could say, Christians on Kesui, a tiny island between the eastern tip of Ceram and the Kei Islands, were attacked unexpectedly by Muslim militias, mainly from the neighbouring islands of Geser and Gorong. Several thousand assailants armed with machetes, spears, and even bows and arrows attacked and burned, each day overwhelming a different village.

"They wore flowing white robes and laughed wildly all the time," one of the women said. She was the eldest of the group who took the lead in telling their story.

"I saw at least nine people lying dead. Their bodies were chopped. Chopped into pieces. There was blood everywhere," said another, younger woman between sobs.

"They had green eyes – the eyes of the devil," wailed yet another woman, making round shapes with thumbs and forefingers for emphasis. Father Xavier looked up to gauge the reaction of the audience. Some of them were his parishioners, but they looked different, their faces taut with apprehension. The wind had died down and the heat was fierce. There was a deathly stillness about the place as if the Almighty Himself had stopped whatever He was doing to listen to the story these poor people had to tell.

The older woman who was doing most of the talking wiped her sweat and tear-stained face with a faded and apparently blood-soaked sarong before continuing with the story.

"Some of us managed to escape by boat to Teor, or further on to the Kei Islands. Others fled to the woods." Father Xavier knew the area, which he had visited on several occasions to see a distant relative. Dense thickets of nutmeg and mace, a pungently perfumed jungle, were matted and overgrown since the end of the spice trade. From his childhood, he recalled it was a place for illicit romantic trysts.

"A few days later, the Muslims came after us, and dragged us to a nearby mosque. Here, there was a large crowd. Some of the people knew each other yet they chanted slogans like "'Death to all Christians'" and their faces were filled with hatred."

"They wanted our money and our jewellery – anything of value," chimed in another of the victims. Her clothes, although ragged, suggested that she had possessions to lose.

"…And they wanted us to leave the island. But it was our home. Where were we to go?"

"After a while, the imam told us that by order of the jihad, we had to come down from the woods and embrace Islam. Those not willing to do so would be separated from the others and killed."

At this point in the story, another one of the women started wailing loudly. Next to her, one of the men from the group shivered uncontrollably. Father Xavier noticed that he had a long gash down one side of his arm. The wound was dark with congealed blood, and probably infected. He did not speak, but stared at the ground, his pale lips trembling, as if he had seen something horrific. As Father Xavier watched the traumatised man, he realised the frailty of the communal harmony over which he presided. It dawned on him also that here was another dimension to the human state, one that would not be so easily coaxed into putting faith in God and His intermediaries on earth. As a priest, he'd been trained not to delve too deeply into the context of human sin, only to trust in how the church defined transgression and know what remedies it prescribed. He saw for the first time a threat to his domain.

After another pause, the older woman who seemed the most composed – she had a steely look in her eye, a look of cold resolve – picked up the story again.

"They told the remaining Christians that they had better immediately convert to Islam to save their lives. Some of them converted on the spot, out of fear. What else could they do? Our men pleaded for their lives, and the lives of their families. I saw hatred in the eyes of the Muslims. They would have preferred to kill us, I'm sure."

"Yes, and we had to give them all our money, after which they forced us to cover our heads," the better-dressed woman, obviously consumed by her loss, repeated.

"Don't believe people if they tell you we entered Islam willingly, which is what they told us to say," added the other woman.

"A week or so later, they attacked again. Among the attackers were former Christians turned Muslim; many houses were burned and destroyed. That was when we were forced to leave."

"We left quietly, at night. This boat is all we had." The woman lifted a limp wrist and pointed vaguely in the direction of the beach.

"If we had stayed, we would all be dead."

"Dead, yes. We might as well be dead. We've lost everything."

As the story trailed off, the women kept up their moaning, rocking gently as they sat. A small crowd of onlookers stood silently, some with mouths agape, others with eyes glued to Father Xavier, who was expected to ask the next question. But he was lost for words. Now, he too was trembling. The act of compassion made him quiver with a mixed feeling of apprehension, which, oddly, he associated with pleasure. It reminded him of the awkward brushes he had with physical love as an adolescent, a rush of blood and bowels that turned to jelly.

There was a long silence. The assembled villagers took in what they'd just heard. Eyes darted from left to right apprehensively as everyone waited for Father Xavier to speak. The priest wasn't sure where to begin. These people needed counselling as well as medical treatment. They had been exposed to the elements for days and were tired and thirsty. They needed shelter and care immediately. Yet they also acted as a valuable conduit of news. Curiosity got the better of him.

"Didn't anyone send for help?" he asked.

"Initially, yes. The government sent an old boat with several policemen. But when the ship docked, the Muslim militia assured the commander that nobody wanted to be evacuated."

"Can you believe it?" one of the North Shore villagers cut in.

"Shh. Let them continue," said another, irritated.

The older woman continued.

"Yes, they seemed friendly, shaking hands and drinking tea together. So the ship went back without taking anyone."

There was a long pause. Then the woman looked up at Father Xavier. She wore a look of contempt for a world not fit to live in anymore, her eyes were dark pools of bitterness and regret.

"That's not the end of it, either," she muttered.

"Tell us, mother," Father Xavier gently prompted. He tasted salt in his mouth, and from the constriction in his throat he knew this was brought on by fear.

By now, quite a large crowd had gathered around the tamarind tree. Everyone in the village knew about the beached boat and its sad cargo. Alicia Gordon was among them. Hearing the commotion, she had left her ironing. Her beloved fiancé, Adam Junaidi, was down on the beach, looking over the stranded fishing boat. There was something very disturbing and unfamiliar about these people who no longer looked at each other and no longer smiled, as if they had come from another world.

"We have not spoken of the circumcision," the woman telling the story continued.

"What is it you mean, mother?" asked the priest softly.

"The circumcision that was carried out on our village using a single razor blade. The blade was as blunt as it was dirty. It caused heavy bleeding, so we were all sent into the sea for disinfecting. Women, too, were circumcised." The woman sniffed and turned away to look at the sea, using her hands to shade her eyes from the glare. Father Xavier put his arm around Alicia Gordon, who bit her lip and held back a wave of nausea. Down on the beach, he saw the men, Adam among them, crouched in the shade of the boat, having a smoke.

He heard their laughter, for they had not heard anything of the appalling story told by the refugees. Everything seemed so normal. The wind picked up again, whipping tufts of spray off the surf, which glinted in the bright sunlight.

∽ ⌒

The two men sat across from each other like Sunday afternoon chess players. Flies buzzed lazily around their table in Hotel Merdeka's forlornly empty coffee shop. Faded yellow oilcloth covered the tables, which were attended by cheap white plastic chairs, the kind that could be stacked. The island wasn't noted for its furnishings, most of which came off passing ferries. A menu, frayed and curling at the edges, declared in Indonesian and poor English that fresh fish was always available – as well as "international cuisine." A dark-skinned girl wearing a yellow frock stood behind the serving counter at one end of the coffee shop, Ghani's hefty presence at one of the tables being the only reason why she had not yet scuttled into the shade of the kitchen hallway.

It would be a little comforting to think that Hotel Merdeka had seen better times. The fact is that it lost money from the start. The building itself, being grander and taller than anything else on the island, was an expensive undertaking. No one had ever heard of reinforced concrete when it was built to what was then a modern design, complete with art deco curves instead of corners, some thirty years back. A building three storeys high was unheard of on an island where dwellings hugged the ground out of respect for the forces of nature that periodically battered Noli. The whole structure looked rather like a shipwrecked vessel left high on the shore by a storm. Roof tiles, window frames, and even light fittings were shipped in from as far away as Surabaya. Ghani acquired the hotel from its Chinese owner and founder a decade back as part payment of the debt the Chinese owner accumulated building the place. Having paid off the building costs on the back of his tuna business, Ghani was content to see the place run on a shoestring. Paint peeled off mildewed walls indoors. Outside, a faded skeleton of bougainvillea clung to the walls like an old scab. The lobby was sparse and unadorned, except for the large ornate grandfather clock left to Ghani's family by the Dutch relatives.

Ghani was beyond regret, having long given up dreams of a tourist haven complete with gourmet restaurants, big game fishing, and all the other trimmings of international sophistication that he read about in paperback novels cast off by the ferry once in a while. He once had fantasies of beautiful people like Ava Gardner and Gregory Peck – she wrapped in silk and chiffon; he in cap and blazer – stepping out of a sleek mahogany motor launch at the end of the little pier that jutted out from the hotel: "Oh, Mr. Ghani, what a wonderful place – we'll come back and do our next picture here...." But the only regular habitué of the pier was old Yaakob hauling in fingerlings with a ragged net to augment his meagre soup bowl. For the most part, Hotel Merdeka served as a haven for Ghani to imbibe liquor, flirt, play cards, and generally flaunt the moral constraints of his faith. The seedy setting worked for him. Somehow being in a hotel put him beyond the reach of moral authority. The irony, which always struck him with a chuckle, was just how little this seemed to bother the priest.

For all Father Xavier's bouts of resentment, the bond between these two rather different men was built on solid foundations. Ghani needed the priest to smother his guilt and the priest needed Ghani to vicariously enjoy his sin. It was a mutually beneficial relationship. Seldom, though, were their meetings as sombre or as serious as this one. Ghani fidgeted and chased a persistent fly that kept returning to the rim of his beer glass. Father Xavier stared, glassy-eyed, out to sea. It was past three in the afternoon and quite a few empty beer bottles lay scattered around the table like victims of a fracas. The priest wore a pair of light khaki slacks and a faded brown batik shirt, which made him look like a local beach bum – something he might have been if his father had not died suddenly, leaving him to shoulder responsibility for feeding the family. Xavier's father was a good fisherman who never gave a thought to tomorrow and raised his family from a distance, spending most nights carousing with his crewmates and coming home drunk after drinking too much palm toddy. For a while, it was a burden Xavier took up gladly. He also was a good fisherman, hauling in tuna off the lines as fast as they could be baited. What he never anticipated, though, was the deep melancholy that set in a year or so after his father died. "The road to priesthood and the service of God is never clearly sign-posted," old Father Sudiono had once told him to dispel a moment of self-doubt.

"Tell me, Father, what does the church prescribe in situations like this?" Ghani asked. Father Xavier stared out to sea and searched the horizon for the appropriate response. The sea had a benign, almost hypnotic effect, absorbing like a sponge all the unpleasant things the priest had to think about right now.

"I mean, don't they have a plan to protect Christians in times of religious conflict? Can't your pope intervene? Look at the Muslims. We have all these militias…."

"They use violence to defend their faith. Is that the path you'd have us take?" Father Xavier cut in sharply.

"An eye for an eye, I suppose," said Ghani. "That's how it is written in the book. Well, actually, your book too."

In the awkward silence that followed, Father Xavier toyed with a riposte to this scriptural provocation. Somewhere inside, somewhere hidden from the calm disciplined parish priest skilled in the art of compassion, a small cauldron of his blood boiled. At seminary, the

Jesuits taught them to submit to authority for the sake of avoiding conflict with the Muslim majority. The Jesuits were skilled operators, using guile and subterfuge to influence the authorities and always shying away from direct confrontation. "Better to have the local military commander in your pocket than on your doorstep with an arrest party," Father Sudiono said. The larger interests of the flock always took precedence over the sufferings of those few subjected to persecution. He was reminded of an old Italian priest who spoke, in a moment of candour one evening after prayers, of the weakness Jesus had as a politician. "You see he consorted with the Galileans; he knew nothing of the Jerusalem crowd, which made it easy for them to do him in." The diplomat in him remained in control. It was the first of many tests he would face in the coming weeks.

"Do you have any cigarettes?" Father Xavier suddenly asked.

"But you don't smoke, my friend."

"I'm thinking of taking it up."

The refugees who landed on the North Shore had spooked everyone on the island; their presence offering tangible evidence of what everyone had tried to disbelieve. The five women and two men were housed near the old Dutch fort in an abandoned house that belonged to a Christian relative of Ghani's, a move widely acclaimed as helping to revive the victims. Their physical health slowly returned, but through their tear-soaked eyes, Father Xavier could see into souls that were seared with pain. One of the women came ashore clutching a bloody bundle. It turned out to be the dark, putrefying remains of a newborn child. The child was born on the boat and died after a few hours. He asked about it with a view to burial, but was told that the woman and her dead infant had disappeared.

Among the islanders, no one said much about what had happened and outwardly things seemed as normal and routine as the waves lapping at the beach. However, small differences became more noticeable as time wore on and Father Xavier observed that the presence of the refugees began to extinguish the island's happy state of languid tranquillity. People brooded and laughed a lot less at meal times; Adam's fishing friends turned serious and stopped discussing how drunk they planned to get at his wedding party. Fear, like a virus, had an incubation period. The first symptoms were innocuous enough; casual conversations cut short, nothing more obtrusive than that – even old Yaakob was less obsequious and more reserved, and something in his eyes conveyed a sense of disappointment with the priest. He no longer came to confession. Yet, in church, Father Xavier counted a swollen congregation at morning mass. There was a collective look of concern on people's faces, and their response to the Eucharist was more pronounced and less casual. With all this, the priest's worries magnified beyond how to replace a burnt altar cloth.

In church that Sunday after the refugees arrived, Father Xavier felt compelled to preach tolerance in the face of provocation. "Remember the way that the Pharisees taunted Christ in the temple," he thundered from the crude wooden lectern that served as a pulpit in the island's church. "There is no need for us to respond. Put your trust in faith. Just like a sudden squall, the storm will blow over our little island without causing any damage." The congregation nodded in appreciation of the priest's soothing peroration. Their faces lit up with shiny expressions of hope. But later in the day, Father Xavier woke up from a sweat-drenched afternoon nap and saw his congregation arrayed before him; they all wore masks. Each mask bore the same smile of faith and contentment. Then someone took off his mask to sneeze and from behind it he saw a face twisted in hatred and rage. He wasn't sure what to make of this uncomfortable apparition.

From his daily perch in the coffee shop of Hotel Merdeka, Father Xavier watched the fishermen sort out their catch with more haste and less merriment. A pall of apprehension hung in the air. Men spoke in hushed tones and made sidelong glances at one another. Every so often, one of them would scan the horizon out to sea. They smoked more and coughed nervously. In the late afternoon, people hurried home instead of lingering in the little square in the shade of the big-leaved breadfruit trees. By dusk, people made sure they were safe at home, which wreaked havoc with the incomes of the mostly Javanese stall owners. Felix Ling closed his shop earlier, often by five, and Ghani had not bothered to replace the broken strip-light over the sign out-side Hotel Merdeka, which flickered on and off like a warning beacon.

The change of mood opened the gates to a flood of bad memo-ries. How little it took to disturb the human temperament, Father Xavier reflected, as recollections of his unhappy youth rushed in. Af-ter his father's death at sea, the family struggled to survive and find happiness. There was his poor mother, contorted with pain, still in-sisting that she was able to cook and do the housework, her body riddled with tumours. His elder brother Francis, laughing loudly as if uncaring and leaving the day of the accident, was never to be seen again. Then, his little sister Agnes married the boy next door, a first cousin no less, and gave birth to a retarded child. The doctor called it Down's syndrome; islanders said the child was possessed. And so the idyllic island life of his childhood gave way to pain and responsibility – something the seminary recognised and cultivated.

"You must go back to Noli, my son," the bishop said.

"But there is nothing but bad memories for me there," the young Xavier protested a week ahead of his ordination. Entering the priesthood proved a legitimate form of escape from family responsi-bilities. He'd entertained the idea of travelling, perhaps applying for the Society of Jesus after a spell of further education. After all, he was named after the great Jesuit saint, Francis Xavier.

"Pain and suffering are the foundations for a strong fortress of faith," the bishop insisted.

Ghani removed his hands from the bulbous head that sat on his shoulders like a great pale onion. His large, heavy-lidded eyes were moist and a little red. Beer did not agree with him, but the bar was out of whiskey. Another thing the ferry would bring; Ghani usually took delivery of a few cases of whiskey as partial payment for the fish.

"I have a proposal," he said at last.

"Surprise me," The priest replied sceptically. He took another sip of beer.

"Listen, my friend," Ghani ploughed on. "There will be trouble, I feel it. There's no government to speak of anymore. No control, believe me. That Cornelius fellow, he told me yesterday that no one pays his wages anymore because the situation in Jakarta is so bad. That's it. He's a spectator now. And Widodo? Come now, Father, you place too much faith in authority. Captain Widodo? Ha! He's no more a policeman than I am. That plump wife of his has him so pumped full of rice and soy beans, he's no good for anything except producing gas – a fart factory."

Ghani sat back in his chair and allowed himself a throaty laugh. For even with serious matters at hand, he was never one to miss the opportunity to pillory his peers.

"And so?" Father Xavier wasn't certain where this was leading.

"So I anticipate anarchy, my friend; a total breakdown of society. Here in Noli there isn't the capacity to govern a pinhead."

"I can calm people in church. I'll use the power of the holy word. They'll see sense." Father Xavier turned to Ghani and fixed him with a hard stare. The phrase "holy word" had come out with the full force of the dogma behind his training and it embarrassed him a little. He wondered what Ghani was driving at. He wasn't exactly on close terms with the local imam, who was the sultan's man. Religious patronage was one aspect of informal island leadership Ghani had abdicated for rather obvious reasons.

"You can try, and I have every respect for your talents as a preacher, my dear Father. But I'm telling you; no holy book will hold back this tidal wave of hate and hysteria. Look at Ambon. Can't you imagine that responsible people on both sides, people like you and me, tried to restore calm? Wouldn't the pulpit and the *mimbar* have been deployed the same way?"

"So, what is it exactly that you propose?"

Ghani raised his glass and downed the dregs of his beer. Then he belched loudly.

"Ah, I'm coming to that," he said. "Sarah?" Ghani hurled the name towards the counter at the other end of the coffee shop.

"Sarah. More beer," he said when the dark girl in the yellow dress peered out of the kitchen hallway. The girl scuttled off and returned with two fresh bottles of beer and the two men drank in silence for a while.

Father Xavier's head was beginning to spin. Outside, he could hear the distant sound of the surf pounding the reef in time with the pulsating throb of his temples.

"I know you'll look after us. That's what you're thinking, isn't it?" Father Xavier spoke slowly and laid a hand on the fish merchant's chubby arm.

"How, I don't know. But yes, that's right. You'll be safe here – that's what I wanted to propose – if it comes to that. After all, where else will you go?"

"We're getting drunk," the priest observed placidly. He felt compelled by a strong feeling of inadequacy to change the subject.

"Of course. Don't you know? Our forefathers always discussed weighty matters under the influence. Our democracy was built on a sea of *arak*." The priest knew that Ghani was only half-exaggerating. Traditional Moluccan councils were built around daylong feasts and island bacchanalia, principally involving large quantities of palm toddy and sago wine. They often ended in altercations that led to violence and the odd death.

"It's getting late. I have to be in church for confession," insisted Father Xavier.

"You'll stay and have another beer. I'll bet no one wants to divulge his or her darkest thoughts at a time like this," Ghani shot back, taking aim at the priest with one watery eye, while with a grubby hand he rubbed the other. Father Xavier felt relieved.

≈ ⌒

A slothful bureaucrat, and a loathsome figure to many, Cornelius Lahatula was nonetheless a God-fearing man who graced Father Xavier's little church each and every Sunday. On these occasions, he wore his best navy blue safari suit, a little shiny from too many pressings. When he was not running what there was of a government on Noli, he was mostly to be found sipping sweet iced lemon tea in a little noodle shop wedged beside his tumble down office.

"Muslim conversion can be undone. I've seen it."

This remark came from the noodle shop's owner, a pale-skinned Manadonese from North Sulawesi by the name of Gus. A blend of genetic and cultural heritage lent Gus an appearance people took to be European. In fact, his grandfather was Chinese, ancestry that revealed itself through a set of sad, almond shaped eyes tilting downwards into a large flat nose that shone like a well-used door-knob. Coming from Manado, where culinary tastes are notoriously adventurous, patrons suspected that Gus chopped desiccated rat into his fried noodles for taste.

"Nonsense," snorted Cornelius. "Once a Muslim, always a Muslim. It's a one way street."

"Nah. Ain't so. I've seen a conversion. Sister of mine married a Buginese trader – son of a bitch crook – she just mumbled a few words in Arabic, and that was it." Gus raised the cleaver and brought it down hard on a head of garlic.

"Those words from the Koran, they're sort of like passwords. Just say you love God three times and you're in, my friend. No argument."

He raised the cleaver.

"Then of course there's the snip – if you know what I mean."

Down came the cleaver again, pulverising the garlic.

Cornelius winced. He felt uncomfortable about this conversation and was very glad to find his Muslim colleague, Captain Widodo, dozing at the table. Although only nominally a Muslim, like many Javanese, Widodo was sensitive about appearances and fiercely defended his faith. Gus wiped his nose with an oily rag and ploughed on:

"Yeah, but after the wedding, my mother made her wash her mouth out with noli."

"And so? What does noli have to do with anything?" Cornelius was growing irritable with the sort of talk that, under strict rules laid down by the government, could be considered an offence.

"I'm telling you, the woman died a Christian giving birth to that Buginese trader's bug-eyed son."

There was a loud crackle and angry hiss as the chopped garlic hit the blackened iron wok in which Gus tossed and fried his oily noodle creations.

"Well, Gus, let me assure you," said Cornelius, raising his voice because of the roar from the gas stove. "Here on Noli you won't see some of the awful things those people from Kesui talked about. Frankly, I think they were overdoing it a bit. Noli is different. Why, I've seen Christians lend out their rosaries as Muslim prayer beads, isn't that so, Do?"

Captain Widodo, not quite alive to the subject at hand, spluttered a blanket agreement with his colleague in authority before allowing his heavy eyelids to come crashing down again.

Inwardly, Cornelius was deeply troubled. What disturbed him most were suggestions he'd heard of official connivance and collaboration. Soldiers, police, and government officials taking sides, or simply standing aside as the killing went on. He wasn't aware that he'd signed up for holy war when he joined the civil service. For a struggle against communism, yes. Communism threatened the republic with all its insidious and tenacious ways. Cornelius had been diligently vigilant in this regard and could truthfully report that the island of Noli was free of communism. There it was in every report: suspected communists, nil. In strict accordance with regulations, there were no casual meetings, no informal associations, and no organised groups of any kind without proper approval – and none was ever given. Nothing was left to chance. When a fishermen's cooperative started operating without seeking official approval (or offering him a stake for that matter) the venture was swiftly shut down. The hapless fishermen were suspected of what official parlance called "unclean personal environments" and barred from borrowing money from anybody – except the agricultural coop that Cornelius ran. As rigid as the system was, he never once interfered with religion. Religion is good, he'd been taught, because it is ritual that becomes instinctive. Instinct is safer than reason. If you have no religion, it's because you question too much and therefore you are a stinking freethinking communist. So what was so wrong with Christians mingling with Muslims, Cornelius shuddered.

Gus wiped his oily nose with one end of his apron and looked pensive. "Christians outnumber Muslims here, if I'm not mistaken," he said.

"Used to, Gus. Used to. Not anymore." Cornelius said, shaking his great head.

"That was before all these migrants came from other islands – mainly Sulawesi."

"Well, don't look at me," said Gus, who himself had come to Noli prospecting for business. Originally, he worked for the Cross and Crescent Insurance company, a Chinese insurer based in Surabaya. But Noli was a desert in terms of personal life insurance. Very few Nolians suffered significant losses over time to warrant insuring anything at all. The most valuable of possessions were boats, and if one of those was lost, the community helped replace it by building a new one. So, instead, noticing a dismal scarcity of good cooked food, Gus called it a day as an itinerant salesman for Cross and Crescent and opened his noodle shop.

"None of this would have happened if there was more discipline," Cornelius continued, waving a pudgy fist in the air for effect. "There must be more control over migration. There are too many people moving around freely; it's an invitation to disorder and criminal disobedience. It all comes down to discipline and control," Cornelius intoned in a slow deliberate voice, the one he reserved for issuing instructions to subordinates. Gus, sensing an indirect reproach, made for the back of the kitchen. Widodo snored.

"Agh. Damn them. Damn them all," Cornelius quietly cursed, hoping that his sleepy partner in administration wasn't listening. "A week since those refugees arrived and still no instructions. How can I possibly do anything without some guidance?"

"The boat is due in this evening." Gus said, returning armed with a steaming plate of noodles for Cornelius and reading the troubled bureaucrat's mind as well as he normally read his stomach. He pitied the bureaucrat for his impotence, but then that's how the government liked things: everything in black and white with no grey areas to encourage initiative.

"That's right," said Cornelius, remembering that the monthly ferry was due and slapping an ample thigh. "The captain will have the pouch for me and there are bound to be instructions."

The shipping company was required to carry government mail

in the service of the Republic. Normally, the pouch for Cornelius came stuffed with trivia – the usual exhortations to foster development, support the ruling party, and embrace the state ideology. There was almost always some high-level order about party discipline based on the practice of "self-control" and maintaining a "clean personal environment." Once, and this was something Cornelius still shuddered to think about, he'd received a high level order from the ministry in Jakarta to explore the possibility of establishing a penal colony on the island.

"Sure to bring news one way or another." Cornelius said, his spirits revived more with the arrival of his plate of noodles. The aroma was inviting and dispelled his woes.

"Or trouble," said Gus, disparagingly. The cook had a nose for trouble, something he'd picked up during his days as an insurance salesman.

"Or help. We could do with some reinforcements," Cornelius added through a mouthful of noodles and pointing to his corpulent colleague with a fork.

≋ ≋

There was considerable activity down at the jetty where the cutters from the big ferry pulled up. No ship larger than a dinghy could actually dock at Noli because of the reef. The reef held the outside world at bay; the gaps were too narrow and the inner sea too shallow. A gap in the reef some five hundred metres offshore let the cutters through, a breach in the island's natural defences. The rising and falling of the tide acted like a drawbridge. It was the same for the old spice galleons from Europe: no shelter and at the mercy of the surf. Early prints, some badly-framed copies of which hung in mildewed splendour at Hotel Merdeka, showed the old galleons riding at anchor, rolling in the surf in the shadow of Noli's then quite active volcano. It was hardly a safe landfall. Seamen were constantly falling from the yardarm or simply overboard, and the little cemetery on Noli is full of touching epitaphs that read: "died, falling from aloft. Much regretted by his shipmates…."

Along the jetty, roaring kerosene pressure lamps augmented the pale light offered by the two fluorescent tubes usually kept on at night. Mangy island dogs, disturbed by all the unusual activity for the hour, howled and yelped in the distance. A larger crowd than usual had assembled, which suggested to Father Xavier, who leaned against a nearby fence, that some people were already planning to leave. In the distance, the ferry's lights, hovering like fireflies above the dark water, hove into view and the horn sounded, announcing the arrival of the island's principal contact with the outside world. The ferry's monthly visit was an eagerly awaited event, but it merited special attention on this occasion because of the trouble on Ambon.

"Let's see what we're in for, Father." Ghani stood at his elbow, peering out towards the ferry lying some half a kilometre offshore. The mood was nervous and grim. There was little of the usual small talk as everyone peered intently at the ferry's lights on the horizon. It was like waiting for relatives to arrive at a funeral, Father Xavier reflected.

"I can't help feeling nervous," the priest said. "I hear rumours of roaming Muslim roughnecks out to evict Christians from these islands. Some of my parishioners want to prepare and arm themselves. I've counselled against it, of course, but I must tell you, Ghani, I'm not certain that was the wisest approach."

"Have you no faith, Father?" Ghani nudged his friend.

"Faith alone is no defence against men with evil in their hearts." The priest found himself struggling with the urge to be militant, which he realised made him no better than the Christian mobs roaming Ambon. The church was simply vague on the issue – damned if you do and quite possibly slaughtered if you don't.

"Then why don't you organise your people? Why haven't you prepared?"

The priest turned to Ghani and gave him a perplexed look. He regretted being so open about his feelings: of course, he wanted to organise them. But he was scared of provoking Muslim neighbours – and also of the possible recriminations if the bishop found out.

"The Church preaches…"

"Agh! I know, I know. Nonviolence is the path to righteousness. If that's the case, how on earth can you explain why two world wars were fought between peoples of the Christian faith? Explain the Crusades. Explain the behaviour of the Dutch soldiers when they massacred our tribal leaders all those hundreds of years ago and turned the sea red. That's no comfort to me," said Ghani, strutting off towards the pier's edge with one hand furiously rubbing his chin. He was sweating profusely and felt sore about the harsh words that came to him in this situation. He only had the interests of everyone in mind.

Coming to an island as small as Noli imposed a burden on visitors. For being the only physical link with the outside, it was hard to avoid being sucked dry of any kind of information. Politics, football, the latest fashions, and, of course, the price of tuna; there wasn't any scrap of news that was deemed insignificant. Ferry captains understood this and usually decked the ship out with every kind of light and invited island dignitaries for a meal onboard. There, in a stuffy wardroom reeking of fish-based chilli paste and stale clove-scented tobacco, the ship's officers enjoyed a few hours of respect and power derived from their role as great seers in physical contact with another world. The more arrogant among them liked to tease the simple Nolians by telling wacky stories. There was a ship's engineer from Surabaya who tried convincing Ghani that the president of the Republic actually stayed in power by driving a nail in the earth each year somewhere outside Yogyakarta. Sometimes, the ship brought medicines that the island's small infirmary had run out of, or took aboard the very sick. Once, the ferry itself was turned into a floating hospital during an outbreak of typhoid some five years ago. The monthly ferry was a lifeline for the island of Noli, but on this trip, no one was sure whether the lights shimmering offshore beyond the surf were beacons of hope or the first sign of trouble.

"Remember, let me handle any Muslim delegation," Ghani reminded Father Xavier as they watched the lights of the first cutter approach the jetty. "Do we have an agreement?" Father Xavier had been tossing over Ghani's proposal in his mind. Too much alcohol and the burden of worry had slowed down his normally keen senses. At first, he protested.

"You can't assume that level of responsibility alone. It's suicidal, believe me," he had pleaded with his friend over the last of too many beers the other evening. But Ghani insisted that he knew these fanatics; that he could persuade them to leave Noli untouched.

"They will claim their mission is holy, but I can tell them, 'Look at me, am I not a man of God? I'm descended from the Prophet!'"

"You fool. They'll slit your throat."

"No. I'll feed them, offer them my hospitality," Ghani continued, not listening to Father Xavier.

"Look, it's a trick I learned from politicians. These people are like sheep; they're all looking for a safe paddock. They crave leadership and patronage. You establish your credentials as a big man, throw around some money – the next thing you know, they're all in your pocket. Yes, sir, no sir, we'll follow you to the end of the world, sir."

Father Xavier looked up and smiled. He was worried about the old sultan, whose activities at the mosque were well observed. Ghani had clout on the island, but the sultan possessed formal legitimacy and he was pious. Once, he was considered dangerous because of his embrace of communism. These days, he wrapped himself in the green flag of Islam.

"And what if they scream for Christian blood?"

Ghani stared the priest in the eye for a moment, then looked away at the deep red bloodstain the sun had left in its wake. The first stars were twinkling in the night sky. The ferry would come, and then leave. Then they would be alone and cut off from the world again, protected by a wall of coral that kept most things out, but which, of course, was no help against the evil within.

"Then I will be the first to die," Ghani said, slowly and deliberately.

◡ ◠

"Hurry, or we'll miss the boat," Alicia said. Adam was dawdling. The drive from the North Shore to the jetty down south would take at least twenty minutes around the tree-lined coastal road that hugged the gentle incline between the shore and the foot of volcano. And there would be people on the road – the island buzzed with life when a ferry came in. A pale yellow moon was already climbing above the tops of the coconut trees when they finally set off on a little Honda motorcycle borrowed from a neighbour. It was an experience that Adam enjoyed because it involved a precocious but permissible proximity. With the warm night air in his face, the coconut fronds shimmering in the moonlight, and Alicia's arms around his waist, he was sure that, right at that moment, there was nowhere in the world he wanted to be more.

Alicia loved meeting the boat. The ferry brought news of the outside world; it was a tantalising connection with a great unknown and made up for the great chasm in her knowledge of the world. Inwardly, it pained her that she had never once ventured beyond the reef. Once, she and the rest of her class had gone aboard for a lunch with the captain, an outing arranged by the island's school. They ate tuna out of a tin, which amused her. A Javanese officer explained that civilised people ate rice, not sago palm. Everyone onboard smelled of cigarettes and engine oil. The experience came as a shock and Alicia decided that she quite liked living on Noli and did not need to stay on the smelly boat to see the capital after all. Now, the throbbing of the cutter's engines drew nearer to the jetty and the lights could be seen. Ghani stood on the jetty, his two legs planted firmly apart to steady himself. Adam was among those who helped bring the cutter along-side the dock, wielding a boat pole with the ease of an expert. The captain of the ferry was the first to disembark.

"Greetings, Ghani."

"A pleasant journey, Captain, I trust," Ghani replied.

"Actually, yes," said the captain, searching his pockets for a cigarette – his first on dry land for three days.

"And Ambon?" Ghani asked. "We've had no news, you see."

"Terrible, my friend. It's a kind of living hell. No one is secure. You wouldn't recognise the place. The shops are all looted and burned, the streets empty," the captain replied, wearing a stern expression he'd rehearsed for the occasion. A small crowd gathered around the captain, whose name was Abdullah, a Buginese from Makassar. He wore a white shirt with ragged, grease-stained epaulettes designating him as captain and sported a small goatee. Father Xavier was there too, tugging at his chin and listening intently. Cornelius Lahatula tried to look purposeful as he waited in the background for his official pouch. Captain Widodo puffed and wheezed, rubbing his eyes because he had just woken up.

Ghani stared over his shoulder towards the cutter. A small group of people was getting off the boat carrying bags and bundles. They had a furtive manner about them and kept their eyes downcast. Strangers, thought Ghani. It was dark, so he couldn't make out what they were wearing or what they carried, but they looked suspicious. Who might they be? he wondered. Thinking that the ferry's captain might know, Ghani tried to pull him aside, but it was hard to disengage the man from the crowd of curious islanders wanting more news about the violence on Ambon.

The captain seemed strangely eager to leave. He explained that he could not linger, that his ship was full of refugees – mostly Muslims from Ambon wanting transport to safer islands, even as far away as Java.

"They are the victims of mass hysteria, mostly. Spend all the time crying or staring out to sea. Won't say what happened to them," the captain explained, shaking his head. There was an awkward silence. Then, someone from the back asked: "How did it start?"

"No one seems to know, except that a few days before the first killing, a bunch of toughs had been sent back from Jakarta. They were Christians mostly, bad elements. You know, Ambon is a small place."

"Not as small as Noli," Father Xavier cut in.

"Oh, you've nothing to worry about here," the captain shot back, his eye fixed nervously on Ghani. He didn't look convinced. Then he slapped him on the back. "Surely not, with a man like Ghani around?" There was a ripple of laughter in support of this notion. Ghani pursed his lips and folded his arms. He was still curious about the group of people he'd seen disembark, and that curiosity was only fuelled by the ferry captain's apparent desire to leave Noli so hurriedly. But now wasn't the time to ask and risk fuelling people's fears. Besides, the captain was already making his way back to the cutter – he hadn't even raised with Ghani the usual issues like the truckload of frozen tuna that waited to be taken onboard, or the whiskey he'd been promised on the last visit.

Hearing this vote of confidence in Ghani, Father Xavier winced, for surely it was his role to maintain calm. Like so many people from the major islands, the priest sensed that the ferry captain had treated him like some kind of pariah. Bad enough that Christians are a minority in this country, which makes their priests people to be wary of. He was aware that Muslim mothers taught their children to steer clear of priests for fear that they would be tempted into conversion; "fishing for souls," as Ghani liked to put it. The sense of insecurity he felt brought a light sweat to the back of his neck. It was a familiar sensation, one that dogged him like a chronic disease: a sense that he wasn't loved because he lacked the capacity to love. And yet love was the currency he supposedly dealt in. There was Ghani, with his rough manners and leering eyes, yet people felt secure in his presence.

To Alicia, the little island of Noli seemed suddenly vulnerable and it stimulated her protective instincts. It occurred to her that a safe passage to the island of Java was only minutes away by cutter. Next to her, Father Xavier stood with one hand rubbing his protruding jaw. The gaunt priest stared out to sea.

"Anything wrong, Father?" Alicia asked.

"No, my child. Nothing." Father Xavier was never a convincing liar. Comb in hand, he tugged at his thick hair to release the tension.

"So why do you look so concerned?"

"It's nothing, really. How's Adam?"

Hearing this, Ghani turned away from the ferry lights and placed one arm on Alicia's slim shoulder. He wore a wide smile and seemed keen to be jolly.

"They'll make a fine couple, don't you think?"

Alicia smiled and turned away, making as if to look for Adam. She felt burdened by the circumstances of their union, as if the island's happiness now fell on her shoulders.

꿈 ꧁

"We need your help," the ringleader said in a soft voice. He was a wiry man with a pockmarked face partially covered by a wispy black beard. A thick line of black eye make-up highlighted the lower lids of his eyes, which burned with the subdued intensity of slow-burning coal. A white skullcap covered his bony, close-cropped head and he played incessantly with a set of jet-black prayer beads. The others, about a dozen men wearing the same skullcaps and black eye shade, called him *Ustad* Umar and treated him with great respect. They all wore at least one item of military clothing and seemed jumpy, nervous, and somewhat dazed. They had with them green plastic travel bags emblazoned with the name of a company in Jakarta called "P.T. Transjihadi." One of them, a burly youth with a pair of wraparound sunglasses perched on his balding head, kept watching the door to the musty room in the old sultan's tumbledown palace where they were all gathered. His hand rested on a small plastic handbag that bulged and looked heavy.

"Whatever I can do," Sultan Tarmizi said with customary politeness. He was afraid because he knew that these men were armed and dangerous. At the same time, he was intrigued by the possibilities. They'd come to him out of the blue, these ruffians dressed up like common thugs, but their timing was good. For Sultan Tarmizi aimed to exploit the troubles wafting over these islands to regain some of his stature. It was a trick he'd learned in the heyday of the Indonesian Communist Party: when people feel uncertain and insecure because of events over which they have no control, they tend to turn to sources of traditional authority. Umar nodded politely and said: "Our friends say you have been conducting missionary activities here on Noli."

The sultan smiled, using a show of coy politeness to buy time before answering. He wasn't sure of the angle here. Had he been doing too much or too little on the missionary front? Was he going to be accused of preaching heresy or the true path? Given the tendency for Muslims to dispute degrees of religious devotion among one another, he thought it best to fudge the issue.

"Well, I do my best in the circumstances. Daily Koran readings, some charity-work. You see..."

Umar interrupted him. His voice was calm and even. It was as though he had a goal to reach but was happy to take time getting there; he showed the patient cunning of a feline predator.

"You have been helped by our friends overseas, no?"

"In a small way, yes." Tarmizi squirmed.

Now he felt like he was being stalked, played with, and worried before the kill. What did they know about the money? Each month, a generous sum was deposited in his postal savings account. He knew very little about where it came from other than a short, stocky man with Arab features and an expensive gold watch who had visited him some five years back with a long story about wealthy foundations in the Arabian Gulf. All he'd done was sign a testimonial. Perhaps this man, and his band of toughs, represented some kind of audit committee come to enforce more prudent disbursement of the funds.

"Come now, brother," said Umar, sensing the sultan's suspicion. "We are helped by the same people. We also have friends in green, if you know what I mean."

"In green?" The old sultan was confused. What did he mean by "green?" The term had military connotations, too. His relations with the army were not so good because of his former communist connections; neither were the boys in green all that tolerant of the far religious right, so far as he knew. If they were, it was a new twist.

"We have come to rid the island of heathens." The softness of Umar's voice was matched only by the economy of his speech, and the sultan strained to catch what he was saying. The overall effect was a quiet confidence that his followers venerated. When he said "heathens," several of his followers muttered a quiet prayer beneath their breath. The way they all looked upon him, Sultan Tarmizi sensed blind devotion, an admirable, though scary, quality in a man. There was a pause and some of Umar's followers used this to cough, shift the weight on their haunches, and light cigarettes. Smoke gathered like a cloud beneath the weak light bulb that lit the room and drove away a pair of buzzing mosquitoes. The old sultan shifted uneasily, his fears confirmed. For these men had come to wage holy war on Noli.

"Does not the Koran tell us, 'God loves not the aggressor,'" the sultan asked, meekly, citing a well-known verse that hardly showed off much scholarly erudition. The man called Umar shot back: "Of course, but does Allah not also tell us to 'fight the leaders of unbelief?'"

Not being an *ulama* or religious preacher by training, it would be hard for the sultan to keep up this textual duel for long. He noisily sipped some tea to disguise his discomfort, and Umar took this as an invitation to continue with his sermon.

"We lived in ignorance for so long, but now we see this holy war as a way to purify our faith. The Prophet, peace be upon Him, taught that jihad is a struggle to cleanse impurity…"

"Ah yes, the greater jihad, perhaps – to fight against immorality and sin," the sultan interjected. He'd reached the outer limits of his scriptural knowledge, but wasn't about to be bullied. Was he not the titular defender of the faith on Noli?

"Of course, my brother, but blood spilt in defence of our faith – this is also jihad. Now it is your duty as a Muslim leader on this island to take up the struggle. Your legacy will be judged on how well you defended the faith!"

At this point, Umar's followers muttered a string of holy words, mostly in Arabic, after which they all waited for the sultan's response, fixing their eyes on him. Sultan Tarmizi stood at the edge of the precipice and hesitated. Below him, he saw the allure of power in this world, and perhaps even paradise in the world to come. Arrayed behind him were the people of Noli, an ungrateful lot who had abandoned their culture and history to live in blissful ignorance of the glorious past. Now they put their faith in priests and merchants. Resistance seemed futile. A part of him was nervous and judged this response prudent in the present company. All the same, he was greatly relieved that this peculiar band of cutthroats had no quarrel with his own missionary activity. They hadn't come for him. In fact, the more he thought about things, they seemed bent on eliminating his enemies, even if it involved some violence. The old sultan resolved to play their game. "About time, thanks be to God," the old sultan said at last. Then he lowered his eyes as a gesture for the others to drink the tea that had been brought in for them. His hands were trembling.

Sultan Tarmizi Shah bin-Shah was a pious man. Religion was a comfort to him in the dwindling years of his long and colourless reign, a sultan in name but precious little else. Even his harem, once numbering more than a dozen in his father's day, consisted of no more than four elderly matrons, two of whom were sisters with severe arthritis. Inwardly, Tarmizi basked in the subdued glow and glory of being the thirty-eighth sultan descended from the same great ancestor, a man the island simply remembered as Arufa.

"The great Arufa was our island's first Muslim convert," the sultan told the band of ruffians drinking tea at his feet. He decided they needed a history lesson in order to light for himself a filament of authority. He sensed that these people answered to some powerful outside force. There was something about them that suggested recent training and indoctrination, something rough and ready about their ways. Umar commanded authority all right, but he seemed to be reading from a prepared script.

"Thanks be to God. Islam is the foundation of our national identity. Nothing should pollute this," Umar interjected with a voice that was confident, although the sidelong glances he gave his followers betrayed doubts and fears. "For too long, our leaders tolerated the Christian scum and gave them leadership positions, but see what they did? They stole from the people and secretly tried to divert us from the path of true faith."

"Ah yes, quite so," the sultan admitted. Despite his sympathy for the sentiment, he was a little shocked and unaccustomed to this kind of prejudice. After all, the Christians on Noli were his subjects as well. For the sultan, religion was about power, not conviction.

"Well, as I was saying, the great Arufa brought civilisation to Noli and laid down the traditions of this once-great island." Then, to be on the safe side, he added, "Arrogant Christians took over and trampled on these traditions."

"We can help rid you of these Christians," Umar cut in, nervously fingering his prayer beads.

"Yes, it is time to liberate these islands," chimed in a companion.

"Freedom is purity of faith!" shouted another from the rear.

"People will surely die," the sultan said in a small voice. He knew there was no resisting these people, with their crazed convictions and simple loyalty to Islam. He also felt his own resistance crumbling. Umar looked him straight in the eye and, using a mixture of poor Arabic and Javanese-accented Indonesian, quoted a verse from the Koran:

"Think not of those who are slain in Allah's way as dead. Nay, they live, finding their sustenance in the presence of their Lord."

"Thanks be to God," they all mumbled together and, for the first time in years, the old sultan recovered a little of his dignity.

The era of the spice trade brought Tarmizi's antecedents untold wealth. Each and every foreigner who managed to find a safe passage over the reef promised the sultan of the day vast riches, titles – even an embassy in great European capitals – so long as he granted a monopoly on the supply of noli. Such were the exaggerated promises made in return by the mesmerised and flattered sultans, encumbered with gifts and trinkets and usually drunk on celebratory palm toddy, that great European powers drew close to declaring war over conflicts arising out of overlapping oaths and assurances.

Under colonial rule, the sultan and his retinue were pampered, but firmly ignored in all but the lightest of matters. Each month, the Dutch resident made a stately visit, calling on the sultan sweating and red-faced under the full plumage of colonial splendour. The outstanding orders were to flatter and honour, but give no ground – and take it all if possible. Gifts and trinkets, usually cheap toys and gadgets, were duly proffered and tea formally taken. In the case of Tarmizi's grandfather, a cure for piles was endlessly discussed, but never found. "Tedium in the extreme; a huge waste of time and money," was how one resident described a call on the sultan in an official report to the colonial capital, Batavia.

Tarmizi's last great attempt to assert authority over his people came with the end of Dutch colonial rule. When the country's founding fathers declared independence and battled the Dutch in 1945, the people of Ambon, who dominated the ranks of the Dutch colonial soldiery, held out for a state of their own under Dutch tutelage. Sensing an opportunity to wield some real power at last, the young Tarmizi sided with the Moluccan rebels. He fell under the influence of new streams of socialist thought that talked about revolution and *merdeka* from oppression. He became a communist and abandoned all pretence of being a religious man. In the spirit of socialist thinking, Tarmizi gave away some land and offered shelter to a few of his poorer relatives. Everyone took advantage and discreetly laughed at him. "See how the old feudal relic embraces Marx!" When the Moluccan independence movement collapsed, Tarmizi withdrew in shame to the dusty back room of his palace. For years, he secluded himself, having everything brought to him and more or less opting out of island life.

Not that he was idle during all these years in hiding. Trading a dog-eared Dutch edition of Marx's *Das Kapital* for his father's leather-bound Koran, Tarmizi taught himself the scriptures. "Man grows older and draws nearer to God," his father once told him in a rare spasm of sobriety. And so, in his sixtieth year, Tarmizi started praying five times a day and became fastidious about fasting. Instead of the forage cap he wore during his revolutionary period, Tarmizi adopted a flamboyant turban in which was embedded a very large pearl encased in filigree silver that was a family heirloom. He wrapped himself in Buginese silk sarongs of the finest quality and endowed the main mosque of Noli with a new pulpit made of the finest Javanese teak. Less well known was the recent visit to the old sultan by an Islamic charity organisation that claimed connections with the House of Saud. The charity offered him money to help pay for missionary activity with very few strings attached – merely a yearly report. The money was substantial – enough, in fact, to cover all his debts.

Little known too was Tarmizi's fondness for the taped sermons of a fiery preacher from East Java commonly called Mullah Zainal. The preacher made popular calls for Islamic statehood and attacked the government for promoting Christianity at the expense of Islam. Mullah Zainal's high-pitched voice and pleading, almost seductive tones were a hit with poor labourers and alienated Muslim students across the country. In poor communities where the only form of affordable entertainment was the dull official media using manipulated Javanese mythology, the earthy words of a powerful preacher enthralled young and old alike. At first, it was more the seductive and inspiring cadence, rather than the preacher's message, that won him a following. But as economic conditions worsened, people began to listen more closely to his insistence that faith was the path to purity and prosperity. For the students, Mullah Zainal's entreaties for purer faith were another way of addressing the country's deep social and economic problems. For Tarmizi, like a powerful talisman, they promised a new lease of power.

Lately, Sultan Tarmizi had taken to strolling in the lanes beside the old central mosque of Noli after Friday prayers. There he encouraged people to kiss the large emerald ring that was reputedly ancient Arufa's heirloom. In the cool shade of the mosque, a large grandfather clock ticking and chiming in the background, Tarmizi drew a small crowd of eager youngsters around him to study the Koran. Everyone in this group had new Korans, supplied by the overseas Islamic charity. Members of this group took to wearing white skullcaps, even though none had been on the holy pilgrimage to Mecca. They also discussed other, more political ideas and the blame for things, large and small, often fell on the government and what Tarmizi liked to call "its Christian masterminds."

Shortly after news reached Noli of the events on Ambon, Sultan Tarmizi stopped greeting his Christian neighbours. A week later, a green flag bearing the Arabic slogan *"Allahu Akbar!"* was raised above his ramshackle palace.

⌣ ⌢

At midday prayers the following Friday, Sultan Tarmizi announced an important visitor and invited him to speak to the congregation. It was a hot day and the worshippers were grateful for the new ceiling fans donated by the old sultan and whirring quietly above their heads. Friday prayers at Noli's whitewashed principal mosque, recently renamed the Sultan Tarmizi mosque, were normally subdued and somnolent. The congregation came to meet their peers, wash, and pray together, snatching a few moments of contemplation on the newly-laid plush green carpet – another recent donation from the sultan. Visitors were rare and a few of the assembled worshippers softly grumbled in the way that people do about departures from routine.

Umar, wearing a white robe and a red headcovering in the

manner of the Arabs, stood up and walked in front of the congregation, before seating himself cross-legged on a carpet, rather than
mounting the mosque's roughly-hewn pulpit. It was a calculated move
to stress his humility before God.

"My brothers," he began, after the customary invocations to
Allah the great and merciful. His voice sounded soft and seductive.
For Adam Junaidi, who sat near the back of the mosque, resting his
weary back against a cool whitewashed pillar, it was an invitation to
doze. There was little any religious homily could do for his line skills
on the fishing boat, so he lost himself in sensual thoughts about his
beloved Alicia. Before closing his eyes, he caught sight of a small group
of newcomers close to the edge of the mosque's carpeted interior. Like
Umar, they wore white robes and were either crouched in fervent
prayer, or sat on their haunches with raised palms, staring into the
middle distance, murmuring. Who were these people? Adam wondered. Refugees, perhaps. There was talk of a Christian militia stalking
outlying islands and wild rumours about knife-wielding priests.

Umar wasted no time getting to the point. "It's time for the
Indonesian people and the Muslim community, which are both now
suffering, to come to a basic conclusion: that, if necessary, we must
drive evil people out of this Indonesia we love." There was a murmur
of assent and ritual invocation from the back, where his followers sat.
The rest of the congregation, accustomed as they were to the usual
exhortations to be pure of faith and morality, looked puzzled. This
was politics, and they were accustomed to official guidelines that
strictly forbade the mixing of religion and politics. Their own chief
ulama, old and nearly blind, had long ago stopped preaching much of
any significance, not even news from the Middle East. In any case,
increasingly he left the sermonising to the old sultan, who was fond
of giving history lessons and castigating Nolians for neglecting tradition. Umar fell silent and Adam opened his eyes. Like others around
him, it dawned on him that this was a new and rather more serious

message. A friend nudged Adam in the ribs.

"Who is he?"

"I don't know. Looks like one of those preachers from Jakarta the rich pay millions for to help their business – you know, like the one always on the radio."

Umar continued now, pitching his voice a little higher.

"Even if we have to rebuild from nothing, even if we lose our loved ones in the process of this struggle, we will build from our own righteousness and the heroism we possess."

At this, more members of the congregation started murmuring, invoking the name of God and encouraging Umar to go on. From the back, Adam heard a buzz as Umar's followers started praying, swaying as if hypnotised. Umar continued.

"We have been purified by adversity. Struggle helps us to face the ultimate test, which is martyrdom."

Now there was a more lively response from the congregation. A few people joined Umar's followers in their chanting and everyone's attention was riveted on the preacher, who broke into Arabic every now and again when he cited holy verses. Most Nolians were poorly educated, so they didn't understand the language of the holy book. There was compulsory religion instruction for everyone up to the age of twelve, but mostly this was conducted in Malay and teachers found that the best response from young students came from readings of *The Thousand and One Nights*. The Arabic language, with its guttural masculinity, was held in awe and had a hypnotic effect.

"Don't be afraid to die," Umar said. There was emotion in his voice, and Adam felt a tingling sensation as these words and the chanting of his followers stirred his emotions. "No one should fear death in the cause of righteousness. Why, hear the words of the Prophet, peace be upon Him: 'The blood of the wounded would smell like musk on the day of resurrection – and nothing would interfere with Allah's reward....'"

With these words, there arose a cry from the middle of the mosque and a young man, one of Adam's boatmates, in fact, stood up and raised a fist defiantly. Umar looked on approvingly, then continued, hammering home his central message.

"We cannot allow the power in this country to fall into the hands of Zionist agents or groups who hate Islam. Who are the enemies of Islam? Look around you, my brothers, see the Chinese and their grasping ways that bring you into debt. And the Christians, how they force their religion on you. You've heard their bells and their rough church songs. Don't they pollute the true faith? How often we find ourselves being asked to tolerate them, even join them? These are the enemy and they must be crushed...." Umar's eyes narrowed as he surveyed the congregation. He paused before continuing: "And you should know that they are abusing our women – why I've heard that just the other day, there was an incident along the beach involving a Christian man and a young Muslim girl. The family is trying to hide the girl out of shame, but I have learnt of this terrible act – and the man goes free and unpunished by his church and his fellow Christians. What kind of morality is this?"

By this time, others had stood and started waving their fists, drowning Umar out. A voice from the back cried out: "Death to the Christians!"

As Adam listened to this sermon of hatred, he felt fearful. His father had always taught him to regard religion as a ritual and a duty, but not as a weapon against his neighbour. Why? he wondered. What have these people done? He had heard nothing about any attack on a Muslim girl. Then there was his impending marriage to think about; his beloved Alicia was now cast in the role of infidel. Around him, people were discussing the sermon as Umar quietly returned to his place and sat in silent prayer. The next thing he knew, one of Umar's followers was behind him, smelling strongly of musk oil. In his hand, he had a sheath of papers and handed Adam one.

"What's this?" Adam asked.

"Survey. Just a few questions," said the follower, moving on to the next row.

Adam turned the paper over and saw a list of questions. One of the questions asked if the respondent would be willing to give his life for the cause of Islam.

CHAPTER FOUR

The trouble hit Noli without warning like a squall. It was mid-morning, some ten days after the ferry's fleeting visit. Father Xavier was crossing the little square on the way to church after drinking coffee with Ghani and Felix Ling at the hotel. This was the quiet part of any working day on Noli. The fishermen were out riding the deep blue swell in their boats. The sun was high and the plump little Noli pigeons, a prized delicacy because they fed mainly on the aromatic spice after which they were named, took to the shade of the large banyan trees ringing the square. Very little stirred, except for the odd object that the gentle sea breeze picked up and blew inland across the dusty square.

Suddenly, piercing the languid tranquillity of the scene, a pickup truck appeared in the square shrouded by a cloud of dust, its engine revving very loudly. The vehicle was full of men, making the rear end sag and lurch as it careered towards Sutan Sjahrir Street and Father Xavier's little church. Leaning out of the back, men waved large cutting knives and wore green headbands. They shouted slogans, some of which sounded to Father Xavier like Islamic exhortations. "*Allahu Akbar!*" He distinctly heard the Arabic for "God is great." There was still some distance between him and the church, and the pickup truck had almost arrived, but there was nothing he could do. In an instant, a torch was hurled and, in what seemed like seconds, the wooden structure was ablaze. The men tumbled out of the pickup and danced crazily around the burning church, waving long knives, spears, and crossbows. One of them carried a rifle and started shooting in the air, the sound of gunfire curiously muted against the roar and crackle of the wooden church. From where he stood at the far end of the square, Father Xavier could not make out their faces in much detail, but none looked familiar and they must have come from the boat, he thought.

Without being instructed, Father Xavier's feet took him behind a large breadfruit tree, one of several that ringed the square and offered shade to late afternoon strollers. He stood with his back against the tree, breathing heavily, and suddenly perspiring. He was certain there was no one in the church and he knew it would be futile to rush over and try and save what was left of the building, for alone and unarmed, he would surely be cut to pieces by the mob. And yet a small voice inside him was questioning why he just stood there and did nothing as an infidel mob burned down a house of God. He'd done nothing to save the Holy Cross, the sacrament; wasn't this his duty as a priest? This was the moment he'd dreaded since becoming a priest: a trial not of his faith, but of his strength to defend it. With his back to the tree, away from the flames he could see the brilliant blue ocean and in the distance a fishing boat riding the waves beyond the reef. He longed to be on that boat, hauling in the lines with only a split finger from a stray hook to worry him. He closed his eyes in the hope that it was all a bad dream. But when he opened them again and looked across the square, he could plainly see the flames and the white-robed mob dancing wildly around the church. Minutes later, the first beams crashed to the floor of the burning church in a shower of sparks. Father Xavier instinctively offered a quiet prayer of thanks for the coffee-drinking habits of himself and his friends – otherwise, Father Xavier would have been inside his little office adjacent to the church. Almost certainly he would have been burned or hacked to death. For it had begun.

Hard as it was to take his eyes off the burning church, the priest knew it wasn't safe to linger behind the tree much longer. Soon the mob would move on, and the square was an obvious place to look for the targets of their anger. The hotel was the nearest and most obvious place for retreat, although he would have to sprint a short distance in the open. He had no choice. By the time he reached the gates of the hotel, his heart was beating so hard it could have been in his mouth and the sturdy muscular legs that once firmly straddled a fishing boat felt like jelly. No sooner had he crossed the dusty threshold of the hotel, he met a small knot of people who had fled the main street and market area.

"Father, Father! They are here… Please, help us!" screamed a bulky woman he recognised as one of his parishioners. Aunt Etty, as she was known, was a widow who sold garlic in the small morning market adjacent to the square. Normally a cheerful woman, always smiling, her eyes were red from the tears that streaked her chubby face. Her screams snapped Father Xavier out of the instinctive daze that had pushed him towards the hotel, like a child returning home after a traumatic beating.

"Inside, Aunt Etty. Hurry now. You'll be safe in the hotel," said Father Xavier. He wrapped himself around Aunt Etty's formidable bulk and buried his face in her shoulder. The physical contact felt good and, for a fleeting moment, he found some relief from the naked fear and pangs of guilt that paralyzed his senses. On releasing her, he found that he'd regained his strength and composure; there was work to be done. He started waving his arms furiously to get everyone to see what they must do. By now, more people were at the gates to the hotel. Some carried belongings, all they could grab as soon as they saw the smoke rising from the church. They seemed reluctant to go in and waited for direction from the priest.

"But isn't he a…"

"Muslim? Yes, of course," Father Xavier struggled to find the right words. "But Ghani is a trusted friend and, above all, a Nolian. You are safe here, trust me."

"They want to drink Christian blood. God save you all, they're coming after us," a gaunt old man with bushy grey hair said as he leaned against the hotel gate and watched the church crackle and burn. It was old Yaakob, and there was sadness in his eyes. The town was a largely Christian settlement, and the flames that consumed the little church spread fear in the hearts of its parishioners. Of course, they had nowhere to go, so Father Xavier herded them towards the hotel as they drifted into the square.

Soon the square was empty. Nothing stirred as Father Xavier stared at the column of black smoke that rose from where the church had once stood. It angered him now that his first instinct had been to seek shelter in the hotel and not rush towards the church and take a stand for his faith. Though he knew this would have meant a swift death at the hands of the mob, hacked down in the burning embers before he could do anything to save people: hardly a fruitful martyrdom. Everything he knew about the meaning of the Scriptures and the history of the church added up to a verdict of dereliction of his sacred duty. Yet the hard pragmatism of his inscrutable Javanese Jesuit mentors was a source of great comfort to him. "God is within you. God is everywhere, but do not think you are God," Father Sudiono would say, citing Javanese homespun wisdom. Beyond the square, Father Xavier could hear the distant screams of people in trouble and the sounds of new fires burning. Already the smell of wood smoke pervaded the air.

"Come, Father. Come inside. People need you here and you'll be safe."

Ghani tugged on the priest's sleeve as he peered with a worried look in the direction of the burning church from the threshold of the hotel entrance. But the priest stood his ground.

"Luckily you were with me, you know. Otherwise…"

"I know, I know. Thanks be to God for that. And this is only the beginning. Do you hear the cries out there? The killing has begun. God in heaven, what have we done to deserve this?" The priest turned to Ghani with eyes filled with tears.

"So come, let's talk, make plans to save our people, save ourselves. We can pray too, if you like. But please, please come inside. You're not safe here."

There was a genuine note of concern in Ghani's voice that touched Father Xavier. Perhaps he had underestimated the fish merchant's capacity for compassion and focused too much on the greed and the lust that so heavily tinted his personality. He turned away from the hotel entrance, clasping one of Ghani's arms. Part of the priest longed for a drink and some solace from his old friend to steady his nerves. Ever since his mother died, Father Xavier's impulse in the face of crisis was to cry out and hold somebody close – though he'd been trained to resist these lay impulses. His duty as a priest was to display courage and have faith – yet at this moment, he felt bereft of both. He felt for his comb. Then he stopped. Something in him snapped, like a taut line that has hooked too large a fish. He knew the feeling and knew when to let go, play out the line. What would he say to the terrified people inside? How could he face them without any sign of courage or faith? Father Xavier turned to Ghani and said: "No, I must go. I have a lot of work to do." The priest spoke slowly and deliberately. He raised an arm and pointed to the square beyond the gate. "Out there."

Ghani nodded slowly and relaxed his grip. As he did so, he noticed that the priest was shaking and there was a distant, fearful look in his eyes, like a man staring death in the face.

⌒ ⌒

With one fleshy cheek resting on his hand, Cornelius Lahatula was dozing at his desk when the alarm was raised. He'd been reading the last of the official documents that the ferry brought in the pouch — something predictable about needing to be vigilant about the return of the communist menace and a drive to root out those with unclean personal environments. Ambon wasn't mentioned. He searched in vain for any guidance on community relations, for a manual of some kind on promoting religious tolerance. Cornelius liked to follow instructions.

"Fire, *Pak*!" It was Latief, his energetic but dimwitted office boy.

"What?" Cornelius raised his head and removed a flimsy official document that had stuck to his hand.

"Fire in the church. Some boys have gone crazy. Come quickly, *Pak*."

Captain Widodo was already there, his service revolver drawn, eyes wildly rolling around in search of a culprit. But the men in the pickup truck had long disappeared, driving off in the direction of the North Shore in a trail of dust and high-pitched taunts. All that remained of the church was a pile of burning timbers and blackened tin roofing.

It was obvious to Cornelius, slow as he was, that something bad was about to happen to Noli. He hailed Captain Widodo, who wandered over with a look of utter amazement on his face.

"Where did they come from?" asked Cornelius.

"Come from? What do you mean?" The policeman was having problems finding the holster for his pistol, which was concealed by a roll of fat.

"This was not the work of local people, surely you can see that," Cornelius sputtered irritably.

"Maybe, maybe not. All as I know is that when people get hot like this there's nothing we can do."

"Nothing?"

"Says so in the manual – riots, mobs, angry farmers; let them blow off steam. Only way to contain it is to let the thing die down. Otherwise, everyone gets killed."

"Everyone *is* going to get killed," said Cornelius, peering up the road, his hands resting uneasily on his hips. "My God, isn't that Father Xavier? Where does he think he's going?"

～ ～

A little further up the road from the burning church, Father Xavier came upon the first corpses. A woman lay beheaded outside her house. Someone, probably a neighbour, was wrapping her fly-swarmed body in a rush mat. A dog sniffed at her bloodstained sarong that lay nearby; the poor animal confused by the confluence of scents, one familiar as the hand that feeds, the other redolent of food itself. In the distance, Father Xavier heard shouts and screams. From inside a doorway, a woman sobbed. He darted in to take a look and saw a middle-aged woman cradling a bloodied corpse. The room was dark and it took a moment for the priest's eyes to adjust from the blazing afternoon sunlight outside.

"Father, Father, what have they done?" the woman wailed as she recognised the priest.

"My God," the priest said aloud.

As his eyes grew accustomed to the gloom, he saw that there were deep gashes on the torso and flies buzzed noisily in the room. The man's head rested precariously on the side of a wicker chair, mostly detached from a body that had been cleaved like an animal's carcass. Father Xavier steadied himself at the door and fought a wave of nausea. It took him a while before he could summon the strength to give the dead man a final benediction. Father Xavier tried to coax the man's wife into leaving for the hotel, but she could not be persuaded to leave her husband's corpse.

"I want to die with him," she said, staring blankly at the priest.

Outside, it was now late afternoon and the sun hung low casting long shadows through the thicket of banana and coconut trees that lined the road. He could see in the distance that another vehicle had joined the pickup now; a small microbus that usually ferried villagers to the main market and children to school was careering up the road in a cloud of bright orange dust. Brown arms clutching knives and cudgels protruded from the windows and the driver sounded the horn incessantly. He recalled that a Muslim owned the bus. He, along with other Muslim villagers crammed in the bus, must now have joined the pack of murderers heading north, the priest assumed. The madness of it all, Father Xavier thought. His hands were covered in a sticky substance and he realised in horror that it had come from the man he'd just given last rites to. Up till now he'd felt afraid, but now he started to boil with anger.

The road to the North Shore was lined with little tin roof and whitewashed houses, once neatly kept and swept, their owners normally bustling outside at this time of day, bringing in sun-dried laundry or a tray of chillies. Now, these tidy frontages were littered with soiled carcasses lying where they were hacked and mutilated. Smoke from burning homes and vehicles, tinged with the acrid odour of burning flesh, invaded Father Xavier's nostrils, causing him to retch constantly; his throat was parched. His ears were filled with the moaning and wailing of the survivors, dogs barking, and children crying. Frozen with shock at all the carnage, Father Xavier was at a loss how to pray over the dead and, since most of the corpses were decapitated or mutilated beyond description, to identify them. He came across a whole family strewn across the road, their innards spilled on the tarmac, dark patches of coppery-smelling congealed blood everywhere. Men's heads lolled where they had rolled, some with bloody pieces of flesh wedged in their mouths, which Father Xavier took to be their genitalia. A child's arm was flung carelessly on to the roof of a car – the words "Death to Christians" were daubed on the windscreen in blood. No one killed had been shown any mercy. In the silence of the scene, Father Xavier could hear in his mind the screams and the hacking of the knives.

The road strewn with bodies, dark lifeless shapes, like bumps on a road, brought the meaning of the word genocide home to Father Xavier. All those pictures he'd seen from Rwanda and Bosnia became more tangible. A picture of a mangled corpse conveys only so much information. It fails to capture the stillness of death against everything that continues to move and live, or the colours and smells of death that reduce us all to something organic and somehow inhuman. The contents of his stomach had long since been thrown up, so that now he just heaved bile and his stomach muscles hurt. At one point, he'd taken down two severed heads from bamboo poles and buried them using Christian rites. He could not be sure whether they were Christian or Muslim. Coldly, he noted that religion doesn't mark a face, for in these parts, men grew beards as a mark of maturity.

Father Xavier wandered from house to house, consoling the few survivors he found – those who'd managed to hide under baskets, piles of nets, or in the thickets of noli bushes that lined the road.

"They came, Father, and chopped. They just kept chopping. They asked for nothing, gave us no warning," said a terrified girl Father Xavier managed to pull out the bottom of a latrine. She was covered in filth, but lucky to be alive – the rest of her family were cut down where they stood and there was blood all over the whitewashed walls of the house. There were signs that the familiar and cosy order of small island life had been shattered. Confronted by sudden and violent death, the people of Noli became unhinged and lost all sense of propriety. A little further on, he came across a teenage boy who was hacking fingers off a dead woman to collect her rings. Father

Xavier knew the boy. The lad was a fisherman no more than sixteen, normally a sweet-natured fellow with an easy smile, skilled at scaling fish and chopping off their gills. There he was, sawing off human digits using the same scaling knife. "I'm sorry, Father. We're all crazy," the boy muttered, before scurrying off with the bloodied loot in his hand and snot trailing from his nose.

In the face of the carnage, Father Xavier struggled to stay calm. He muttered prayers and spoke the soothing language of hope and faith. His right hand trembled as he held it upright in the classic pose of benediction. Outwardly, he upheld the dignity of faith in the face of so much chaos. Inwardly, though, his soul was on fire, throwing up huge clouds of doubt. How had the faith and morality of these people been rewarded? With murder and the loss of innocence. What would the bishops say to that? What's more, all the evidence pointed to the motives of these killings being faith itself. The Muslim rabble screamed the name of their God. Wasn't religious faith supposed to protect the order of our world and prevent neighbours from falling on each other? How could faith protect these people from fear and guide their actions when they had just seen loved ones cut to pieces before their eyes? These were the questions Father Xavier asked himself as he stumbled through the landscape of horror unfolding around him. A numbing anger welled up deep inside, an anger that fuelled an urge to chase down the killers and bash their heads in, mutilate them, and stamp on their broken bodies. The urge grew stronger with every step he took and compounded his doubts. Eye for eye and tooth for tooth – there was no escaping the simple formula for revenge, which the Holy Scriptures cited, then immediately contradicted by saying it was wrong to take revenge on someone who wrongs you. Yet, just at this moment, revenge seemed such a natural compulsion: resisting it seemed like holding back a sneeze.

By nightfall, the little island was fully in the grip of terror. The smell of wood smoke and burning rubber hung in the air, which was eerily still and quiet. Soon after word of the church burning spread, some Christians on the South Shore took matters into their own hands. Not waiting to be slaughtered, they seized the Muslim headman and hacked him to death together with his family. Very soon, a Christian band, armed with spears, swords, and a purloined plaster image of the Virgin went marauding in the back of a light truck. They passed Father Xavier on the road as he made his way back into town, exhausted and blood-spattered.

"Father, Father! We'll kill them, kill them all!" screamed a young man from the back of the truck as it passed. The priest at first didn't recognise him, his face daubed white and bisected by a blood-red mark of the cross, his eyes concealed by a pair of sunglasses. Then he realised that the fellow had only just left the church choir. The violence knew no boundaries now, reflected Father Xavier, as he stared into the night after the truck. Every now and then, cries of pain and despair not unlike the natural sounds of the jungle pierced the dark. It took hundreds of years for the seeds of civilisation to take root and grow, he thought, and barely twelve hours for the jungle to take over again. Through the trees along the road on the way back to Noli's main square, he saw the flickering shadows of people running on the beach and the flames of burning property. It was like the vision of hell he'd once seen portrayed by a European painter from the Middle Ages. No one could be blamed, the priest thought to himself, because everyone was involved. The truck passed, leaving him alone in the eerie the stillness of the night. He found a perch under an abandoned fruit stall and hugged himself because there was no one else to turn to. Then he began to cry.

꒰ ꒱

The telephone line was bad and Ghani had to shout: "Have they reached the North Shore yet? What? Already? *Wa-Allah*." He listened for a moment or two, running one hand through his thinning hair, now damp with anxiety, then let the receiver fall clumsily from his hands as the news sank in. The apparatus clattered on the counter, a voice at the other end still shouting, terrified with death at the door. This was the moment he feared would come, the sum of terrible fears nurtured over the past few weeks by the rumours filtering in from other islands. Ghani was certain that they'd come with the ferry, these outsiders bent on killing. If only he'd paid more attention to the suspicious group at the jetty the night the ferry arrived. Worse still, he'd turned away some suspicious-looking characters who came looking for rooms at the hotel. The thought crept up on him and gave him a fright: could he have prevented all this from happening? A marauding militia had sown terror all over the island, destroying in an instant a community whose complex harmonics had been established over centuries. An object of immense natural beauty, like one of the island's great fan corals, a thousand years in the making, was crushed in an instant.

"What? What is it?" Ghani said, looking up from the reception counter where he had gone to make the call to a cousin who lived up on the North Shore. One of his employees, a wide-eyed girl with short hair, stood and stared. "Well?"

"The people inside," she stammered. "They are hungry and thirsty. What shall we do?" Under normal circumstances, the ever-watchful Ghani wanted every plate and glass consumed by his paying guests accounted for; his staff was nervous and even kept a tally of Father Xavier's prodigious bill, which was the only exception because it was never presented.

"Feed them, of course!" Ghani roared at the girl. "Give them all we have. Do you think this is an ordinary time?" The girl ran off towards the kitchen. Seeing everyone flock to his hotel for safety,

Ghani hurriedly established something of a command post in the coffee shop; it was a move he had anticipated and broached with the zeal of a responsible community leader. These were his people and they needed help and protection. There was little he could offer except shelter and the dubious comfort of a few tables and chairs.

The grimy coffee shop was filled with the sobs and groans of misery. There were wounded and bleeding survivors and people shivering in terror relieving themselves and vomiting where they lay, incontinent with fear; the stench of human misery had displaced the usual aroma of stale onions. In one corner sat Felix Ling and his wife Sonia, surrounded by a stack of bags and hastily packed cardboard boxes. Felix sipped tea from a flask and one leg was pumping furiously up and down as he stared out to sea clutching a brown leather bag. It was stuffed with all the money he could grab from the safe before abandoning the shop. Sonia wept softly into a large handkerchief. She was afraid of the mob, but also angry. She was furious with the wretched existence that her puny husband seemed incapable of escaping, and now it would lead to a horrible, painful death at the hands of a crazed mob. Around the Chinese shopkeeper and his wife, a small crowd of terrified townsfolk, mostly Christians, had gathered together a few belongings and set up temporary shelter on the grounds of Hotel Merdeka.

Slumped on a chair, Cornelius Lahatula looked at Captain Widodo, who in turn stared at the ground despondently.

"The situation is hopeless," he said to a terrified family of four nearby. "It's hard to see any help coming from Ambon in the immediate future. You see the phone lines are down."

"That's right," chimed in Widodo. "Cut by criminals. The radio is out as well."

"Does anybody out there know what's happened to us?" asked a man.

"Perhaps in Ambon they have intelligence, but who knows? I

cannot contact my superiors, so how am I to make a report? If there's no report, how are they to know?" said Cornelius, clearly agitated by the breakdown of the tenuous chain of command that defined his role as a government official.

"Oh, but don't worry," Widodo chimed in with more certainty: "the army will come soon. The troops will come. Mobile Brigade, I imagine as well. They're suited to the job. Fine men. Order will be restored, I'm certain of it."

"That's right," Cornelius added, "and when they come, these hoodlums will get a taste of discipline under the law. Without law, there is only anarchy."

The two officials continued on this way, imagining grand plans for the restoration of order, but convincing no one within earshot that salvation was at hand. They had to have something to hold onto, for the island's only government officials were suddenly cut off from the bureaucratic world that bound them together in an awkward partnership. The Christian bureaucrat and Muslim policeman cooperated outwardly, but inwardly, they were wary of one another. Even if they could trust their sense of duty, they feared pressure from their respective communities. In search of assurance, and perhaps a patch of neutral ground, they'd headed for Hotel Merdeka, taking Gus the noodle seller, who they found shaking with fear among his blackened pots and pans at the back of the noodle shop.

"Well, I think we're done for," moaned Gus, drawing heavily on a kretek and letting out the exhaled smoke in fierce bursts. "Who will bother to save us? The government forgot about us long ago." A woman next to him coughed and broke down in tears.

"Where is the law? Hasn't word been sent? Surely the army will help," muttered her husband.

"God has abandoned us, to be sure. There's no hope." It was Aunt Etty. She had planted herself in a large wicker chair and found an old newspaper to fan herself between fainting fits.

The sun sunk low and threw an incongruously-peaceful golden glow through the picture windows of the coffee shop where everyone assembled because it was the largest space and people could eat and drink, at least for now. The room was also a cauldron of misery and fear. The assembled refugees feared the mob would burst in and cut them to pieces at any moment and it was all Ghani could do to prevent a wave of panic. "Look, we're safe here," he told a group of men who were all for barricading the hotel using the rickety furniture. "This is a Muslim household and you are my guests. There's nothing they can do about that. Don't you know the custom? A guest in a Muslim household is treated like family. Please, you have to believe me."

The men weren't convinced – and nor was Ghani.

There was a stir in the room when Father Xavier returned shortly after dark. He looked gaunt and was covered in dried blood. On seeing him, people fell silent, their mouths hung open; no one could find any words. Finally, someone said: "Thank God you're alive, Father." Father Xavier collapsed on a chair that someone hurriedly vacated for him and buried his head in his hands. From the movement of his shoulders, everyone could see that he was weeping. To everyone's astonishment, it was Sonia Ling who came over to him and laid a hand on his heaving shoulder.

"There now, Father," she whispered in his ear. "We're all fine here. Rest for a while." He'd never heard Sonia speak like this. There was an unnerving air of intimacy about her voice – far from the shrill commanding tone she reserved for her hapless husband. Father Xavier had often heard the tone of voice used in the Lings' shop and it stimulated a surge of appreciation for the difficult act of celibacy. But this was different, and, without thinking, Father Xavier allowed his hand to find hers as it rested on his shoulder. The sensation this sent to the roots of his hair was beyond anything that his trusty plastic comb could deal with and, for the first time since he'd seen the church burn, Father Xavier found a measure of inner peace to douse the fire that burned within him.

After a short while, Father Xavier roused himself and took stock of the situation. The hotel was full of refugees, most of them Christians. They all looked anxiously at him for advice and support.

"Father, they are murdering us and we have no defence. What shall we do?" asked one parishioner, his hands trembling.

"Yes, we've been attacked for no reason. Father, we have to defend ourselves," chimed in another. There was panic in their faces, but also anger; Father Xavier felt he was staring at a mirror of his own feelings. Act? How?

"We are ready to defend our homes – just lead us," bellowed a man from the back of the room.

"Lead us, Father. They have killed our children and raped our women."

Father Xavier's head was spinning. Images of corpses lying where they had been mutilated swam before his eyes.

"Wait…wait," he said. Someone helped him to climb unsteadily onto a chair. The coffee shop was filled with the moans and cries of terrified people. He smelt their fear and tears now ran down his own face as he searched the room for the right words.

"People. People of Noli, listen to me," Father Xavier began. His legs felt unsteady and he rested one hand on the shoulder of the nearest person. People stopped whatever they were doing, mostly nursing wounds and caring for wailing children, and looked up at him. "We have been attacked for no reason, our church burned and many people savagely cut down in innocence. I was out there and saw everything for myself." With these words, the crowd in the room erupted. People shook their fists and men stood up with defiant cries of "Revenge, revenge…kill the Muslim scum!" Father Xavier felt his blood rise, too: "My brothers and sisters, I share your anger. I do.

Like you, I want this outrage addressed in some way – we all feel the same way." The crowd erupted again. In the far corner of the room, Ghani frowned and felt uneasy. As a Muslim, he could very easily be the first target of an angry Christian mob. What was the priest up to? he wondered.

"But first, first of all, good people of Noli…" He paused and stared at the sea of angry faces around him. It would be easy now, he thought. Just go with the flow, let their anger find some release, and perhaps achieve a measure of justice. He was tempted, sorely tempted – especially after everything he'd just seen. Then he caught Ghani's eye and saw fear in his friend's face, an expression of one who is looking at a monster, a monster he now had the power to unleash. It brought the priest reluctantly to his senses. "First, my dear brothers and sisters, first we must stop the violence. Then we will seek justice."

There was a groan of disappointment. "Too late, too late," came a voice from the crowd. "They must pay with their blood. Father, lead us…." Father Xavier paused and looked around. His throat was parched and constricted with fear. The moment was poised for him, offering a choice between leadership and responsibility. Somehow the two were in conflict, which didn't make sense. His mind raced to find the right words.

"Have faith. You must have faith in the words of our Lord. He will save us," he said finally. Looking down from where he stood, Father Xavier saw Ghani with a worried look on his face and beckoning him to step down from the chair.

"It's no use, Father. These people are afraid. They can't think. Save your strength."

"Perhaps, Ghani, but if we keep our faith in God…"

"Father, right now their fear is feeding on faith. Don't you see that? Because they are afraid, faith offers a fortress to hide behind, and becomes a weapon too. What do you think this killing is all about? Look, if you ask me, talk about God and justice just makes it worse."

Father Xavier pondered Ghani's words with difficulty, numbed as he was by fear and exhaustion. Faith and fear; he wouldn't have drawn the same connection. Right now, all he could see was the blood of the victims; all he could hear were the cries for help.

As the night wore on, the mood of panic subsided somewhat and the debate at Hotel Merdeka focused on possible reasons and causes. Was it the Christians who had provoked the outbreak of violence? Had Muslim extremists infiltrated the island? As it turned out, both explanations applied.

"There was this fisherman from the village just outside of town. His engine broke down, so he was unable to take his boat out. That meant he was idle." Father Xavier related the story as he had heard it some hours previously from a parishioner. "So, there was this local beauty, in fact, the daughter of a Muslim immigrant, strolling on the beach…."

"Don't tell me. One thing led to another," Ghani cut in impatiently, and a little too knowingly.

"A little more than that, I'm afraid," the priest continued, lowering his voice. "He raped her."

"*Wa-Allah*." Ghani said, bringing both hands to his face in an expression of shock.

"So the girl's relatives came looking for the fisherman," the priest continued.

"Who is a Christian, of course."

"That's right. Odd fellow. No one seems to know very much about him – a recent immigrant. They couldn't find him, so they assumed he was sheltering in the church." There was a pause as everyone took in the odd chain of events that had sparked off this catastrophe.

"So all this is about a woman?" Ghani asked.

"And a broken-down engine," Felix Ling added dolefully from the next table.

"I think this is the same fellow who came to me with the bent propeller blades the other day. I took back his engine to have it fixed." Felix Ling sighed and sunk his head deeper into his hands; so much for his grand plans for a chain of stores.

"Look," said Ghani. "A broken outboard motor and a strolling beauty on the beach: these are two rather ordinary events, events which one might think commonplace on an island like Noli. Under ordinary circumstances, the issue would have been easily dealt with. A meeting with Father Xavier here, appropriate punishment and compensation, nothing would have got out of hand. But things are different now."

"How so?" Felix asked.

Ghani touched Father Xavier on the elbow and indicated that he wanted a quiet word. When they found a quiet corner of the coffee shop, Ghani lowered his voice and said:

"I have not mentioned this before, but the day after the ferry left, I received a visit from two men."

Around them, the forlorn little coffee shop, normally empty, was alive with refugees and survivors from the violence. It was hard to be discreet. As they spoke in hushed tones, everyone stared at them.

"They said they represented something called the "Front to Protect Islam," I've never heard of it. They arrived with the ferry and were looking for rooms," Ghani explained.

"Go on."

"Well, I was suspicious, see. They looked strange – and this is hardly a place for the religiously pure. I told them the hotel was booked up, which was kind of hard to make look convincing, as you can imagine, Father. One of them, the leader, I think, a thin man with shifty eyes and a beard, he was very pushy and turned aggressive when it was clear I would not let them stay. So I asked them to leave."

"That's great," Father Xavier said, sounding irritated. "Now we don't know where they are."

"Odd thing too, now that I think about it. There was something about them that suggested military discipline or training. There was a clear chain of command, which is odd because we Muslims tend to treat each other as equals, more or less. Not them; they almost looked on me as the enemy for not putting them up."

Ghani looked behind him to see if any one was listening and said: "I heard they went straight to Sultan Tarmizi's place."

"Oh. Meaning?" Father Xavier gave the old sultan a wide berth to avoid kissing his hand.

"They asked me if the church was actively converting people from the faith. They wanted to know if we Muslims had a missionary programme. I took them to be wandering holy men, not killers."

"Well, that suggests trouble. Old Tarmizi has been trying to get a missionary programme off the ground for months now."

"Yes, and what's even more disturbing is that I heard that he was seen walking with a band of roughnecks who all wore military gear and carried long knives in their belts. No one around here needs knives except on their boats." Ghani nodded in Felix Ling's direction and said, "Ling's discontented customer may have added a spark, but I'm afraid the fire was already kindled."

Around them, women mostly cried or moaned, pressing sweat-drenched sarongs to their faces to hide themselves from the cruelty and tragedy they had been so suddenly subjected to. The men sat staring blankly out to sea, as if they expected a ship to arrive and take them away at any moment. They stared and waited in vain.

⋅ ⌒ ⌒ ⋅

Up on the North Shore, in the village that Adam Junaidi and Alicia Gordon called home, no one was prepared to resist the onslaught. A shared sense of security built up over generations had made walls redundant and doors flimsy. Land was commonly held and villagers shared boats, lines, nets, and other important tools of daily life. Suddenly, a brutal divide descended on the place. You were no longer from a village up on the North Shore, but were either a Muslim or a Christian. Depending on which mob you met, you were either spared or cut down and killed. Island people are used to sudden changes in nature, a still sea that can become a churning cauldron with a passing squall; a clear sky that can turn dark with the rage of a thunderstorm. But as a close-knit community, they are accustomed to constancy in human behaviour, so no one was prepared.

"No. You will not see that woman," Adam's father sternly ordered. It seemed to Adam that he had spat at the mention of his fiancée. His son had just returned from his boat – which he shared with three Christian neighbours. They had come up from the beach laughing and joking, until stopped in their tracks when they saw houses burning and met the first angry mob, which happened to be Christian. Adam sensed something was wrong and ducked down. He headed straight for home, crouching low and skirting the coconut trees that fringed the village.

"Papa, they were dragging a corpse. I knew the man. It was old Arifin," Adam cried as soon as he burst through the door. Arifin, the former merchant seaman with a gammy leg; the poor fellow couldn't possibly defend himself. So the whooping mob cut him and he died quietly, his body jerking in protest from loss of blood before being dragged out as a trophy.

Adam's first thought was to find Alicia, but now he was ordered to stay home and guard his family. A rock landed on their roof and there were cries outside.

"Come, let's eat some pork!" someone in the crowd outside shouted.

"Yes, bathe them all in pig fat...." said another.

"Why?" Adam asked his father softly. "What's all this about?" He was terrified. "Madness, son; the madness of mankind," he said, as he shielded his wife's ears from the blasphemous taunts outside and gently chanted verses from the Koran. She sobbed and her shoulders heaved. Adam had never seen his mother cry, knowing her only as a strong woman. At that moment, every member of the Junaidi family believed they were about to die and so they all instinctively sought physical contact with one another. Adam's bowels weakened and he had the urge to evacuate them. There was a smell of urine and a damp spot on his mother's sarong. Adam's father recited holy verses over and over again. "You had better confess your sins to God, son," he said at one point through chattering teeth, his eyes glazed over with fear. Yet for all the physical signals of imminent danger, somehow Adam could not grasp the idea that this was the end. Here, now, with happiness only weeks away.

By the time the Muslim rabble arrived at the North Shore village, several Muslim houses had already been torched and a few people had been killed. The Christian mob had moved like a tornado through the village, leaving murder, destruction, and a trail of severed body parts in its path. Adam and his parents listened, horrified, as a Muslim neighbour was dragged out of his house, moaning and pleading for mercy. Moments later, they heard primal screams punctuated by the dull sounds of hacking until they stopped altogether and the crowd moved on. Just when they thought their house was next, the opposing Muslim mob arrived, heralded by great shouts and a honking of horns. Then the real fight began. Someone in the Muslim camp managed to find a shotgun, which kept the Christian mob at bay. A few shots found their mark, judging by the screams of the wounded. The air was filled with shouts and taunts, obscenities, threats, and primal screams. In a village where just twelve hours earlier neighbours stopped and traded gossip to be polite, now they swore to murder each other. Yet even as his family cowered in fear for their lives, Adam seemed strangely detached from it all. All he was thinking about was the safety of his beloved Alicia, whose fate now lay in the hands of the recently arrived Muslim mob that had just saved his life from the crazed Christian mob.

As evening approached and the light failed, both sides withdrew and the noise subsided. In the space of barely twelve hours, the little world of Noli had been turned upside down and the North Shore village was effectively partitioned: Christians in the red zone, Muslims in the white zone. Marking off their territory, Christians hung a shirt stained red with blood on a pole close to the old headman's house. Nearby, someone had placed a severed head on a pole, its features mutilated and a bloodied piece of genitalia stuck between the lips. On both sides, young men and boys grabbed anything they could find to use as weapons, mostly knives and blades tied to long poles. The stench of blood and viscera hung about the air. Only a few hours earlier, the day had dawned with a fresh breeze blowing off the ocean and the clear brilliance of a cloudless sky. The new day began full of the promise of abundance and the sweet spicy aroma of the noli flower. It ended with carnage and the scent of burning flesh. The abrupt transition was savage and unnatural, something nobody could comprehend.

Unharmed but shaken, Adam and his family sought refuge in the little village mosque along with other Muslims from the village. The mosque, a stout building made of brick and stucco, was heavily defended by people, some of whom Adam recognised from the previous Friday when the visiting preacher came to the island's main mosque. They were mostly armed with spears, knives, and even bows and arrows. Somebody carried a two-way radio and was communicating with a man called "*Ustad* Umar." Everyone smoked heavily and little was said. Adam noticed quite a few of the young boys had glazed eyes and runny noses. They appeared to be on some kind of medication. Or were they intoxicated by murder? he wondered. They didn't seem interested much in talking. One of them came up to him and thrust a makeshift spear in his hand.

"Here. Kill the Christian scum," he said and then laughed.

"Kill, kill. Kill the Christian scum…," chanted a group of boys nearby. Adam shuddered and retreated to the shadows at the back of the mosque, where he hurriedly dropped the spear. It clattered and awoke an old man asleep on a grass mat against the wall. "What is it boy?" he asked: "Are we going to die?"

"I don't know, Uncle," Adam replied: "I'm scared."

There was no organised strategy of attack or defence on either side of the religious divide. Rocks hurled at the mosque were hurled back. Taunts flew in the night. Someone thought to boil a cauldron of water using scraps of firewood, into which a few packets of instant noodles were stirred. But no one was very hungry and a lot of people shivered with fear. A few people prayed; the rhythm of the holy verse with its accompanying body movements had a strangely calming effect. It was only after three in the morning, once everyone was quiet, either passed out through exhaustion and anguish, or gently sobbing, that Adam was able to slip away in search of his beloved Alicia.

෧ ෙ

The island fell silent in the hour before dawn. All that previous afternoon and deep into the night the killings had raged, the cries for help and muffled screams of the dying fading only in the early hours. The lull in terror brought solace to no one, though; it only amplified everyone's fears. No one slept. The islanders huddled in the hotel coffee shop mostly stared out to sea waiting for the new day and praying it would somehow bring relief. Just as the first light of day appeared, a grey smudge in the sky, Ghani came across Father Xavier sitting disconsolately across a fallen coconut tree along the beach in front of his hotel.

"You should be careful wandering about alone. You're a target, you know," Ghani said as he approached the priest.

"I know. I'm sure they'd love to have my head as a trophy." Father Xavier glanced up and rubbed the back of his neck, stretching in the process. Ghani sat down heavily beside him and sniffed. The scent of smoke hung in the still, cool early morning air.

"You know, this smell reminds me of when we were kids. People used the beach for a family barbecue and the next morning the air was laced with the smell of burnt wood and you had to watch out for fish bones in the sand."

"Yes, but God only knows what manner of carbon matter has contributed to this morning's bouquet."

It had been a long night and only moments before Ghani arrived, the priest had muttered a quiet prayer offering thanks that he was still alive. Staring out at the thick blackness of the night, his mind wandered off in search of an explanation. He watched a bat fluttering in the darkness, expertly avoiding obstacles, including him, and hunting down its insect prey. How perfect nature can be, endowing the bat with such skills – whilst mankind, in broad daylight with a huge brain, gets lost and stumbles.

"Are you trying to figure all this out, Father?" Ghani asked.

"Did you ever read any of those old Portuguese accounts of the Moluccan islands from hundreds of years ago?"

"Well, only the bits about Noli. I'm not good with words, as you know, Father."

"The Jesuits, God bless them, they faithfully recorded all the blood spilt in the name of God and spices. These chroniclers, roughly-hewn men from the worst parts of Europe, had an eye for the violence they encountered. They observed that the natives of these islands were constantly waging war and enjoyed it. I remember one detail in particular. Why? Because it seems to match precisely the inexplicable horrors I've witnessed these past few hours. The combatants never spared each other; they immediately cut off the other's head. I remember one specific phrase: 'And after having plundered their enemies, they do so to themselves.' Doesn't that tell you something about us?"

"You should get some rest," Ghani said, his own voice cracked with stress. Ghani had relatives and friends everywhere on Noli – he'd had no word from any of them. He couldn't bear to think of the friends he'd lost that night.

"There can be no peace or refuge from this hell, so even if I had a bed, how could I lie down?" the priest replied, staring at the sand that cooled his aching feet.

"Point taken. I'm on patrol myself," Ghani said, finding a new perch for himself on the fallen tree beside the priest.

"My guests are terrified, so I dug out this…" With a theatrical flourish, Ghani produced a bulky pistol from the folds of his shirt. In the dim grey light of early dawn, the gun looked black and ominous. Father Xavier instantly recoiled and shot Ghani an angry look.

"You fool, shoot them and they'll fall upon you. Can't you see? It's a mad mob."

"Let them try," said Ghani, holding up the gun and squinting at an invisible adversary out to sea.

"What do you plan to do?" he asked the priest in a tone just short of contemptuous, "Pray?"

"Praying helps. Although I've prayed all night – mostly over the dead and dying."

The faces of all the dead people Father Xavier had seen the previous night swam before his eyes; it was hard to imagine their souls finding peace after such a violent end to their lives. "Remember our brothers and sisters who have gone to their rest in the hope of rising again; bring them and all the departed into the light of your presence…."

"What's that?" Ghani asked.

"A prayer."

"I suppose there were many."

"Many. Too many."

"Did you see…did you manage to reach the North Shore?"

Father Xavier knew what was on Ghani's mind; he had family all over the island.

"Too late, I'm afraid. The Christians have already hit back. We're all in it now."

The priest felt helpless in the face of so much concerted evil. Much as he always feared, and quite against the teachings of his calling, the circumstances of this tragedy exposed the limits of faith – any faith.

"You'll see people grasping for their religious identity like a life raft in a storm-tossed sea. What they don't see is that while clinging to faith may save their lives, their souls are lost."

"I don't understand," Ghani said, puzzled by the priest's provocative riddle.

"Simple. You can't hold on too much to values because then you lose sight of what makes us free."

After a while, Ghani sighed and said: "Well, you remember my proposal."

Father Xavier stared at Ghani for a moment, his mind desperately trying to review recent events before this calamity.

"Yes, I remember, vaguely," Father Xavier said. It was hard to recall what normal life was like before hell descended on the island so suddenly a few hours before.

"I meant it, you know," said Ghani, pocketing the gun and throwing his friend a watery look of sincerity. Yet Father Xavier felt awkwardly impotent in the situation; he had no gun and no plan – both of which his friend Ghani possessed.

"That's the problem with faith," he said, managing a weak

smile, "it comes without detailed instructions."

Just then, the first rays of dawn broke through the band of grey cloud that hung over the horizon like a thick blanket. Father Xavier raised his head at last and wondered at nature's audacity; sticking stubbornly to an unchanging routine in the face of so much evil. This was no day for the sun to rise. He stared at Ghani, desperately trying to muster a smile or some sign of faith and trust. Instead, he reached for his comb.

After a while, with the weak morning sun glancing off their stubbled and dirty faces, both men got up and returned to the hotel, just up the beach. Behind them, waves lapped at the shore, the rhythmical sound sending a comforting signal to the pair that nature's heart was still beating, even with the traumas wrought by mankind.

"You must eat, Father. You'll need some strength today," Ghani said, clasping the priest's bony shoulder.

"I can't, Ghani." The priest's voice was weak and sounded, at least to him, like the plaintive bleat of tethered goat that already knows its time is near. The threat seemed so real; would he see the day out? Or would his head end up on a pole, the gory trophy of some half-crazed Muslim militant?

"Can I offer you a room, then?" Ghani seemed genuinely concerned. Every bone, every sinew in Father Xavier's meagre body cried out for him to take the offer. He desperately needed sleep. Still swimming before his eyes, though, were the images from last night. Oh Noli, oh once happy Noli, Father Xavier thought, will you ever recover from such venal carnage? Inwardly, he was concerned about what to do next. All his training as a priest was based on a solid pillar of faith; his ministry depended on other people sharing in that faith and the promise of paradise to come. Yet he'd heard people on both sides of the killing this past night cite faith in the belief that what they did wasn't evil but devotional, in the name of their God.

"Only a few hours earlier we were planning a wedding," sighed Father Xavier just as they reached the hotel.

"A wedding that joined our faiths," Ghani replied.

"As it should be."

"Always."

"But no more, my friend." Father Xavier sighed. Overnight, Father Xavier had seen Christian boys scratch crosses on their foreheads so they wouldn't be mistaken for Muslims and give themselves names like Jesus and Gabriel. Their Muslim adversaries recited the Koran and collected the genitalia of the Christian dead.

"No," he sighed, "I can't imagine a wedding now."

For the bulk of ordinary people on Noli, superstition and magic filled the spiritual void between the formal rituals of the Christian and Muslim faiths. The average Christian went to church on Sunday, while the average Muslim attended Friday prayers; in between, they inhabited a world filled with spirits of place and their associated omens, whose origins predated the coming of either religion of the book. Just a week before the violence hit, a rumour swept the main market in Noli that the spirit of the dead child brought ashore by one of the refugees was stalking the island in the shape of a fire-breathing monitor lizard. It didn't help that a few days later, a large monitor was caught stalking chickens on the edge of the North Shore village.

"It was like this before, you know, when the army came looking for the communists. Once the violence erupted, people believed that carrying dismembered digits – noses, ears and even genitalia – protected them from bullets, spears, and arrows." Ghani rested his weary bulk on a stool that one of his staff had wedged against the hotel reception counter, since the hotel coffee shop was now overflowing with people. Someone had brought him a cup of milky tea to calm his nerves. Father Xavier paced the reception area. In his mind, he was preparing for the service he knew he must give for all the people taking refuge in the hotel. By the second day of the violence, their terror had intensified, expecting the mob to arrive at any time to finish them off. But where to begin? For Father Xavier, the challenge was to bridge the huge gap between the moral and the profane.

The people of Noli possessed few reference points in the modern world, apart from what pierced the static on their radio sets. Besides, the mundane spiritual dimensions the islanders grew up with served them pretty well. There was the old man whose goat foretold the violence – a prophecy disclosed in the colour and content of its vomit. Then there was old Mama Fatima. Distantly related to a long-lost princely line on the nearby island of Ternate, Fatima was the island's most well-known soothsayer. Eschewing goats and other forms of animal trickery, Mama Fatima claimed she was the reincarnation of a once-great warrior queen who had tricked and defeated a gullible Portuguese captain, briefly restoring Ternate's glory until the next year's galleons arrived from Goa. Mama Fatima's transformation could be witnessed every Tuesday after sundown in a little hut on stilts near the beach. Great things were expected of Mama Fatima, who smoked fat cheroots and wore a feathered headdress when she was in her trance. Supplicants, both Muslim and Christian, came to the door of her little house with a vast array of problems ranging from mundane domestic problems to matters of great psychological complexity. Although not given to believing in spirits, Ghani nevertheless paid Mama Fatima a modest yearly stipend, just to be on the safe side.

⁂

Only the faint smell of burning wood and gasoline reminded Adam that things were not as they should be on a peaceful Noli night. Around him, people were pretending to sleep, shivering with fear and excitement. Nearby, he heard a few of the militants discussing plans for the next day in hushed tones.

"The Christian scum will regroup and attack the mosque in the morning."

"Yes but we can stand our ground here, the walls are strong and we have the guns. Let them attack, I say."

"Brother Isa is right…"

"Shh. Who appointed him leader? What would *Ustad* Umar say?"

As Adam listened, he felt tears welling up and stinging his eyes and cheeks. Time to go, he thought; there is nothing but death here.

On the marble-floored porch in front of the mosque, a white-robed militant standing guard with an old shotgun challenged him. A young man with Javanese features, he clearly wasn't from the village and wore a fearful look; the look of a lost child, or someone who had just decided that this wasn't something he wanted to do. Adam motioned that he needed to use the bathroom. Once inside, he saw a window that was open and easy to climb through. Although it was dark, he paused for a moment, his back flat against the outer wall. Once he was sure everything was still, Adam scampered across a small open yard in Muslim territory to the scrub that skirted the village. With every step, he expected to be challenged, or worse, cut down by a bullet or spear. But now he confronted a new geography. The village was divided and from where he crouched panting in the scrub, he could see the Christian lines that he needed to cross in order to reach Alicia's house. Although the night was quiet, he sensed the presence of people, awake and watching, around him. There was no wind but a few leaves rustled. There was no moonlight, yet shadows stirred. Suddenly, a shot rang out and a voice screamed: "Bastards, we'll slit your throats and fry your testicles…." The only way to reach his lover's house was to skirt around the place using the tangled scrub of noli trees as cover.

On reaching the house, Adam stared up at the window and

noticed that it was broken, which made his heart leap. He thought the worst, of course. The Muslim mob must have taken the family and slaughtered them. Alicia? What would they have done to such a beauty? He had visions of her slashed and broken body, probably violated as well, lying around the corner in a pool of blood. In the distance, he could hear the muffled sound of sobbing. Was that Alicia's mother crying over her body? Tears welled up in his eyes and he clenched his fists to overcome a wave of nausea. Oh Alicia, such innocence and committed to join the faith out of love! Adam felt the anger in him well up and there and then he renounced his faith – all faiths, in fact. From now on, he would reject religion. After all, it was love that sustained him as he rode the swell and faced the dangers of the open sea. It was Alicia that brought him home safely each day – he was sure of that.

"Alicia."

There was no response. The house was dark and Adam heard only the rustling of some chickens kept at the back. In all this carnage, the chickens had been left untouched.

"Alicia," he called again as loud as he dared. He was standing directly beneath her bedroom window, gazing at which from across the village yard, Adam had imagined many a night of passion in the arms of his beloved Alicia; there was still no reply. A gecko croaked nearby, startling Adam. The night was hot and still, enveloping and dulling the senses as if nothing had happened.

What happened next startled him beyond belief. There was a rustle behind him and something tugged on his shoulder. Everything he had heard and seen over the past day or so made him expect an attack, so he quickly threw up his arms in defence, but it was only Alicia. Her face was dirty and streaked with tears; her dress, only a few hours earlier a neatly-pleated yellow cotton outfit, was torn and filthy. In her hand, she carried a small flashlight. They stared at one another for a moment, taking in the despair and tragedy of their predicament; their whole life had collapsed around them. Then they embraced.

"I thought they had come to get you," sobbed Alicia.

"The same. I saw the Muslim mob move towards your house," Adam replied through a mouthful of Alicia's sodden hair. She smelt of wood smoke and naked fear.

"Your parents?" Adam asked after a moment or two.

"Safe. They left for the hotel in a convoy. Yours?"

"Yes. They are all at the mosque. *Allhamdu' lillah*."

"Yes. Thank God." She looked up at him and saw that his eyes were filled with tears.

"Whose God, I wonder," Adam muttered.

They pulled apart and Alicia led him behind the house to a small grove of noli trees that offered some shelter. Then they embraced again and kissed, violently. There had been almost no opportunity for this kind of passion whilst courting on the steps of the headman's house in full view of the village. Now that they were free from scrutiny, there was urgency about the way they held each other. There was no time to explore the contours of each other's body, and their display of mutual affection was clumsy. It felt more like the primal embrace of a parent or sibling, rather than of a lover. Breaking away, Alicia pointed to a bag stuffed with things lying on the ground.

"Food. A few things just in case."

"Why? Where are we going?" Adam asked. Her prescience overwhelmed him. The first light of dawn was painting the side of Alicia's house with a dull grey hue. A cock crowed somewhere, oblivious to the renewed tragedy that the new day would bring. Otherwise the place was still, as still as might be expected at daybreak.

"We've got to leave. There is no place for us here now.

Everything is destroyed." Alicia spoke calmly; her voice had acquired an air of authority. All her energy was now focused on their survival. Adam knew he would obey even though it meant abandoning his family.

≈ ≈

Captain Widodo was on his knees, his mouth gagged with a strip of oily rag and his hands tied tight using a strip of inner tube. He wore a ghastly expression that suggested intense pain and sheer terror at the same time. A crowd of mostly boys surrounded him, whooping and chanting. They were Christians; enraged, bereaved, and blind drunk on palm toddy and desire for revenge. Some wore bandanas soaked in blood. One of them, clearly their leader, wore a crown fashioned of thorny noli branches. "Jesus the Redeemer," the slogan on his T-shirt declared. All of them came from the North Shore village.

"What shall we do with him?" asked one, waving a long knife.

"Kill him, of course. Filthy Muslim brute," said another who wore dark glasses and a checked shirt and looked like a circus harlequin. Stuffed into the right side pocket, as carelessly as a pen or spectacle case, was a human child's hand, its fingers gently curled. A boy, no older than twelve, was playing with the hapless policeman's pistol, spinning it around and around with exaggerated bravado, emulating the movies, then probing the fleshy recesses of Widodo's ear with the stubby barrel. Each time he did this, the policeman's fearful eyes swivelled wildly in their sockets, then squeezed shut. His bowels gave way and his clothes reeked of excrement. Nearby, lurking in the early morning shadows, the noodle stall owner, Gus, watched with suppressed horror as his former patron sweated his last minutes. For surely, Gus knew, Captain Widodo would die. He watched, distraught with fear and a hefty measure of guilt. For it was he who had suggested leaving the safety of Hotel Merdeka at first light and checking on the police station by way of the noodle stall. Selfishly, he craved the policeman's cover to check on his belongings. On their way, a Christian gang riding around in a pickup truck with a chipped plaster statue of the Virgin strapped to the radiator grille had stopped and apprehended them.

Gus wore a gold crucifix on a chain, but everyone knew Widodo was a Javanese cop. The terrified policeman quickly drew his gun and wounded one of the gang. But he was a terrible shot, so they pounced on him all the same, beating him almost senseless, then trussed him up like an animal bound for the spit.

"Oh, Gus, tell them," Widodo pleaded before he was gagged. "Tell them that I eat your fried rice with pork fat…please, tell them. I'm not really Muslim. I am Javanese. My wife is a Christian. Please, Gus, Please, I'm begging you." The fat policeman sweated profusely and the whites of his eyes shone with fear. His khaki pants were soaked in urine. But his fate was sealed. There was nothing the noodle seller from Manado could do, even if he had tried.

As a Christian, Gus felt compelled to take sides. But now, as he watched Widodo in the hands of this band of Christian thugs, he realised that there was no real difference between the gangs that roamed the island. Christians and Muslims had blood on their hands in equal measure. Only the dead were innocent. From outside the now heavily fortified mosque in town, Gus could hear the sound of chanting; inside men rocked back and forth in prayer, holding themselves as if to contain their rage. Nearby, Christians had gathered on the beach around a large bonfire, in which burned everything they could drag from the houses of their Muslim neighbours, dead or missing. The community that once slurped the noodle creations Gus made with all manner of meats and condiments was now divided along lines that appeared in each village separating Muslim from Christian. In some villages, one side had driven the other out. Gus trembled as he watched the policeman squeal with terror.

Father Xavier shook Cornelius Lahatula by the shoulder. The bureaucrat was hiding in one corner of the coffee shop, asleep with his head on the table beside the warm dregs of a beer, lost without any guidance.

"Come, Nels," Father Xavier ordered. "They have Widodo."

The bureaucrat woke with a start. His face, painted a pallid colour by the shock of all that was going on around him, looked like a wax death mask. The sole vestige of government authority on the island felt helpless and deeply ashamed. Without a phone, he could not call for help. The lines were cut soon after the church burned. There was a simple ship-to-shore radio set on his official boat lying offshore, but the feeble signal would never reach Ambon. Even then, he knew, they would tell him to standby for further orders. Waiting – the watchword of bureaucracy; waiting allowed the higher-ups to decide what was the safest way out of a problem. In normal circumstances, waiting allowed serious problems to dissipate before anybody could screw up trying to solve them. The people of Noli had always seemed content to wait; for a better school, for a new pier – even for streetlights. In his experience, people showed patience and a great deal of respect for authority, which is what so surprised Cornelius about the speedy breakdown of order after the church burning. No one came to his office with a plea to sort things out; there had been no seeking of advice. People just took matters into their own hands and the killing began. Experiencing this complete breakdown of order had destroyed him. There was nothing official about the man now; even his brass badge of office hung upside down from the lapel of his crumpled safari suit.

"Who has Widodo?" he asked, bleary-eyed, after a long uncomprehending pause.

"The Christian mob, I'm afraid – just outside the hotel."

"He's a goner, then," Cornelius said, averting his eyes. He made to scuttle back into his corner, where he thought he could sleep until the government sent relief in the form of a battalion of troops and a legion of bureaucrats.

"He will be if we do nothing," Father Xavier insisted, tugging at the terrified man's sleeve.

They were too late. Not five hundred metres beyond the hotel gate, Captain Widodo's headless corpse rose like an earth mound off the roadside. His head, pale and streaked with blood, lay on its side on a hemp sack in the back of the pickup as it raced towards Noli's stuccoed city mosque, not far from the burned-out church. Father Xavier, with a clearly panicked Cornelius in tow, found Gus retching in a nearby ditch. At Father Xavier's prompting, the three men eventually knelt and prayed.

⌣ ⌢

Just before first light, Adam and Alicia left the village, passing through the tall stands of razor-sharp grass that covered open land behind the village bordering the old noli garden. The grass cut Alicia's arms and tore Adam's shirt; it was as if something, perhaps the souls of their murdered friends and neighbours, was trying to hold them back. Further up the slope, the grass gave way to stands of noli. Hardly tended at all, for the nut fetched no price a tub of tuna could match, the trees were a mess of thorns and cobwebs. In some villages, the little trees were used to shade coffee and pepper. But here on the North Shore, the fishing was too good and the spice gardens were derelict and untended. The dense tangle of vegetation looked like a natural jungle and offered good cover as they escaped. The ground was soft underfoot, a springy mattress of rotting vegetation. Here and there, a fern caught a shaft of morning sunlight and gave off an incandescent glow of chlorophyll. The sweet smell of noli displaced the acrid fumes of human tragedy and soon they had put the village behind them. Once they judged it was safe, they circled around back down to the shore. Their plan was to wait out the day, sleeping mostly, then load the little boat Alicia had found with the provisions they had collected and head out to sea.

The beached vessel listed to one side close to the shoreline, but Adam thought he could fix that. The boat looked old and poorly maintained, but sturdy nonetheless. Adam was good with boats, and proud of his ability to wrestle a heavy fishing boat through the surf that pounded Noli's outer reefs.

"Will it do?" Alicia asked as they both peered at the boat from the thick undergrowth that skirted the shore. Adam had never seen the vessel before, a typical daytime fishing boat, about five metres in length with a rudimentary plywood cabin.

"Sure. With luck, I can rig up a single mast and a canvas sail. There should be oars on board, too. I've not seen a boat like this before. It must have come from one of the other islands." Adam tried to sound measured and confident. Actually, the open sea scared him because he had some knowledge of the wild forces of nature that waited out there beyond the surf. He was used to feeling the strong swell through his leg muscles, tensed to keep him steady as the little fishing boat he shared with friends rose and fell on the back of the waves. Then there was the wind that blew spray off the tops of the waves into his hair and made his eyes sting. These were good reasons to head for home and the safety of the reef, not away from it.

"Perhaps it brought refugees," Alicia suggested, remembering the group who had landed on the North Shore bringing the first eye-witness news of the trouble. "You remember their stories, their terrible grief-stricken faces. They were the ones who brought this plague of hatred; they were the messengers of death. We should have left then. Before they came, nothing like this ever happened on Noli." She shuddered and clutched Adam's strong forearm as she remembered the story about forced circumcisions. Then they embraced because there was no other refuge from their sorrow. It was past midday and the searing glare off the white sand on the beach in front of them was painful on the eyes. Nothing stirred, as if nothing had happened.

Adam resisted the idea at first. "Okay. The boat looks seaworthy, but where an earth are we going? The nearest island is about a day's sailing away, and for all we know there's trouble there, too. Isn't that what the refugees said? I don't think this is a solution."

"Perhaps we could go to Ambon? The police and army are there." Alicia said.

"No way. There's trouble there, as well. Where do you think all this came from? And besides, I should think of my family; they needed protecting."

"And what about me?" Alicia snapped back. "What will happen to me if the mob finds us together? Can't you see how hopeless things are? There can be no more quiet evenings on the headman's porch; our families are at war."

"Nonsense, we're in love, everyone knows that. We'll get married and live at home. Once you enter the faith, everything will be okay, you'll see."

"Easy for you to say, but have you seen what's going on around you?"

"Father will understand," Adam replied, weakly. No sooner had he said this than Adam knew he wasn't sure that he would. Right now, his family was cowering in the mosque, protected from Alicia's Christian relatives by a crazed mob. Right now, they would kill her, and he knew it. He recalled the scene at home that day he got back from fishing when all the men from the mosque were conferring with his father. It was shortly after the refugees had landed on the North Shore. His father did not understand then; and that was before there was blood on anybody's hands.

"Adam. You know that even if they spare us, we'll never be able to be together. We're doomed if we stay on the island. Can't you see that?" Adam looked away, staring into the dense green of the forest. The faces of his parents swam before his eyes; his father's kindly smile and his mother's deep, dark eyes. It was hard to leave. They had sent him away and he had come back; he was happy on Noli. But now Noli was destroyed. He realised that all he had left was his love for Alicia. Finally, he looked back at Alicia and said in a tender voice: "You're right, my love."

So they planned to escape, trying not to think about where they might escape to; anything was better than persecution, perhaps even death, on the island. The two lovers were driven by the probability that they had a better chance of survival on the open sea. They spent the rest of the day planning to provision the boat, which meant a trip back into the village. For this, they waited till dusk. Skirting the village in the long grass, the young couple passed the ransacked ruins of a neighbour's house on the perimeter. They shuddered to imagine the fate of their former neighbours, a Christian couple. The shrill shrieks of fear and agony still filled their ears from the day before. But necessity stiffened Alicia's resolve; she was fighting for her life now. Grabbing Adam's hand, she stepped gingerly over the scorched threshold. Inside, they managed to find most of the provisions they needed – some sheets, a few tins of food, dried fish, and chilli; things the crazed looters had overlooked. Adam went back to lug a large plastic jerry can of fresh water. There wasn't a sound from the village and not a soul to be seen. Overhead, a Noli pigeon cooed from its perch in the palm fronds. Noli, oh Noli, Alicia thought as she nestled against Adam's still heaving chest; when will we ever see you again?

꙳ ꙳

The new Muslim stronghold in the centre of Noli was focused on the town's main mosque where, on the morning after the violence had erupted, Sultan Tarmizi held court before a growing crowd of people angrily demanding that every Christian be slaughtered and their bodies flung in the sea. Bright morning sunlight streamed through the unshuttered windows of the mosque as Sultan Tarmizi, dressed in his finest sarong and wearing a fresh white turban, did his best to look wise and in command. Of course, he wasn't quite in command. Seated behind him, Umar, the militia leader, fiddled with a two-way radio and worked a tape machine that played Mullah Zainal tapes over and over to keep the crowd pleased. Throughout the long and bloody night, Muslims had shown up at the old whitewashed mosque – some to seek shelter, others to join the cause. It was a nervous, fearful assembly and everyone had their eyes on the unlikely pair who now assumed leadership of the Muslim community. There was no time for blame, no urge to explain, only a collective desire for decisive action. Every so often, Umar whispered in Tarmizi's fleshy ear.

From Umar's point of view, everything was going very well. In less than twenty-four hours, the island had been divided and the two religious communities were at war. Now all he needed to do was to throw the Christians in the sea and his mission was accomplished. His masters would be pleased. Umar knew that he'd earned his reward in paradise; he wanted to be sure of more immediate compensation in this world. If he and his new friends needed any more help, it came in the form of a bloodied bundle of burlap that came hurtling over the walls of the mosque and landed in the courtyard with a dull thud. A few of Umar's followers rushed out, thinking it was a bomb. When the assembled crowd inside saw Widodo's bloody head, a terrible cry went up. "It's time," Umar whispered to the sultan. "Hmm? Time?" he asked sleepily, "Time for what?" Umar fiddled with a button on his radio then spoke into the speaker: "We're moving out now."

"It's going to be a stinking hot day," Ghani observed, addressing no one in particular. Around him, exhausted refugees lay like beached fish, stranded in an alien environment and unable to move. Most of them wore dazed expressions and fanned themselves with whatever came to hand. The electricity supply was down and Ghani's tiny petrol-driven generator was only strong enough to power the light bulbs and keep the food from spoiling, which meant the ancient ceiling fans stood idle. A large air-conditioner – tilting precariously out of a window as if about to escape its mountings – gave up the ghost long ago. The air was still and hung with the smell of stale cigarette smoke and fear.

A few people gathered near the counter where bottles of boiled water were available and those who were not so dazed and immobilised by shock gathered to drink and escape the heat near the window.

"If only I could sit down with these people, these fanatics, I might be able to talk some sense into them," Ghani said as he dispensed water in a variety of chipped glasses and old chinaware.

"I'm sceptical, but there's no harm in trying, I suppose," offered Felix Ling. He had already resolved to leave Noli the next available opportunity and was past caring about the place. Things would never be the same, he reasoned. Sonia was inconsolable. She sat across the table from her husband, eyeing him malevolently. She was past sobbing; everything was this silly man's fault for not getting her off the island sooner. As surely as Noli's society crumbled around them, so did what was left of the marital bond between the Lings. Having given up on her husband, Sonia felt like a hermit crab in need of a new shell.

Father Xavier opened his eyes and stared out of the coffee shop window. Squinting in the bright morning light, he was surprised to see a cloudless sky and flat calm sea, as if, somehow, the elements should reflect the dark human tragedy unfolding on Noli. Coming inside at some point as dawn broke, he'd sat with his back against an upturned table that served to fence off some space for a sleeping family, and drifted in and out of a fitful sleep. From outside, he heard strange, primal sounds. There were angry commands, periodic moans and screams, and the whimpering of excited dogs. The eerie aural backdrop prompted him, in a semi-dream state, to imagine how things must have been for the first European settlers on the island. Huddled inside their crude stockade, staring into the jaws of death, he imagined how they must have gone nearly mad waiting for a relief ship that could be months or even years away. He saw the haunted looks on the rough faces of the settlers, stinking men; their clothes ragged and torn; their water rancid; their only food gnawed at by every imaginable vermin; and mouldy to boot. The air hung with the stench of confined, unhealthy humanity. Periodically, there would be fights, some resulting in deaths or a mortal wounding, after which the small band of ruffians would have recalled their faith in God.

Wandering like a participant through this historical tableau, it took a while for Father Xavier to realise that the vividness of his dream was derived from the surroundings in which he found himself. The people around him were terrified and the stench of their fear filled the room. Outside the hotel, there was death and destruction. There was no relief ship in prospect. Yet, unlike his ancient forbears, he wasn't blindly reassured by his beliefs. How the island had so easily reverted to this carnal state both perplexed and fascinated Father Xavier, who took it as another sign of man's imperfection and further gnawed at the moorings of his faith. He was roused from deep thought by the sound of his name.

"Good morning. What are you thinking, Father?" Ghani asked. In his hand, he held a glass of water, which he offered the priest. Father Xavier looked up at his friend and saw deep lines in his face, grey stubble, and great dark circles around his eyes. Staring at a mirror of his own weariness, the priest desperately wished he could do something. But all he could do was shake his head. He was too weak even to drink.

"The truth is, I have no idea what to do next," he said at last. "This is all beyond me now; I'm a priest, but I have no answers. How can I explain to these people that after everything that has happened in the last few hours, the world moves on – the sun rises and nature shines in all its glory." He waved weakly at the dazzling sunlight streaming through the verandah's windows, then pulled up his knees, folded his arms, and buried his head. He wished there was more he could say, but the words wouldn't come. Ghani touched him lightly on the shoulder and said:

"I won't let them destroy what we have, if it's the last thing I do."

From the dilapidated and now overcrowded coffee shop at Hotel Merdeka, Ghani had assumed responsibility for the refugees. If nothing else, he possessed a pistol. The old British-made Webley revolver occupied a prominent position in the hotel owner's bulging waistband, where it sat at a rakish angle pointing disconcertingly towards his groin. A part of the priest wanted to seize Ghani's revolver and rush screaming out of the hotel over to the mosque, where he knew the ringleaders were based. Would he shoot? Oddly, he was dying to be offered this choice; it motivated him so much that he felt exhaustion ebbing from his weary frame and almost leapt to his feet. Then reality hit, like a net full of stones landing in his lap. The only viable strategy was one that required resisting one's instincts and to fall back on ritual; saying mass was pretty much all he could do in these circumstances. Unlike the forces of nature, which follow predictable paths, man is capable of resisting and overcoming instinct. That, he realised, was what constitutes the essence of faith.

"I want to say mass," he said, lifting his head.

"Where?" Ghani asked.

"Out there, on the beach."

"You must be mad. You'll provoke an attack."

"Then where? The church is gone. Out there belongs to us, the people of Noli. We must reclaim the island from the dark forces of evil."

"Right here, then, in my hotel. Do it here. Make this place a house of God — it sure could use a little cleansing." Father Xavier smiled; not only was Ghani managing the situation well, he also found room for his sense of humour. Just then, there was a commotion at the entrance to the coffee shop and a short man wearing a blood-stained white coat burst in. It was Doctor Sudarpo from the polyclinic, what passed for the island's hospital.

"I take it this is all that passes for government here," the doctor said, addressing Ghani and casting a watery eye over the assembled crowd. Normally, Sudarpo possessed the self-assured manner and impatience typical of doctors: always certain of a situation and eager to move on to the next patient. He'd come to the island only the year before, part of a government healthcare programme. He'd come full of hopeful talk about smallpox inoculation, malaria eradication, and birth control. He'd come clutching rolls of colourful posters printed by the government, which promised all these things. "Two children are enough," he'd chirp in the freshly painted clinic, where the posters hung. He held up first two fingers, then a full five, mimicking the official birth control campaign that used simple sign language; two fingers for the number of children, the full five signifying enough. There were no condoms, though; nor was there any smallpox vaccine. And an old stock of malaria pills was green with mould. Soon the posters started to fade and curl as well.

Dr. Sudarpo's smooth brown Javanese face and prominent nose suggested good breeding and possibly an aristocratic background. His thick black hair, usually stylishly swept back, was uncombed. Very few people knew that, like the late Captain Widodo, Dr. Sudarpo's presence on Noli was the result of a monumental political transgression — in his case, the failure to offer a financial incentive to gain admittance as a resident at one of the major hospitals in Jakarta.

"Er, that's right, Doctor," said Ghani, hesitating at first.

"That's right," he added with more emphasis, one hand resting on rusty hilt of the aged pistol. "What are your needs?" Ghani asked, doing his best to project an air of authority.

"Needs?" Dr. Sudarpo bristled. He was unusually blunt and abrasive for a Javanese. "Needs, you ask. Well, since you ask, here…" The doctor made his way over to where Ghani sat. In his hand he clutched a sheath of papers. "Here is a list of the drugs needed to treat all the wounded," he explained, stabbing the air with the papers. Father Xavier roused himself and wandered over to the doctor to examine the list.

"Look, I have wounds that even the textbooks don't cover," the doctor continued. "Do you know what it's like to worry about whether you've stuffed a pile of guts in the right body? They don't carry labels. I've seen people walk in carrying their own limbs. It's medical mayhem out there and this place doesn't even have a hospital. These people need serious care." Sudarpo spoke as if somehow the critical situation made it more likely that help would arrive. Like the hapless Cornelius, he placed an inordinate amount of faith in the distant apparatus of government, a government that, just at this moment, had not the slightest inkling of the chaos on Noli.

Under normal circumstances, serious cases of illness warranted an evacuation flight to Ambon aboard a naval seaplane. The service was part of the military's much-trumpeted programme of "social responsibility." In fact, patients often found themselves asked to pay fees; the higher the fee paid, the faster the service. These were not normal circumstances, however.

"Excuse me, doctor." It was Sonia Ling. She approached the doctor with a bundle wrapped in brown paper in her hand. "I have some medicine here." Father Xavier gave her a smile, and she returned it, weakly. "Let me see," the doctor said brusquely. Sonia handed the doctor the bundle and gave Father Xavier another smile, and this time, it seemed to convey something. Father Xavier wasn't sure what.

"Aspirin and antacid tablets. You think we're treating the common cold out there?" Dr. Sudarpo snapped. He looked around at everyone with an exasperated glare.

"Just trying to help, Doctor." Sonia looked faint and, finding himself nearest her, Father Xavier put one hand under her arm to support her. Sonia gave him a grateful look, and something stirred the priest's feelings.

"Whatever, whatever. Look, can you spare some people to help out at the clinic? We have bodies to move, people to bury. The whole town is empty and I have cadavers stacked up like meat…" Dr. Sudarpo stopped and stared at the priest, his mouth open in mid-sentence. "I'm sorry, Father," he said. "Look, I'm a doctor. I deal in the reality of flesh and bone." Then, leaving the list of requests on the table in front of Ghani like a votive offering, the doctor mumbled something about having to return to his patients.

"I feel sorry for him," Father Xavier remarked as the doctor stalked out, his stained white coat flapping in his wake. "At least he's trying." What he meant was that he admired the doctor for upholding the dignity of his profession, which, he felt, was more than he could say for himself. Despite the faith these people had put in him, and the comfort they derived from his presence, Father Xavier still found it hard to imagine he was doing anything the slightest bit useful. He felt somehow naked without his vestments and the physical paraphernalia of faith – as if merely burning a candle and some incense would have made a difference.

෩ ෪

As soon as the doctor left, a large rock came flying through one of the coffee shop windows. The missile shattered the glass and made a noise like a large explosion. The crowd in the room gasped. Men embraced their wives, mothers hugged children, and the sobbing, which had subsided, started all over again. Another window broke. Then came the sounds of taunts and screams outside. A hotel worker rushed in, panic-stricken with news that a large mob had gathered outside and threatened the hotel. Evidently a Muslim mob, judging by the cries of "*Allahu Akbar!*" Father Xavier's heart sank. "We're trapped, Father. The only way out is by sea." It was Sonia. Now she clung to the priest for dear life. Her sharp nails dug into the sinewy flesh on his arm. He could smell her sweat and feel her heart beating. It was the closest he'd been to any woman in years and it made his heart race even more. Around him people sobbed and wailed. "Oh, dear God, we're doomed," screamed a woman from the back. The priest's own assessment was pretty much the same. Only a miracle could save them and, for all his faith, Father Xavier wasn't sure one would come along. Unconsciously, he pulled Sonia closer to him and, inwardly at least, prepared for the worst.

From outside came chants and calls for the Christians to come out. "Give yourselves up! It's no use." The terrified occupants did the only thing they thought they could, moving tables and chairs to fortify the windowed section leading onto the verandah. Men crossed themselves, women sobbed uncontrollably, and children screamed. Everyone smelt death close at hand and started acting on instinct. Some of the refugees made their way upstairs in search of places to hide, locking the flimsy doors and hiding under beds in the vain hope that they would not be found. "Get out!" screamed a desperate father at a lost and bewildered child who stumbled into a room where he and his family cowered. Downstairs in the coffee shop, Ghani peered at the mob outside over the top of a table pushed up against a window which overlooked the beach. Their leader, the wiry man with a wispy beard, led the mob in a chorus that called for Christians to be burnt. He wore a green camouflage jacket with the words "Front to Protect

Islam" emblazoned in orange across the back. It was Umar.

"It's hopeless," said Father Xavier, now at Ghani's side.

"No, it's not," Ghani shot back. "Remember our agreement?"

"You're a fool…" Father Xavier began saying, before another missile crashed through a window and interrupted their exchange.

"No, I must go out there and talk to them. Otherwise, we're all doomed."

"But they want blood – our blood," Father Xavier said, allowing a note of terror to creep into his voice. In spite of himself and what he stood for, the priest was angry and wished he had the means to defend all these poor, terrified people. At the seminary, they talked about the sword of God, but they never taught self-defence, only sacrifice. He scanned the room behind him looking for possible weapons and his mind raced to calculate some form of defence. He wasn't about to go down without a fight, but all he saw were the faces of terrified people preparing themselves to be slaughtered. Women crossed themselves, clutched their children, and looked helplessly at their men who wept and prayed, some of them on their knees. Without saying a word, Ghani pulled himself awkwardly to his feet. There was a sad look in his eyes, Father Xavier noticed, a look of resignation; the look of a condemned man who has exhausted all appeals and faces death calmly. The hotel owner scratched the back of his head then turned to the assembled islanders. Their anxious faces seemingly urged him to go outside to meet the mob – what choice did they have?

"You can do it, Ghani," Felix Ling said, "Go on. Please."

"Yes, and you have a gun," Sonia added, suddenly animated. The room was filled with encouraging murmurs of approval. A herd of animals corralled for slaughter, they saw only one escape route and they all headed for it. Nobody knew where it would lead. Ashamed of his resistance, Father Xavier backed down and nodded quietly in approval. Where was the strength of his faith when he needed it? he asked himself.

As a boy, Ghani enjoyed a spell as the school bully. Bulky, with piercing eyes and dark eyebrows that failed to divide at the nose, the young Ghani possessed a fearsome, somewhat Turkish countenance. In the schoolyard, he was respected, but only because he could give anybody a bloody nose. Ghani grew up considering himself a leader, but life dealt him a rather different card; trading fish with passing ships and stewardship of the most remote hotel in the Spice Islands. Even so, he was never one to stick his oar into very much besides making sure that a good deal of the day's catch passed under his protuberant Arab nose. Selfishness got in the way. "I don't know, I don't care. Do what you like," was the refrain he mostly commonly used when confronted with the petty squabbles of his large extended family, which included more than thirty cousins on the island. Now, as he turned to face the angry mob outside, he wondered how many among them were distant relatives; perhaps he could sway them.

The terrible events of the past few days had changed Ghani. In part, it was the hotel, where people had come to seek refuge. Their presence conferred a responsibility on him; it made him feel proud after a lifetime of underachievement. Then there was the love he felt for the island. The legacy of his long and colourful heritage was under attack; this simple idyllic island, with its deep blue waters and emerald green gardens – how could anyone think to destroy such beauty. Something rather deep inside him reacted to all this, something that recalled the simple idealism of his desert forefathers; a binary view of the world that calls for complacency in the face of what God provides, but demands action when it is violated. Ghani walked out of the coffee shop and reached behind the reception counter, rummaging for something. "What are you looking for?" Father Xavier asked. The priest stood right behind him. He found himself following the hotel owner, as one follows a natural leader. Ghani ignored the question and continued with his search. "They will storm the hotel and all will be lost, anyway," Father Xavier said. "Why not save your strength? We can try and fight them off."

"Nonsense. This will work. You'll see," said Ghani. He lifted his head from behind the counter, clutching in one hand a dusty and, by the looks of it, barely opened copy of the Holy Koran. "It belonged to my grandfather. He wasn't a pious man, but he believed."

Outside the hotel, the mob's anger was boiling over.

"Bring out the Christian filth!" they demanded, chanting in unison, as if directed.

"Cut off their heads – I want to play football," screamed a single, high-pitched voice. It sounded like a teenaged boy. All this to the general accompaniment of spears and machetes banged together. The crazed crowd originated from Noli's main mosque where, not twenty minutes ago, the bloodied head of Captain Widodo had been lobbed over the wall. Incensed by this act of murder and desecration, the Muslims moved out of the mosque in a body like a swarm of angry bees. Led by Umar and his band of thugs, they headed straight for Hotel Merdeka, which they knew had become a haven for the town's Christians.

When Ghani appeared, the crowd outside at first cheered. Perhaps they tasted victory in the shape of surrender.

"Give us the Christians," they chanted. The mob had gathered on the beach adjacent to the hotel – presumably, the ground they favoured to do the killing. Slowly and unsurely, Ghani advanced towards them, holding the Koran up above his head. His feet were leaden, his hands shook; his body was telling him that this wasn't such a good idea.

"I come asking for peace," he shouted towards the crowd. Then, for good measure, he threw in the basic Islamic call to prayer: "In the name of God the merciful…." The crowd was in no mood to be swayed by protestations of peace and piety, however. "Turn them over.

Give us the Christian scum," the crowd chanted back. They banged their weapons more loudly and got ready to advance. Ghani wasn't used to praying so fervently, but now he found himself pleading with God, any God – even the spirits of the island he so carefully propitiated through donations to Mama Fatima. Now they were advancing again and Ghani closed his eyes before deciding whether he should run or stand his ground. When he opened them again, he saw Umar, their leader, approaching. His face was grim and determined, but he held his arms open to embrace Ghani as a fellow Muslim. Now, thought Ghani; now is the time to act. He tucked the Koran under his shoulder and pulled his pistol. Umar stopped in his tracks. He wore a look of pained surprise.

"Leave. Leave right now," Ghani demanded. The pistol was either heavier than he thought, or naked fear had drained his strength. He waved the pistol as menacingly as he could in the direction of the mob and swallowed hard in a desperate bid to find his voice.

"You'll leave these people alone."

"Are you out of your mind?" Umar screamed, pointing to the mob at his back.

"I said, these people will not be harmed. They are my guests – doesn't the Holy Koran teach us to respect the rules of hospitality?"

Ghani stood his ground, even though a voice within that sounded very much like his shrew of a mother told him to call off this nonsense and either run for his life or agree to hand over every last Christian in his hotel.

"In the name of God, they will die," came back the defiant reply.

"Over my dead body, then," said Ghani. At this point, he wasn't sure where his courage was coming from. Then, raising the pistol and pointing the barrel skywards, he squeezed the trigger, screwed up his eyes and fired a single shot in the air. The loud report sent the mob scurrying for cover in a cloud of dust, but they were soon up on their feet again and advancing on Ghani.

"Again, I ask you: Are you mad?" Umar fearlessly stepped closer to Ghani and brought his face up close. With his large dark eyes locked on Ghani, Umar lowered his voice and said: "You know you'll be killed."

"Kill me, then. I don't have enough bullets to keep your mob at bay. But you'll have to kill me first."

"We're doing God's work here; we are waging a jihad. These people must go," Umar shrieked.

"Sure you are. Where does it say in the Holy Book that Christians must be killed?"

"They have killed us. Their gang killed a government representative – the policeman. For that alone, they must be punished. Don't you see what's been happening around you?"

"You started this thing. Now be gone, and we'll go back to living our lives."

Both men were sweating profusely and their faces drew very close. Ghani felt a tug at his arm as one of the younger hotheads leapt out from the crowd and tried to grab his gun. Quickly, Ghani squeezed off another shot in the air. He had worried that the bullets were old and would misfire in his face. The gun gave him the courage he needed to stand there and face the mob – at the very least, he thought, he could shoot himself before they hacked off his limbs.

The confrontation became a standoff. Ghani barred the way, pistol in hand and bareheaded under a hot sun. Umar stepped back then approached again with a different offer.

"Get out of my way, and I promise you the island will be yours," he said in a softer tone of voice. Ghani looked at Umar for a while, then sneered.

"The same offer you made to our sultan, no doubt."

"Ha! The old man is a fool. Leave him to his aging concubines.

You have everything to lose."

"I am an islander. I belong here and these are my people. I lose them and I lose everything."

Behind Umar, the mob chanted and waved their long knives and spears. From the back came a low ululating sound, a war cry of sorts. Ghani was losing his nerve and the gun, which weighed heavily on his arm, started to droop. But there was no going back now. Turn and he would be killed; say yes to the mob's demands and they would doubtless cut him down, too. The only option was to stand his ground.

Umar retired to confer with his followers. One of them spoke into a two-way radio. They argued as the sun beat down on them. Ghani trained the gun on Umar as best he could, though it was hard to concentrate because of the glare reflected off the white sand of the beach. Sweat dripped from his skull and burned his eyes; without a hand free to wipe them, he was forced to blink the perspiration away. After a while, to his utter surprise, Ghani's aggressive posture started to work. Some of the crowd had already settled down on their haunches in the shade of some nearby trees to await the outcome of the standoff. Slowly the mob's anger dissipated, and they began smoking and chatting among themselves. Finally, Umar walked back towards Ghani. He wore a smile meant, it seemed, only for him, because he was careful to keep his head down. The militant leader came up close, or as close as Ghani's unsteady outstretched arm would allow.

"Look, I have a proposal to make," Umar said. He looked nervous now, and his eyes blinked a lot.

"I'm listening." Ghani's voice was weak, but his eyes stayed fiercely trained on Umar, which unnerved him.

"What if we withdraw, but only on condition that the Christians leave the island. I can arrange a boat to pick them up."

"Where will they go? This is their home."

"Who cares – just away from here. Away from Noli."

"I'm a Muslim. I don't want that to happen."

"Do you want them all to die?"

Umar was angry again and Ghani knew that he needed to concede something. He alone, armed only with a rusting pistol and sweat-drenched copy of the Koran, wasn't going to be able to hold the mob off indefinitely. At some point, he reasoned, they would lose their patience and rush him.

"You think they will be safe on a boat? What guarantees do I have that you and your men won't slaughter them all once they get beyond the reef?" Ghani played for time. Not for one moment did he believe the Christians would be allowed to escape unharmed.

"Fine. We can arrange for a military transport to come and pick them up," Umar replied, brandishing his walkie-talkie. Clumsy of him, thought Ghani, somewhat taken aback by the easy way he'd just alluded to support from the military. What hope can we have if the army is sponsoring these thugs!

"Ha! That's hardly a guarantee," Ghani snorted.

"Perhaps you would prefer to take your chances with us?"

Ghani stood there for a moment, not knowing how to handle the concession he'd been offered. Just a few metres in front of him, Umar's men waited, their rough faces squinting in the sunlight. They looked as if they could wait all day, like patient vultures waiting for a dying animal to give up the ghost.

The two of them stood there, face-to-face, pondering the next move. It was Ghani who broke the silence.

"Who are you? Where did you come from?" he asked.

"I was sent to cleanse this island; to rid the place of the infidel."

"Sent by whom?" Ghani asked, waving the pistol in Umar's direction.

"This is a holy war and only the righteous would understand that I and my followers are ready to lay down our lives in the name of

God." Umar spoke calmly, and the barest trace of a smile lingered on his dark face. He might have meant this to project a calmness of purpose, but to Ghani, it came across as the personification of evil.

"Nonsense," said Ghani. "You're being paid. You and your gang are nothing but mercenaries; it's written all over you – down to that silly name you give yourselves. You're being used. That's how our leaders play politics; they use people like you to create chaos so they can justify seising power. Don't you see that?" Umar's nostrils flared and he looked at the gun, as if wondering whether it was worth the risk. Instead, he shrugged and walked back over to his followers. After a few paces, Umar turned and shouted so that everyone could hear.

"You have only a few days, maybe a week, before the boat comes to take them away. Till then, no one is to leave the hotel. No one – is that clear?"

Then it was over. After twenty minutes or so, much to the relief of everyone huddled in the hotel, the mob beat a reluctant retreat. For a long while afterwards, Ghani just stood there, the gun in his hand, not quite believing that the mob had gone. When he finally lowered the gun and relieved his aching arm, he stood a while longer, allowing the tears that had welled up inside him to pour forth. Slowly, he turned towards the hotel. He was still crying when he fell into the arms of Father Xavier, the gun falling from his hands, but still clutching the holy book under his arm. The priest found himself crying too as he stared across the dusty square, now emptied of life save for a few of the island's dogs, which lay sprawled and satiated in the sunlight.

PART TWO

The next day being Sunday, Father Xavier said mass. Two tables placed together against the bar at the back of the coffee shop served as the altar, a soiled yellow tablecloth as the altar cloth. Somebody dug out a small plaster statue of the Virgin. A plateful of stale bread rolls and a dusty old bottle of Portuguese rosé from a shelf behind the bar were all that could be found for the Eucharist. Father Xavier, without his vestments, brought out the gold crucifix that usually nestled underneath his shirt. Sonia Ling surprised everyone by helping with the preparations.

"Father, will you pray for a ship to come?" she asked, searching the priest's face with eyes stained red from sobbing and lack of sleep. Although a Buddhist, Sonia believed that all religions offered a spiritual shopping service: order what you want and pay later.

"Have faith, we will all be saved," Father Xavier said soothingly, but somehow without conviction. There was scant evidence that faith had saved too many people from the hatred that stalked the island like a sudden plague. There was hope, desperate hope for some kind of rescue effort; but little faith in the earthly forces that needed to be marshalled. He felt rather like a doctor prescribing an aspirin for some unknown and possibly fatal malady. And there were alternative remedies on offer. Not far away, in the ramshackle house on stilts by the beach that served as Mama Fatima's grotto, a large crowd had gathered to implore the restless spirit she invoked for peace and calm. Most of the supplicants were terrified villagers afraid of what may happen if the violence continued. Some were freshly initiated in terror and murder; they came to enhance their vigour and seek immunity from physical injury, something the church no longer offered to crusading warriors of faith.

Ghani emerged from his room on the first floor of the hotel and watched the preparations discreetly from the lobby entrance to the coffee shop. His face was creased and his eyes were red from lack of sleep. He no longer wore the pistol in his belt. Father Xavier made a point of embracing his friend, and Ghani gently asked if he might attend the mass.

"Only as a spectator, you understand," Ghani added with a wink.

Father Xavier eyed the hotel owner, now a local hero, and searched for any outward sign that could explain his actions. But he saw nothing that marked this man apart from others – wasn't it the same with old Yaakob, who had saved all those men in the floundering fishing boat years ago? Ghani reached with one hairy arm and scratched the back of his shoulder, yawning at the same time. Father Xavier concluded that all men are capable of heroic deeds – even the greedy and imbecilic. It's a thought that should have reinforced his faith, but did not. Then he said:

"We're all spectators, my friend. I have no control over what we're witnessing." Ghani felt the urge to ask: What? Your church has no answers? But instead, he fell silent and gestured to the priest to continue with his work.

Inside the coffee shop, people gathered for mass. They moved with more purpose because of their familiarity with the ritual. The room was filled with people coping with tragedy. There was an air of bleak despondency, which made them forget the reason for their despair. There were mothers who had lost children, men who had lost wives, and a number of children who had lost both parents. Attending mass offered these people something to do other than stare out to sea waiting in vain for a boat to reach the island and take them away before the mob returned to slaughter them. For many, the mass offered an interlude of normality on a mundane, earthly level. Others sought supernatural intervention. Somebody produced a portable tape recorder and started playing some badly recorded church music. No one seemed to notice the incongruity of Christmas carols: "O Come All Ye Faithful. Joyful and Triumphant…"

"Father, will you preach today?" Ghani asked as he surveyed the preparations.

"If the words come," Father Xavier replied, giving his friend a weak smile. Ghani reached for the priest's shoulder and squeezed it. "They will," Ghani said tenderly. Father Xavier tensed under the burly merchant's friendly grip. He had resisted calibrating Ghani's heroic action against his own feelings of inadequacy, but the urge was there and it was hard to suppress.

"Whatever I say will not match what you did for us yesterday. All I can do is pray for divine guidance and protection, and the word of God isn't so easily translated into action. Still, it's my job to look after all these people." He turned and looked at the congregation gathering in the coffee shop; an elderly lady clutching a rosary looked at him and smiled. He smiled back sweetly, but inside he was in pain.

"My God, I feel so weak and useless," said Father Xavier. He moved away from Ghani and leant over the reception counter. He felt tears coming, so he hid his face from Ghani, embarrassed by this display of emotion. "What can I really do for these people? Ask them to sing to the glory of Christ the Redeemer and hope the power of their voices will drown out their pain? Yes I could, and I probably will. The people of Noli sing well. What else?" Ghani moved towards the priest, who looked pale and drawn. "You know?" Father Xavier continued. He spoke slowly and quietly. "The church has prayers for the dead; we say that the sadness of death gives way to the bright promise of immortality

– just like the promise of paradise for you Muslims. It's the same; a reward for life lived in the way of the Lord. Yet there's nothing for the death of children: their passing is too awful for us to contemplate. Their lives are cut short in this world, only to enter the next for all eternity in innocence…." The priest's hand came smashing down on the counter. They both stood for a while in silence, reflecting on this profound flaw in their respective faiths. After a while, Ghani said: "I think I may have managed to close the wound. It's up to you now to begin the healing." Then he pushed the priest gently towards the coffee shop and makeshift church. "Now go, Father. The people need you."

The congregation was large, so large, in fact, that many worshippers were forced to sit in the sweltering heat under a tattered awning lowered over the terrace. Overcoming their fears, people came with a profound desire for spiritual comfort, their souls wrung dry by primeval brutality. They came with pale, drawn faces clutching rosary beads and bottles of water for benediction. "So much needs cleansing, Father," said Sonia, who was at the priest's side as he greeted them; "one bottle seems hardly enough." Father Xavier turned and looked at Sonia. Her face was lined with worry and she had abandoned all pretence at hiding her age. Hair that was once carefully coiffed now fell straight from her scalp in greasy strands. Yet there was a confident radiance about her that attracted the priest. Faced with adversity and the need to survive, Sonia Ling had forged a new character which radiated compassion. She seemed to have found a new purpose and that was to find solace in faith. In another situation, Father Xavier would have anticipated a new member of his flock. He smiled and looked into her dark eyes where he saw something unfamiliar and disturbing that stirred him. Hurriedly, he resumed his greetings, focusing instead on the eyes of his parishioners, where he saw deep sadness as well as a longing for an answer why.

People quietly found places and settled down. There was a lot of fuss over chairs and other places to sit. It looked like an orderly rush to the lifeboats; if people were missing, it wasn't noticed. One couple fussed over a child they hadn't seen in a while. "And your parents? How are they?" The child fell silent and buried herself in the folds of an aunt's dress. "Gone away" was all her aunt said, looking away. Some people embraced quietly, allowing tears to flow, but many in the large congregation avoided eye contact and only shook hands briefly, as if fearful of contagion. To Father Xavier, it seemed as if they were people who had never met before. As he clasped and embraced members of his own church or people that he knew, he felt their limbs stiffen, a resistance to compassion that puzzled him. Was it simply that the horror of what had happened was unbelievable and beyond contemplation? Or was there blood on their hands? A few days ago all that worried the priest was a hole in the altar cloth; today the fabric that held together this community was in shreds.

Aside from the comforting ritual of the mass itself, people came with a more tangible purpose; they came in support of something more earthly that gave hope for the future. News of Ghani's brave, if reckless, act of repelling the fanatical mob had swept the entire island and there was deep gratitude felt towards him for helping to tear down the newly-erected barricade separating the two religions. A Muslim saviour of Christian lives; Ghani, the island's rogue male and canniest businessman, was now its undisputed hero. Where he was feared or ridiculed before, now there was genuine affection for the former schoolyard bully. People came to thank Ghani as much as they did to find God, a distinction that didn't evade the priest and added to the burden of his doubts about himself. Their gratitude was expressed in unspoken ways, with respectful stares and bowing gestures, warm handshakes and a few long embraces. All the same, it struck Father Xavier that this was a good day for a new beginning: a brief morning rain shower had cleared the dust of the past few days and left the trees sparkling as if covered in varnish.

Ever the perfectionist, Father Xavier worried that the service would be awkward and disjointed in this unfamiliar place. The make-shift altar, plastic flowers, and tinny Christmas carols playing on the tape player seemed to cheapen the setting. How much the rituals of the church relied on the grand formality of a physical place, he thought; confound the Holy Spirit for being so invisible!

"We're ready, Father," Sonia Ling announced sonorously.

"Give me a moment, please, Sonia," Father Xavier replied curtly. The kitchen behind the bar served as a makeshift vestry where he sought refuge to collect his thoughts among dishes and pans redolent of nicer things in life, not the tragedy before him.

Deep in contemplation, Father Xavier kneaded his knuckles and stared at a battered wok hanging on the wall, stained black by the grease of ages. The faint smell of coconut oil triggered a flood of fond memories and broke his concentration. He recalled the simple things his childhood stood for: a hot sun, a sparkling sea, and fish baked in banana leaves on a beach bonfire at night under a rising moon, pale as a sago biscuit. The idyllic island life, where tragedy was defined by a sudden bad squall catching the fishing boats by surprise beyond the reef and the odd one going missing; where disputes over dislodged dignity were discreetly dissolved on verandahs over tea and cakes; and where the only blood spilt was in a childhood tumble was no more. Father Xavier perspired copiously beneath his shirt, a discomfort he longed to relieve by plunging headlong into the nearby surf – or into a good cold bottle of beer. How could this violence have happened here? How, he asked, when we are so blessed with such uncomplicated beauty and abundance? He took out the comb and soothed his troubled scalp one last time before emerging to face the congregation.

A sea of faces gazed at him expectantly. The sadness of the moment brought another lump to his throat and for a minute or two, he lost the ability to speak as he fought the urge to cover his face and weep. Then he began: "Father in heaven, we have all sinned."

Throughout the mass, people sat mostly in silence, now and then muttering responses to the liturgy through half-parted lips like a half-forgotten song. There was an uncomfortable, embarrassed air about the makeshift church, as if people had come to the wrong place. Nolians were generally good churchgoers. Church was the focus of social life beyond the boundaries of the village, an opportunity to meet, to gossip, and, of course, for the young, a chance to flirt. On bright Sunday mornings after mass, Javanese hawkers lined up outside with sticks of grilled meat dipped in sticky sweet soy sauce and steaming bowls of broth at the ready while old Maria the blind organist pumped the old Dutch harmonium for all it was worth. Even funerals were rarely sombre occasions. Everyone gathered after the service to swap cheerful stories and play cards. This time, things were different. There was a lot of dry hollow coughing and shuffling of feet. The heat was stifling, yet no one got up to leave. They waited, bathed in sweat bitter as vinegar; they waited to be scolded in the eyes of God.

With his back to the congregation, Father Xavier prepared the Eucharist on the stained bar counter, the stale bread crumbling in his shaking hands. "Remember, Lord, those who have died," he cried as he raised the chipped vase that served as the chalice. "May these and all who sleep in Christ, find in your presence light, happiness, and peace." From behind, the priest heard only a thin murmured response and a lot of faint sobbing. The wine was bitter and had long ago turned to vinegar – though it seemed appropriate that the Blood of Christ tasted so bitter on this occasion. "This is the cup of my blood, the blood of the everlasting covenant. It will be shed for you and for all, so that sins may be forgiven," Father Xavier said through trembling lips. Then, one by one in a quiet, shuffling line, they came, approaching the priest with eyes downcast.

Father Xavier turned for one last time to face the crude altar with his eyes clasped shut. On any normal Sunday, he executed the ritual almost unconsciously. But today was different. Each step of the way seemed to him as fresh and challenging as if he was still a novice. All the teaching and Bible study, months of lonely contemplation, nothing had prepared Father Xavier for this supremely challenging moment. Finally, he turned back to face the congregation. "Brothers and sisters," he began.

His voice trembled and he felt it must have come across as a tentative opening. What was he to say? How do you wash out the indelible stains of murder with the spoken word? Perhaps a sign would help. Now more than ever, he needed some tangible sign of the higher being he'd sworn to serve. His upbringing on Noli taught him to trust in nature; his training as a priest was grounded in assumptions about the supernatural. Outside, he heard the sound of the waves gently breaking on the beach and felt a soft breeze waft in through the open windows of the coffee shop. Just then, the wind stirred some of the refuse of the past two nights scattered on the floor at the feet of the congregation. Somewhere upstairs a door slammed shut. For just a moment he felt he was being watched by a higher being and this was His sign. All right, good enough, he thought.

"We have peered into the heart of evil these past few days and found a lot of us living there," he said keeping his voice low. "Please don't think that this calamity was unavoidable. None of us, not one, was incapable of stopping this tragedy." There was a stir and a rustling of clothing as the congregation prepared itself for the priest's message. Someone coughed. They expected to be chastised but they also wanted guidance.

"God delivered the Israelites out of Egypt by parting the waves of the Red Sea; He saved a people who kept faith with the Lord and rained plagues on the idolaters. But which side would the Lord have taken here on Noli these past few days?" Father Xavier searched the room and spied Ghani near the back slumped in a chair, his chin resting heavily on hands clasped to his chest. Perhaps he wanted to keep a low profile, the priest wondered. In fact, still exhausted from his feat the previous day, he was asleep. "I ask you all: where was your faith? Where was your faith in the Lord?"

Father Xavier's hands shook and his mind raced. Normally, his sermons were quiet, low-key affairs. They dwelt on mundane themes of family life and the natural world encased by the reef out there. Neither profound, nor too far removed from the sun-drenched and idyllic environment beyond the bleached wooden swing doors of the old church. Absolution usually covered petty transgressions like a purloined boat hook or badly controlled temper. But these were altogether different times, calling for something more profound and stirring. The gust of wind prompted him to recall a verse from the Old Testament, which seemed fitting for the moment. "When the Almighty came from Mount Sinai, the nations were trampled, the earth shook with every footfall, and leaves on the trees quivered at God's passing, and the mountain trembled at the advent of God. My fellow Nolians, do not take the chaos around you to mean that God has abandoned us. Far from it: He has sent a sign to remind us that we need to be vigilant in our ways – we cannot expect the way to Grace to be always so easy to find. It takes discipline and courage…." As he stared into the faces arrayed before him, he saw fear and a great deal of uncertainty.

"I know that many of you question the need for rules, that we have all felt secure because of the very intimacy of our surroundings. Who would steal a neighbour's net when you depended on the neighbour to help you cast it? What was the point of stealing a friend's shirt when he would see it on your back the next day? Our island's tiny size and bountiful natural state has lulled us into a false sense of immunity from sin, and insulation from evil. Our mistake was to think that because of all the natural beauty that surrounds us that somehow as humans we are different, made as perfect as our surroundings. But we're not. We all have our weaknesses; we are not – none of us – pure in the sight of God until our sins are forgiven, which is why we must confirm each and every day our faith in the Lord. Surely, we might have remembered our faith in these past few dark hours. None of us can escape blame. Not one!"

The priest trained his eyes on everyone in the room, allowing his words, which ended on a crescendo, to sink in. But clearly, they weren't strong enough. All the faces in front of him were blank. They wore the masks of his earlier dream. Was that a gleam in your eye, Mrs. Gordon, or a glimmer of the hatred that burns in your breast? He noticed that Alicia wasn't sitting next to her mother the way she normally did in church and breathed a prayer for her safety before pressing on. "We are a violent people. It's in our nature. Don't be fooled by the beauty and perfection of our surroundings. We have fooled ourselves into thinking our society is perfect, that we live in harmony – and yet I have seen people killing and maiming with ha- tred in their eyes. Some of you are here today. Yes you are. Don't try and hide yourselves." His eye fell on the former choirboy who he'd caught stealing rings from a woman's corpse. The boy had washed his face and combed his hair, but he had a faraway look in his eyes. "Brothers and sisters, we have become blind to our own nature. We are a warmongering people. We like to fight and kill to take revenge. It is stamped on our history, written in the wind that blows across our island." This time, a few mouths gaped open.

The room was silent, but Father Xavier knew the art of preach- ing well enough to know that if a point is worth making, it's worth driving home with repetition. "There is surely much work that needs to be done now to rebuild what we had – and it must begin in our own hearts. For it is not enough this time for us simply to repent. We cannot rely this time on the mechanisms and rituals of the church alone." Here, Father Xavier trod on dangerous ground, but anger rose in him now and he couldn't stop. "What we built here in Noli was, yes, almost a mirror image of the paradise that awaits us all – we had something unique and ideal. We built a fragrant and bountiful paradise, then tore it down with our own bare hands! Yes, we did it all on our own when we allowed the agents of evil to find company here. Good people of Noli! We must all resolve here today to turn back the tide of evil and restore what is good."

There was an audible gasp from somewhere in the congregation. Someone started sobbing and blew his nose. Lacking anything to wipe away the sweat from his own brow, Father Xavier used a sleeve. He paused and looked over towards Ghani, who was still asleep, and dropped his voice again. "And then finally, the Lord found someone to trust, someone to bring us all back to sanity. Who is our saviour? Who is he? No Christian, my friends. Oh no, not in the formal sense." Father Xavier took a few steps away from the counter that served as his altar. He walked among the congregation, over towards where Ghani sat, slumped in the chair. Necks craned to follow his progress. Gently, the priest shook the older man, who awoke with a grunt and a start.

"This man, brothers and sisters. This man, whom I doubted all these years because he came from another faith and followed a dubious path, has now shown himself to be our guardian. Oh, how I doubted him, and may the Lord forgive me for doing so. Yet today, he stands before us, our friend and saviour."

There was a burst of applause, and suddenly everyone was on their feet, staring at an astonished and blinking Ghani. Father Xavier embraced him and as he did so, his head buried in the man's shoulder, he let go. There was no need to say anything more and he allowed the tears to come, sobbing into the ample shoulders of his friend. Ghani smiled modestly and patted the priest's back. Father Xavier was happy now, for he had found his real feelings and expressed them. In the process, the bonds of his calling loosened and he would never look at himself, or what he represented, in quite the same way.

Two days passed and Umar and his followers had not shown up to make good on their threat to evict the refugees from Hotel Merdeka and throw them in the sea. There was still little sign of normality, though. The square remained silent and empty, save for the scampering of island dogs and plump pecking pigeons. The little town was divided; the Christians huddled in the hotel, and Muslims camped at the mosque. Those who had locking doors stayed inside. From behind their makeshift barricades, Christian and Muslim hotheads shouted taunts and looked for opportunities to kill or maim. The militias spawned on both sides of the religious divide gave pubescent boys the chance to strut out their barely-formed manhood; they bossed around their elders, emboldened by crude weapons and liberal doses of palm toddy. The loudspeaker system atop the spindly minaret in Noli's main mosque broadcast Mullah Zainal's sermons and was intermittently given over to a torrent of abuse aimed at the Christians cowering in the hotel. "Give up. Surrender. Spare your women and children. We only ask that you join our faith – or face death," ran the repetitive refrain.

The beleaguered Christians occupied every nook and cranny of Hotel Merdeka and breathed new life into the place. Dusty corners were transformed into makeshift living quarters for whole families, evicting long-residing lizards and cockroaches. Voices filled once empty corridors and the stench of human excrement testified to a major plumbing crisis. "Renovation is long overdue," noted Ghani, as he supervised some emergency work in one of the first floor bathrooms. "Honestly, we'd never have thought of staying here, but who knows, if we survive this, we could meet up for reunions," quipped a garrulous fisherman who had escaped from the North Shore. Supplies of everything were running low, but once it was evident that Umar and his mob were not sticking to their deadline, the atmosphere relaxed somewhat, and there was even a move to open up the coffee shop windows onto the terrace that ran along the seafront and let in some air. Ghani promised to make everyone a round of Noli cocktails. Much as the old sultan had predicted, Hotel Merdeka had become the island's de facto seat of government, with Ghani as its informal leader. Father Xavier's makeshift mass amounted to a consecration of sorts, and the hotel became a centre for spiritual relief, which was Father Xavier's department.

Meanwhile, no one seemed to know what had become of Umar and his so-called defenders of the Muslim faith. They had melted away after the confrontation with Ghani outside the hotel. Diligent investigators, if there were any, would have quickly discovered Umar hiding out at the tumbledown residence of Sultan Tarmizi, where he burned with anger and plotted his revenge.

"This priest has turned the heart of a good Muslim against his faith," Umar fumed as he paced the dim and dusty room that the sultan used as his salon. "He was there the whole time, goading the Christian scum and blackmailing the hotel owner into sheltering them!" Sultan Tarmizi nodded in agreement, but tried to steer Umar in another direction.

"The priest is harmless – it is Ghani who you must deal with. He wants to take over the whole island, and when he does, you won't find things so easy for your people around here."

"Hah! Takeover? Takeover? There was almost no control over this island when that sorry excuse for a policeman was alive…."

"…may Allah bless his soul."

"Amen to that…," Umar and his followers mumbled.

Sultan Tarmizi felt compelled to remember poor Captain Widodo to his maker, and hoped this would divert Umar's attention long enough for him to drive home his point about Ghani.

"Don't you see? Ghani is respected by everyone, so you'll find it difficult to influence the people without his backing."

"Nonsense, don't the people already follow me? Look at the

army we've assembled – an army of God! Its members are devoted to carrying out God's will and dying if necessary. No. We must hunt down the priest because he has an influence over Muslims that diverts them from the true path and he must be crushed. I have friends who can help us. Trust me. They will come soon."

The sultan trembled when he heard this. What friends could he be talking about? From what he heard on the radio, he knew that these were tense times, even at the centre of everything in the capital, where it was reported that competing political factions harnessed ethnic and religious chauvinism to advance their causes. In the absence of real democracy, factions fought wars using unwashed proxies. The liberals writing newspaper columns and attending seminars spoke of freedom and representation, but the elite preferred provocation to process to achieve political ends. Probing the matter a little deeper, the sultan would have discovered that Umar was not acting alone: as Ghani correctly surmised, he was no autonomous, self-made militant. Like others employed by the faction in question, Umar and his Front to Protect Islam was a creation of backroom scheming in some Jakarta salon. He was paid for with money tapped from a slush fund and delivered to a hotel room stuffed in instant noodle packets.

Not the slightest whiff of this despicable political alchemy made Ghani any less presentable. Somehow, news of Ghani's act of heroism had spread beyond the shores of Noli. A small group of Christians managed to limp into Ambon on a crippled and overcrowded fishing boat and told stories about how they were saved from the angry mob by a Muslim fish merchant and innkeeper brandishing a rusty pistol. A local newspaper ran the story, which in turn got picked up by the national news agency. In difficult times, with the nation's integrity threatened by dark and anarchic forces, such stories offered rare good news for the masses. Unknown to him, Ghani's moment of bravery in the face of the mob brought Noli into the spotlight, if only momentarily, prompting the authorities to wonder whether there was any semblance of government authority on the tiny speck of an island.

Elsewhere on the island, tensions still ran high; villages remained segregated, and there were sporadic acts of violence. Dr. Sudarpo reported that forty-seven corpses had been delivered to his clinic in the days after the violence flared up. The day after Father Xavier's sermon, the Muslim mob managed to trap three wandering Christian youths near the mosque and wreaked a terrible revenge for the death of Captain Widodo. Their heads were flung into the courtyard of Hotel Merdeka, prompting a renewed wave of panic. On a visit he managed to make to the clinic, Father Xavier found Dr. Sudarpo swamped with anxious family members seeking news of missing relatives.

"Too many corpses, not enough heads," he informed the priest on his way through the crowded surgery with its posters of happy smiling mothers and healthy newborn babies from another era. "I've never seen so many ways to carve up a body," he added with his head tilted so that he could see over his spectacles. "Quite creative. Where do you suppose such savagery comes from, hmm?"

Father Xavier was at a loss to explain the violence, but was determined to track down its causes.

"It's not over, is it, Father?" muttered Felix Ling over tea that same afternoon. "Felix, you could really help to resolve this tragedy," suggested Father Xavier.

"Oh? How might that be?" the Chinese shopkeeper asked sullenly. He'd watched his wife busy herself with church duties and wondered what she was hoping to get out of it. Perhaps the priest was fishing for souls again. Felix was sure that his wife would be just as shrill and hectoring a Christian as she was as a Buddhist.

"After all," Father Xavier continued, "you've always offered your help during our festivals…"

"You plan a festival now? After everything that's just happened?" Felix interrupted with astonishment. These priests, he thought to himself, they could sell anything with all their optimism. Just as well that they're not in business.

"No, my friend. I mean you have always helped the community."

"Sure, Father, well…" Felix pondered for a moment. "Of course, I'm behind Sonia, all the way. I asked her to help you, you know. She had to be pushed. Hasn't she been helpful?" Felix glanced nervously around the room in search of his wife. As on most days now, the coffee shop was filled with listless Nolians, staring at their hands or out to sea with deep sadness and a sense of despair written all over their faces. The place had the look and feel of a mental ward. And except for Father Xavier's daily little chat with each family, no one dispensed any therapy.

"That's not what I mean," the priest continued.

Felix removed his spectacles and began polishing the lenses on what was left of a tablecloth. One of the lenses had cracked in the hasty move to the hotel on the first day of violence and it bothered him, so he was always cleaning them.

"What do you mean, then?" Experience taught Felix that when people asked him for favours, it was usually about money. He felt vulnerable; everyone knew how closely he guarded the worn leather valise at his feet these past few days.

"It's not about money," said Father Xavier, reading the Chinaman's mind. "It's about that outboard motor a certain fisherman man asked you to repair."

"What?"

"I was thinking. The man stormed off and later fooled around with one of the girls on the beach, right?"

"That's what I heard, yes; because he couldn't go fishing that day. Probably got drunk."

"And you're sure you agreed to fix his motor for free."

"Ah yes, because it was still under warranty– except I was going to charge him for the cost of the part." Felix couldn't help himself, and added: "Business is business, after all." He had not the slightest idea where this was going. The priest gnawed away at his knuckle and wore a deeply pensive look, which is why so many people believed he knew everything and had all the answers, when in reality he did not. Cornelius Lahatula wafted past their table in a daze. The poor man had turned quite odd and took to muttering aloud about duty and discipline. Like Gus the noodle seller, who also witnessed Captain Widodo's brutal decapitation and had not spoken a word since, Cornelius wore a perpetual expression of surprise, like someone who has been woken up suddenly from a deep sleep, hair all tousled. Father Xavier watched him for a while and then returned to the subject, fixing Felix with an intense stare.

"I want you to find this man."

"You what?"

"Yes, find him. He will come back for his motor, won't he?"

"Yes, but why? How can he help?" Felix sounded perplexed and was worried he was being drawn into something that his merchant's instinct told him wasn't good for business.

"I'll tell you when you find him. He must be found."

CHAPTER SIX

Adam cradled the lovely Alicia in his arms and watched the oncoming waves, a blue-black as dark as velvet, rise and fall towards the stern of the little fishing boat. For the three days they'd been at sea, the weather was generally fair, so it was with some concern that Adam noticed the swell grow in size and felt the spray come off the tops of the waves. Tasting the sea salt in his mouth reminded him that their supply of water was dangerously low; although when it rained, he could rig up a spare sail to catch the water. Adam checked the knotted painter holding the tiller in place and stared up at the sky. A high bank of clouds loomed on the horizon and the wind blew stronger in his face. The fading rays of the sun tinted the dark grey clouds a deep pink, for it was already early evening and in a few minutes the sky would darken. The clouds looked as solid as a range of mountains. There was a storm on the horizon.

Adam checked the compass that swung drunkenly in its gimbals from the edge of the cabin. By his reckoning, on this southwesterly heading, they should reach the Flores Sea and the outer islands of the Timor chain within a day or two. The problem was that even if he kept to this course, there was almost no chance of making landfall until after the storm overtook them. There was no reef to dash behind; no welcoming palm-fringed shore, the sand a dazzling white and the water turquoise against the grey bank of storm clouds. Oh Noli, Adam sighed; where shelter from the storm was only a few powerful oar strokes away, and then the warm feeling that gave him goose bumps as he enjoyed his mother's fish curry at home in the cool of a thundery squall. He missed home badly.

"Alicia, Alicia," Adam murmured gently in her ear.

Earlier, they'd made love. Sex was as much a voyage of discovery for them as the flight from Noli. At first, Alicia was hesitant; she'd underestimated the time it could take before they reached dry land. Morality, in her mind, was terrestrial and she did not want to feel ashamed when they came ashore. Alicia felt there was still a chance that they could salvage their marriage plans and all that this meant to them. Adam, ever the obedient lover, reluctantly sheathed his ardour. He distracted himself with what were, after all, more pressing priorities. The little boat needed constant attention because the poorly-rigged sail was inadequate and they were constantly drifting off their course. Eventually, as two nights became three, it was Alicia who relented, surrendering to him at last in the reflection of a blazing sunset the colour of pure copper.

Adam was sleeping with a red sarong pulled loosely over his loins after one of the frequent seawater baths they took to cool off in the close confines of the little boat. The cabin was cramped and stuffy, so they had taken out the rush mats that served as their bed and spread them on the open deck in front of the tiller. They would lay side by side, staring at the stars, trying to ignore their racing hearts and aching desire for one another. Alicia turned and stared for a while at Adam's heaving chest and fought for breath. What am I doing? she wondered. We may never see land again and perish. Something snapped, a lingering bond with her island-bred prudish sense of propriety, and she started stroking his taught belly with the tips of her fingers. She smiled as the tautness in her chest that had made it difficult to breathe disappeared. Adam stirred, his mouth opened, and he uttered a gentle murmur. She continued stroking, watching Adam's lips twitch; his eyes were still closed, but now a smile appeared. She felt encouraged, driven now by an urge to give pleasure to her lover; the movements of her hands, the areas she chose to stroke, she knew them instinctively and without having to explore or experiment. Before she could stop herself, the sarong was loosened and Adam's powerful hands had grabbed her arms, pressing her against his awakened gland. Alicia gasped as she looked up in search of Adam's face. He wore an expression she'd not seen on him before, one that lent his smooth features a wild look, nostrils flaring, eyes dilated. Their mouths met in a bruising kiss that brought their teeth together and his tongue crashing around the roof of her mouth. For a moment he released her and stared at her face; his eyes seemed to ask: is it okay? She answered by pulling him towards her. "Yes," she moaned. Now she could no longer resist and, after some frantic fumbling and the mutual infliction of sharp pain, he plunged inside her.

It was more than a physical release. For a few moments, as they writhed on the crumpled mat and called out each other's name, the memory of the whole terrible tragedy of the past few days was momentarily erased by a powerful surge of pleasure. Afterwards, they took long shallow breaths and stared into each other's eyes: Adam swore that he would never wash the sarong that was now soaked in their fluids. Alicia stroked Adam's sweating brow and smoothed his wet hair. She knew then that whatever happened, they had made the right decision to leave Noli. It was as if the island had been swallowed by the waves and no longer existed.

"What is it, my love?" Alicia asked, with her eyes still closed. She felt the warmth of his loins and the gentle rise and fall of his chest as he breathed and she might have been anywhere so long as the man in her life stayed just as he was. Love can be so simple and yet so profound, she reflected.

"A storm is coming, we must get ready," said Adam, as gently as he could.

"Will it rain?" Alicia asked.

"I'm afraid it will do more than rain." Already the little boat was pitching more and Adam worried that the sail was set too loosely.

"I should see to the sail," he said, lifting Alicia gently off him.

It looked like the night would be long and treacherous. Already the waves had grown in size and towered over the little boat. There was nothing quite as helpless as a small boat on the high sea. Adam's uncle, a great fisherman, had taught him never to point towards land using his fingers, always use an elbow out of respect – and never refer to land by name. Still now, he had no regrets about leaving. With wind and spray slapping at his face and keeping him alert, he recalled the horrific bloody battle he saw the day before leaving Noli.

It had started in the late afternoon as a Christian counterassault against the Muslims holed up in the mosque, which included his mother and father. With Alicia by his side, they hid in the undergrowth within sight of the beach. Having collected their supplies, they were waiting for night to fall before making their planned escape. Adam heard gunshots and screams as the bullets found their mark. One or two bullets swished through the long grass nearby. How had so many guns suddenly reached the island? People on both sides were so inexperienced in battle and blinded by rage they easily exposed themselves to enemy fire. As the battle wore on, Adam felt guilty for not rushing to join in and help defend his family. He felt ashamed of his chosen course of action, which was to turn and run. As if sensing his unease, Alicia held his hand firmly in hers. At one point during a lull in the battle, several Muslim villagers broke out of the mosque and headed for the beach, where they swiftly took to two small boats and headed out to sea. Within minutes, they were headed off by a larger launch manned by Christians. One of the smaller boats capsized. From where they lay, hidden in the dense vegetation along the beach, Adam and Alicia watched in horror as the Christians leaning off the launch used fishing spears to harpoon the Muslim villagers as they swam back to the shore. Close to the beach, where the white sand turned the water clear and inch-long fingerlings normally darted in sparkling silver schools, there were cloudy patches of deep red, marking the spot where the spears had found their mark.

With both hands hugging the tiller, which bucked in the swell, Adam started into the stormy darkness ahead of him and searched for some answers. All their lives, Muslims and Christians had lived side by side in harmony; all of a sudden, they were tearing at each other's throats. Now that he'd fled the island, his greatest fear was that his relationship with Alicia would fall into the great chasm between the two religions.

"Look at us, are we so different? What is it about you being a Christian and me being a Muslim that should divide us?" he asked.

Alicia, who was practical and down-to-earth, blamed outsiders, blamed the refugees.

"They came on a boat, like a disease. These people, they came with their misery and sowed hatred. Then others, they brought guns and knives. It's simple."

Adam, who was something of a dreamer, imagined something more internal and spontaneous, rather like a cancer. How else could he explain why his father had turned that day with a steely look in his eyes and forbade him to see Alicia? Something had changed inside him. In school he had learnt that cancer was not a virus you could catch like the common cold; it was a riotous and uncontrollable burst of cell-growth entirely generated within the body. The question was what defined the abnormal situation here.

"I saw hatred in my father's eyes, and in the eyes of all the other men who went to pray – as if this hatred had always been there, dormant and ready to explode. As if, somehow, the way we had always lived together in harmony was actually abnormal."

"But all those plans we had for the wedding and the Feast of the Virgin. What about that?" Alicia asked, starting to sob again. Adam pulled her nearer to him, putting one arm around her while still keeping both hands on the tiller, for the waves grew bigger still. It was comforting to talk and take his mind off the approaching storm.

"It was all for show. It wasn't really what people wanted at all. Our whole lives, the whole village, right down to the silly headman in his silly house – why that's all a façade. Can't you see? Rituals and customs hold this island together that none of us know anything about, except that we respect them. There's Christmas, then Ramadan and Idul Fitri; we send each other greetings and politely respect each other's holidays. Year in and year out we do the same thing, without questioning why. But ask yourself? Why are they so respected?"

Adam paused and swallowed. His throat was parched. They were short of water.

"The way we behave and how we conduct these rituals is all about respecting each other's faith, surely. This is the glue that holds our society together. Come on, Adam. I feel no hatred towards Muslims. For God's sake, I'm marrying a Muslim," Alicia said. Her eyes were downcast and there was uncertainty in her voice. Adam stared out to sea; it was surprising to him how clearly he had begun to understand things.

"Well of course, that's how it seems. Respect, tolerance, harmony – all those words we use in such a forced way, rather like when we talk to people we don't wish to know: their meaning is exaggerated. But behind closed doors, we actually all hate each other. So we pretend, and reinforce that pretence with ritual, silly stuff like the Feast of the Virgin. You think my father actually liked to mix with Christians?" Adam felt conscious that he had spat out the word "Christian" like a bad piece of fish or fruit. "The slightest hint of something *haram* in the food and he would retch; do you know he would not swallow his own saliva when he fasted?"

Alicia understood, of course. Her mother used to warn her not to dawdle back from school because, as she put it: "those Muslim boys have no morals." Her parents and their Christian friends and neighbours were conspicuous about the precision of their rituals; Muslims pray on Fridays, we Christians pray on Sundays. There was a kind of demonstrative air about Sunday churchgoing and little things like: "Oh, but you can't possibly play with me on Friday. Don't you have to pray?" Nevermind that nobody could explain to her why the Christian Lent and Muslim fasting period sometimes coincided. Yet no matter how hard she tried to understand her Muslim friends and neighbours, no matter how much she wished the boundaries away, she knew that there was something fundamentally different.

"These people, the ones who came on the ferry, they said what exactly when you heard them talk in the mosque? You know, the day you heard them speak." Adam looked out to sea; the storm was catching up fast and would soon be upon them.

"There was a lot of talk about sacrifice. One of them asked me if I was prepared to die for the faith. I wasn't."

"But some are."

"Yes, I suppose some are."

"What kind of religion allows people to surrender their lives so blindly?"

Adam was silent because he knew that every possible combination of the answer he wanted to give involved denying his faith. He'd already abandoned his family, which was bad enough; now with the dangers ahead, he wasn't leaving everything to chance. When he could no longer feel the blood pounding in his temples, Adam turned to Alicia and said: "Look, we all want a reason to hate and to kill, to make room and survive. It's so basic. Religion is a convenient way of dividing us up into categories. Categories are useful ways to divide communities so that they fight and compete. Competition helps our leaders to hold on to power. It's all there beneath the surface. But you're right, something changed and it came from outside."

When the storm hit them, Alicia was installed below in the snug little cabin. There was a small oil lamp but she blew it out to save the wick. Outside, Adam took the precaution of lowering the sail to a bare minimum since the wind already favoured their course. As the rain fell and the wind picked up, he hoped that the square piece of sail he had rigged to catch the water near the bow would hold. Then the storm grew worse and Adam started to seriously worry. The rain fell in sheets, stinging his face and threatened to swamp the boat, which actually rode the towering waves quite well. Adam frantically bailed with a plastic oil canister that he'd cut in half. Alicia did the same. She'd abandoned the cabin because if they were going to drown, she wanted to be in the arms of her lover.

"Are we going to die?" Alicia asked, holding Adam's face in

her hands and looking straight into his eyes, as if they were the last things she was going to see. Adam bit his lip and stared back. He shook his head, but his eyes communicated fear, a fear of dying.

They were both crying. There is nothing more humbling than the open angry sea because death by drowning seems so close at hand.

Drowning in his own misery, Father Xavier took long walks every night along the beach beside the hotel. The confrontation between Ghani and the mob had brought a lull in the violence, and although tensions ran high, a semblance of peace reigned over the island. The hotel bulged with people who ate, slept, and washed their laundry within its shabby confines, giving the place an uncommon air of habitation. "I know things are different because the cockroaches behave less arrogantly," Ghani joked. Father Xavier shared a room with old Yaakob and a pair of scruffy teenage boys from the North Shore who slept on the floor; they proudly claimed to be protecting the priest. There were constant demands on his services as people struggled to make sense of their shattered lives.

To get away from people, Father Xavier would wait till everyone was asleep and slip outside in the early predawn hours. The air was cool, which calmed him. For his heart burned with anger and frustration. A part of him longed to make peace with the Muslim mob, to sit among them and discuss the merits of tolerance and forgiveness – just as he'd been trained. But deep within him, a passionate hatred raged. These fanatics had burned down his church and mercilessly killed many people of his faith. During the day when he as busy dealing with other people's pain and suffering, he managed for the most part to suppress and forget about these sinful feelings of vengeance. Only when he went to bed and tossed to the accompaniment of old Yaakob's rhythmic snoring did he feel the hatred rise within him. It sometimes came in the form of a searing pain to the temples; at other times it knotted his gut. Each time he knew what it was which drove him hot and perspiring outside to the gentle lapping of the waves at shore.

This particular night was no different and he was just heading off down the shoreline in the direction of the jetty when a tremulous voice called out in the darkness.

"Father, Father." The priest was startled and crouched low on the beach, straining his ears.

"It's only me, Father."

"Why, Sonia," said Father Xavier. There was no moon and only the dim lights from the hotel against which he made out the pale, willowy figure of Sonia Ling as she made her way towards him. She wore a lace shawl, which could have been a tablecloth, over a pale cotton slip and had no shoes on. There was something ethereal about her, like one of the spirits the islanders believed stalked the beach after dark. The breeze tossed her lanky hair and in the dim light her lips looked blue, as if she was a living corpse. Her appearance startled the priest.

"I couldn't sleep," she said, coming close to him and wiping strands of hair away from her face. Father Xavier stepped back, though he was close enough to smell a medley of scents; there was newly-splashed cologne, masking a trace of body odour and something of the communal meal of fish and rice they'd all shared earlier in the evening.

"I never sleep much these days," he said, turning to face the sea. He was breathing faster all of a sudden.

"Come now, Father. You need some company. We can't have you wandering the beach alone like a madman."

"I'm fine, Sonia. You should go back in. It's dark and certainly not safe."

"Absolutely not. Leave you alone out here?" Sonia said, thrusting her hand through the priest's arm and tugging him along. Father Xavier froze, though only for an instant, before following. Something within him stirred; it was something unfamiliar but definitely pleasing – he felt blood rushing to his head and fought the urge to sneeze.

A few paces more and they would be out of earshot from the hotel. He thought it best to turn back. What if someone saw him with Felix Ling's wife?

"Really, Sonia…" The priest began, stopping again.

"What? Are you worried about being seen with me?"

"Only for your safety," Father Xavier lied, hoping to convince himself. He knew that this encounter was fraught with danger, and the blood pounding in his temples throbbed like an alarm. He was conscious of a dull pain in his abdomen and desperately fought the urge to put his arm around her, finding instead that she had taken his hand. They walked on in silence. Father Xavier felt out of breath and a strange constriction in his stomach. His throat was dry all of a sudden. Sonia pumped his hand, sending warm blood racing through his veins.

"Father," she said at last.

"Yes, Sonia." Father Xavier's voice trembled. The tips of his fingers now caressed the soft surface of Sonia's hand.

"You probably think of me as a harsh, selfish woman…"

"No, I…"

"Let me finish, please. You see, I have been greatly misunderstood and I would like your advice. You are a priest, a man of faith – I need my faith in life restored."

Father Xavier relaxed and felt a curious mixture of relief and disappointment, rather like someone without the right shoes who is not asked to dance. It seemed that Sonia wanted some private counselling – not at all what he feared, or even secretly desired.

They continued walking along the beach, the darkness enveloping them like a soft silk curtain. Sonia spoke in breathless short bursts, relating the passionate dreams of her childhood and the agony of her loveless marriage. As he listened, Father Xavier realised how much a prisoner she had been, hunched behind the grimy counter of the Noli Superstore, a prisoner of circumstances with a desperate desire to escape.

"You see, there was a large sum of money involved. It's not easy to come across good family matches in the islands. We Chinese are so fussy and I was the only daughter, something of a burden. His family was respectable – his grandfather was a Manchu scholar, you know. I was young with fine pigtails – Oh, Father, can you imagine my pigtails, ha-ha!" She squeezed the priest's hand even harder and nudged him with her shoulder.

"My buttocks and thighs were firm. Oh, you should see them now, Father – still so firm. I am no less a woman than I was then, only bitter and sad on the inside. That's why I appear so, well you know, so hard at times."

"Indeed, Sonia. It would appear there is a lot more to your nature than meets the eye – a lot more."

"Yes and Father, I am so happy to be free now…." She skipped away from him and kicked the sand beneath her feet. Father Xavier stumbled as a he followed.

"Free?"

"Yes, it's over with Felix. You can see that, can't you? This tragedy has released me. He won't stay here after all this is over – he'll leave and I plan to stay. This is my home now, and everything that's happened has brought me closer to the people."

"But…"

"Nothing to worry about, Father. We weren't married before God – though I've always wanted that, you know." Sonia stopped right in front of the priest and searched for his eyes in the darkness.

In awkward situations like this, priests normally feel constrained by strict vows and the conscience of faith, but Father Xavier had momentarily misplaced his moral compass. Just as the violence and the killings had released Sonia from her miserable marriage, it seemed that the tragedy had loosened the bonds imposed by Father Xavier's priestly vows. So he lurched wildly in a direction guided only by an acute desire for physical stimulation. There was an elderly Dutch priest at the seminary in Semarang who was fond of drinking. "There's only one thing that man steers by, and that's his wee-wee," Father Xavier recalled him saying: "Don't let people fool you with all this nonsense about will-power; one way or another, your wee-wee will overpower you…." For this old priest, the beauty of the church was that men, imprisoned by their vows, were forced to think using other organs. Father Xavier shivered at the recollection, then turned to Sonia and said:

"Then why come to me? What is it you want? I'm not much of a priest these days. I'm lost myself, to be frank, at a loss to know what to do about all the killing, so what is it I can do for you?"

Sonia shook her head and let her hair fly in the breeze. These words, with their mixed meaning, thrilled her and her dark eyes flashed.

"Why do you say that, Father?" She stood opposite him now, her body only inches away from his, and searched his face intently. The breeze flattened the thin slip against the gentle curve of her belly. Without his trusty comb, there was little Father Xavier could do to prevent himself from grasping Sonia close to him, which he found himself doing, sinking into her arms with exhaustion and an explosion of desire. The long battle with his senses was over.

CHAPTER SEVEN

Colonel Wahyu arrived one day, about a week after Father Xavier's sermon, poised like the great American General Douglas MacArthur on the lip of a landing craft's ramp. The ramp came creaking down and the colonel came storming up the shore towards Hotel Merdeka where a perplexed and startled Ghani offered a glass of lime soda to him and his spindly adjutant, Dibyo.

"I have orders to secure Noli," the colonel declared, flourishing his military walkie-talkie with its stubby antenna. His chest, all puffed up like male bird of paradise on display, was festooned with military insignia, badges, and ribbons. A pair of gold-plated aviator sunglasses hung from one front shirt pocket, a black nametag from the other. There was a large, nickel-plated automatic pistol strapped ostentatiously to his waist in a polished leather holster. The radio squawked and sputtered static every two or three seconds and Colonel Wahyu constantly fiddled with its knobs. Dibyo stood by, his hands locked together in a submissive perch around his loins, slightly stooped with his eyes fixed on the colonel.

"You and whose army?" Ghani politely inquired, giving Dibyo a queer look. Etiquette on Noli was rough and minimal, mostly revolving around a handshake or slap on the back. Respect was reserved for holy men, sorcerers, and men who wrestled big fish onto their boats. Dibyo's submissive posture bothered the rough islander.

"My men," the colonel said, gesturing towards the beach where a squad of troops wearing green fatigues and red berets were making their way through the sand towards the welcome shade of the hotel.

"It's only a company, but they're the best; Special Forces, you know."

"Oh, I know," said Ghani. He'd read about the red berets. They were supposed to be somewhat less corrupt than other units of the army, but also more ruthless.

"Actually, I'm quite surprised to see you, Colonel." Ghani said after they had taken a few sips of their drink and he felt more comfortable around the uniformed guest on his verandah. Colonel Wahyu lounged, swinging one booted leg over the side of one the wicker chairs while he fiddled with his radio. Dibyo retreated but stayed poised and slightly stooped, ready to dash to his Colonel's side. Ghani observed the scene with contempt; he felt goaded by the man's arrogance. "You see our little island isn't large enough to warrant much attention from Jakarta. Politicians almost never come. Frankly, I don't think they care less whether Noli was inhabited or abandoned to its pigeons and monitor lizards." Just once, a few years back, the president himself had stopped by on his way to a national scout meeting in Ambon. In fact, he came to inspect the possible site of a pearl farm, one of his children's many get-rich-quick schemes. The portly president's only conversation had been with a simple fisherman who had been handpicked by Cornelius's predecessor and thoroughly vetted. The president asked the astonished man whether there was any money to be made from farming noli.

"Oh really, sir? Is that so?" Colonel Wahyu stared at Ghani intently. The intensity of his gaze unnerved Ghani. So did the patina of courtesy that barely disguised his impatience. "That's not how the army operates. It's our duty to defend every corner of the Republic. You'll find us everywhere – from Sabang to Merauke, as they say. Can't trust the civilians, you see. Sure I don't need to tell you that. Always screwing things up – always leaving us to clean up the mess."

"Quite so, Colonel." Ghani replied, averting his eyes to escape the colonel's manic glare.

"Things are getting worse, you know. Ever since the student rabble forced the president to resign, there's all this talk of democracy." The colonel seemed to spit the word out like a bad piece of food. "Since then, things have gotten out of hand. There's no discipline, and people take the law into their own hands." The colonel's hand slammed onto the table and startled Ghani, who wasn't sure why this haughty soldier felt so inclined to confide in him about the army's lack of respect for civilian government and contempt for democracy. Was it so easy to win popular support for military rule?

Quite possibly, given the desperate desire for security on the island. All the same, he felt compelled to answer back.

"Well, I don't know, Colonel. I'm a simple islander, but as far as I'm concerned, democracy's quite a good thing. You see, even on this little island it's hard to get everyone to agree to the same thing all the time. Democracy allows decisions to be taken fairly and for the good of the community – it's a good way of dealing with our imperfections as human beings."

The conversation died right there, leaving Ghani wondering what to say next. Colonel Wahyu tapped the tabletop impatiently, as if waiting for a cue. Here was a man who locked out what he didn't want to hear, thought Ghani; a dangerous man.

"Well," said Ghani finally, "you've certainly come just in time. There's quite a mess that needs cleaning up around here. You've heard, I'm sure, about the troubles, about the killings and the visitors who started it all."

Colonel Wahyu beamed and stabbed the air with his radio set, reanimated by Ghani's apparent approval of his presence.

"Yes, these religious troubles. Damn Christians stirring things up…"

"Well, not quite…" Ghani rushed to correct the colonel, but he waved his free hand dismissively and continued. "Yes, of course, of course. Each side blames the other. That's for us to determine. We'll get to the bottom of everything – we have ways of doing that." With that, the colonel leapt to his feet. Instantly, Dibyo rushed to his side, eyes turned upwards to receive a command. The colonel took a moment to arrange himself, handing Dibyo the radio, which he cradled in both hands like some family heirloom. Slowly and with the kind of deliberate movements made by someone who likes to be watched, Colonel Wahyu slipped on his sunglasses and stared out to sea. By now, all his men were resting on the verandah, smoking and chatting amongst themselves. Their thick Javanese accents wafted indoors. Before leaving to attend to his men, the colonel turned to Ghani and said: "Our job is to stamp out the violence and ensure that traditions are respected. You'll see, sir, everything will be fine. *Insya'allah*. Oh, and I need a room. Okay?"

In vain, Ghani explained to the colonel that refugees with nowhere else to go occupied all the rooms. He suggested that the colonel and his men make their camp in the old fort. "You'll be safe there, Colonel. I assure you." But from the look on the colonel's face, this offer had gone down badly.

"You'd have the army hide from the people? You think we need protecting? Ha! You need a little education, sir," Colonel Wahyu fumed.

In the end, Ghani was forced to displace a family of seven, offering them a dusty corner of the coffee shop instead. The rest of Colonel Wahyu's men pitched tents on the beach.

Later that same afternoon, Father Xavier, Felix Ling, and the rest of the informal island council gathered in the hotel coffee shop. Colonel Wahyu surveyed them all as though observing a pile of garbage that needed removing. It astounded Ghani how he managed to remain so puffed up. Was it a breathing trick, he wondered? The colonel grunted and the ever-present Dibyo simpered.

"I'm sure I can see to all your needs, Colonel," Felix offered, with a heavy coat of obsequious slime applied to his voice. Colonel Wahyu eyed Sonia warily – she'd regained a lot of her composure over the past few days and had taken to wearing a large wooden crucifix. When Father Xavier appeared, she threw him admiring looks and made him blush. It was a small island and everyone noticed. Still, these were unusual times and no one said anything. Dragged out of a dark corner of the hotel lounge he now more or less permanently occupied, Cornelius Lahatula reported sheepishly that the island's administration was intact: only law and order was questionable because of the loss of the island's only, and much-lamented, law enforcement officer. Cornelius blinked rapidly and shifted his weight from one dusty sandaled foot to the other. Something had snapped since Widodo's brutal demise and he seemed eager to scuttle back into his corner like a wood louse, allergic to light.

"Have you secured the island's resources?" Colonel Wahyu asked the hapless bureaucrat. The colonel's well-manicured hands rested arrogantly on his hips. The question puzzled Cornelius. "Resources? What resources, sir?" Colonel Wahyu grew irritated and looked the other way.

"Logistics, man. Come now, where is your sense of initiative," he snapped.

"Logistics, sir?"

"Rice, sugar, cooking oil – all the essentials. The people must be fed, and so must the people's army." Colonel Wahyu's face clouded with anger. Cornelius turned to Ghani with a look of utter puzzlement. Logistics never came up; it wasn't a department he was familiar with. Ghani's expression looked just as helpless. It was Father Xavier who stepped in with a response, throwing a life belt to Cornelius, who was now drowning in shame and embarrassment.

"Look, Colonel, if I may. This is a small island. We don't grow rice. We eat sago. It grows everywhere in abundance. We beat the plant to a pulp by our own hands when and if we need it. If we cannot buy cooking oil, we do what has been done for centuries; take the blubber from beached whales or the fatty tissue of the tuna. We make do. As will you and your men."

The colonel stared at the priest with a look of surprised stupefaction. His well-shaved jaw dropped open and his tongue rolled around his lower lip for a moment, less certain about leaping off than the colonel had been on the edge of the landing craft earlier in the day. For the colonel was a good Muslim from East Java, unused to assertive Christian clergy. Where he came from, the church was obliging and submissive. It played power games discreetly, behind the screen, usually led by Jesuits and involving kickbacks and trade-offs.

"I see," the colonel said curtly, turning towards the verandah and his men. Their voices could be heard floating up from the beach where they had pitched their tents. Some of them smoked, wiping green-coloured towels over their nearly shaved heads, which were shiny with sweat. Others arranged equipment, stacking their automatic rifles in neat pyramids on the terrace of the hotel. It wasn't quite an invasion, more a polite insertion.

"Be careful," Ghani whispered to Father Xavier while the colonel attended to his men. "He's real army."

"I can see that," the priest replied, irritably.

"I mean, he's political."

"Meaning?"

"That he's dangerous. I've read about people like him."

Father Xavier was less a man of the world than Ghani when it came to politics. His training as a priest, although it had taken him as far as a seminary in Semarang on Java, rarely exposed him to the secular world. A lot of his friends at the seminary had been Chinese, and were not too well plugged into politics. The bishop always advised them to steer clear of politics. "This is a country we will never rule; God's work is done at the parish level. Rule your congregation and we will deliver these people to heaven." Ghani, on the other hand, well knew the machinations of military politics. He had a cousin in the army, another in the navy. On rare visits, they brought him contraband liquor and cigarettes – stuff from the black market. "We don't get paid much of a salary," his cousin, a captain in the army, used to say, "but we sure get to taste the good life...."

"You see, these soldiers, they're not really paid very much, so they live off the land," Ghani explained to the priest as they settled down to one of the last cold beers on the island.

It was precisely for this reason that Colonel Wahyu's first official call was on Felix Ling, who had recently returned to his looted but still-intact store.

"Colonel, please don't think I'm a man without means. You find me at a disadvantage right now," said Felix, gesturing at the once-proud, now ravaged, Noli Superstore. The main showroom was a sea of empty containers and broken glass. There was a strong smell of stale beer, which offended the abstemious Colonel Wahyu.

"I'm interested in provisions and some information," said Colonel Wahyu, his eyes scanning the wrecked premises with practiced precision.

"And what…"

"Packets of noodles, soy sauce, tinned fish, that sort of thing," the colonel cut in, before lunging at a stray box of cough drops, the sort favoured by his men. He scooped up a handful of the loosely-wrapped confectionary and stuffed them in a pocket on the side of his tunic.

"I'm sure we can come to an arrangement," Felix said in a fawning tone he reserved for his very best customers or the highest officials. The response he was rewarded with was immediately gratifying: "You will be rewarded with our protection. Later, we'll talk." With that, the colonel summoned Dibyo, who was lurking in the background writing in a notepad, and marched down the street to find his men who were out on patrol.

Colonel Wahyu's stride was confident and purposeful. His was a sensitive mission, but one he felt more than capable of executing. That's because he had trained his men well and spared no expense in outfitting them with the best equipment, making sure that they and their families were well looked after. Even at the company level, there was a special foundation that managed the income from an array of businesses, which included a gambling ring in North Jakarta, a hotel in Ancol, and a clove concession in North Sulawesi.

"Wahyu," his commanding officer had told him before embarking for Noli, "Phase one of the operation has gone well. Your job is to secure the island and make sure all the achieved objectives are protected and maintained."

"Yes, sir."

"The army's aims are pure, so no matter what you encounter, or how you deal with it, be assured that you will be serving the nation's highest purpose."

"Of that there is no doubt, sir."

"Sometimes sacrifices must be made in the name of unity, Wahyu."

"Clear, sir."

"Good luck."

Colonel Wahyu came from a family with a long tradition of military service to the Republic, and with this mission, he was sure that his star was in the ascendant. This potentially destabilising trend towards democracy needed checking, and he was at the forefront of making sure that happened. "The last time this country experimented with democracy, it almost came apart," his lecturer at the army staff college used to say. "The result: Indonesia's communist party became the largest outside China." Like many officers of his generation, Wahyu believed unflinchingly in the army's role as "stabiliser and unifier" of the nation. He swore a soldier's oath to protect the nation, not its government. He recognised that left to their own devices, politicians would drag the country down the road to communism. "The army must stay at the centre of power, or the country could collapse," Colonel Wahyu told his men as they prepared for this mission. "That's the lesson we learnt during the revolution when the civilian leaders abandoned the Republic's capital ahead of a Dutch advance. It's the same today, with civilians offering concessions like independence and autonomy for rebellious provinces." The colonel believed, and so did his men, that with the dictator now deposed, it was now up to the army alone to protect the nation. And if that took a little intrigue and upheaval in the provinces to protect the centre, well, that was the price to be paid.

It did not take long before the effect of the military presence was felt. The angry mob in the island's main mosque was persuaded to leave and no one was arrested. In fact, Father Xavier heard reports that the soldiers had exchanged handshakes and cigarettes, patted them on the back and wished them all luck. "They were smiling and laughing, like they knew each other," someone reported. There was no sound or sight of Umar. By contrast, when the soldiers reached the North Shore, the besieged mosque was relieved and Christian youths were rounded up and beaten. By now, mobs on both sides of the religious divide had formed into distinctive militias. Christians wore rosary beads and crucifixes with red cock's combs pinned to their shoulders; Muslims wrapped themselves in green cloth and wore black velvet *peci* hats or white haj caps normally reserved for the mosque. Each side was sworn to die in the defence of their religion. Father Xavier fretted and sought the army's help to disarm the militias even-handedly.

"These people need separating. They need cooling off. How is it that the Muslim militia escape detention, and even get to keep their weapons?" the priest asked. But Colonel Wahyu stared right though him. He would have nothing to do with the meddling priest, and, if counsel was needed, turned to Ghani, who was his host at Hotel Merdeka.

"In about a week, we'll have this place cleaned up," Colonel Wahyu said between mouthfuls of deep-fried butterfish garnished with coriander and lemon.

"Indeed," muttered Ghani, who resented the full and tasty meal he was asked to provide for the chubby Colonel whilst everyone else in the hotel lived on packets of bland instant noodles supplemented with tinned sardines in chilli sauce every so often. No one had been out fishing in ten days, and Ghani's last consignment of frozen tuna was rotting in the power-starved freezer.

"And how do you define 'cleaned up,' Colonel, if I may ask?"

"Restoring order and discipline, stability," the colonel replied after delicately removing a fishbone from a back molar. "The fish was good," he added.

"Thank you. We've never had trouble before…"

"Christian troublemakers, I know," he said through a mouthful of fish. "We expelled them from Jakarta. They came here to cause trouble and we think we know who paid them…"

"Actually, I think it was the Muslim mob that started things," Ghani cut in.

"Nonsense," the colonel snorted. "That's not what our own intelligence hears. Actually, I understand your sultan – what's his name? I've heard he played a constructive role keeping the religions together as a community. Admirable work he has done, really. Shows the power of tradition – good Muslim tradition." Ghani felt his jaw muscles slacken and he struggled hard to keep his mouth from dropping open in amazement. He was on the point of protesting when the colonel stopped eating and looked around the room, waving with one hand.

"Good to see that you managed to bring the Christians together under one roof. That will help calm things down. Oh, by the way, we've arrested the ringleaders, you know."

At this point, Ghani gave up. The colonel had clearly concocted his own scenario and wasn't to be diverted from it. With the last of the butterfish eaten and armed with a toothpick that he wielded like a sword, the colonel continued.

"In fact, they will soon all be deported."

"The Christians? Deported? Where? And why, in the name of God?"

"Look, this is a Muslim island, right? It's always been a Muslim island. The Christians don't belong here. They'll be sent to other islands, where there is a Christian majority – Flores or West Timor, even. We'll call it transmigration. Haven't you heard?"

Neat. Very neat and tidy – and all within the law, just as the army liked it, Ghani reflected. He disliked this Colonel Wahyu intensely. His puffed-up arrogant demeanour, beady dark eyes, and faintly-perfumed pudgy extremities repelled him. So this was the army standing with the people! This was the army reflecting the purely revolutionary ideals of unity and diversity upon which the Republic was built! Colonel Wahyu's approach was to bulldoze over the people using clumsy social engineering and assert control. The army had a term for this kind of thing: they called it socio-political engineering.

"Isn't that what they call ethnic cleansing?" Ghani said bitterly.

"Rubbish. It's all about stability and order: the army's civil mission. You see, those dissidents in Jakarta, they call us names and drag us through the mud, but they don't really see what we do. They can't appreciate our role because they're not out here, on the front lines, defending the unity of the nation. Tell me, what would have happened if I hadn't arrived with my men?"

Ghani sensed an opportunity to set things right and began telling the colonel about the role Father Xavier had played, noting in particular the calming effect of his sermon. Then, in a modest way, he threw in his confrontation with the mob.

"Yes, I read about that. It was a brave thing to do – reckless, but brave," the colonel allowed. He said nothing about the priest's role.

"Damn civilians, they think they can run this country alone. But you see that fellow, what's his name? The administrator here –

why, the idiot hasn't even got an emergency contingency plan!" From his dark corner at the back of the room, Cornelius Lahatula stared malevolently at the two men having lunch. This wasn't right, he thought. The army should not deal with businesspeople; they should respect mandated civil authority.

"And as for the priest," Colonel Wahyu continued, "I consider him one of the troublemakers."

"What?" Ghani couldn't stop himself; his blood was up. "Father Xavier? You're badly mistaken, sir. I assure you."

"You know that he was plotting with the Chinese shopkeeper to protect the fisherman who raped the Muslim girl."

"I can't believe that." Ghani was amazed at how quickly the colonel had managed to pick things up.

"Ask the Chinaman, then."

Ghani was speechless. Colonel Wahyu took out his aviator sunglasses and put them on. The effect was to make him look like one of the mischievous clowns from the *wayang*, Bagong, perhaps. In Jakarta, they talked about this man as a troublemaker, which was why, Ghani suspected, he'd been given the Moluccan assignment. Yet he was an effective enforcer of stability and order and a former adjutant to the president. Colonel Wahyu was going places and he knew it.

"You know what this country needs?" Colonel Wahyu asked, his face turned away from Ghani. There was a dreamy tone in his voice. Ghani stared up at the soldier who got up and stood over him, hands planted firmly on his hips. He stared out to sea, a toothpick rolling around between his lips. Ghani watched the shoreline reflected in the man's sunglasses. Take away the pale brown skin and he could be taken for a Dutchman, Ghani thought contemptuously. Then the penny dropped.

"Someone like you, perhaps, Colonel?"

Inwardly, Ghani convulsed with anger, but he knew better than to show his hand and lose the advantage of proximity to this dangerous man. If he was to save Noli from this little dictator and protect his friend Father Xavier, Ghani needed to retain his confidence.

"Ah, *Pak* Ghani, you're too kind – and your cooking is excellent." Colonel Wahyu smiled broadly, distending his fleshy cheeks and lifting the sunglasses from his pudgy little nose. "I should be back for dinner, by the way. Now, where do you suppose I can find that priest?"

ꜱ ꜱ

On a regular Tuesday evening, Mama Fatima could count on maybe a dozen supplicants attending her séance, but these were trying times for the people of Noli and the little yard in front of her hut overflowed with people. A pall of sweet clove cigarette smoke hung over the crowd, which was mostly seated cross-legged in front of the roughly hewn door to the house. The flickering flames of crude oil lamps wedged into bamboo stakes illuminated the area and threw constantly moving shadows, like those of animated spirits, up against the side of the little house. People murmured to one another, smoked, and sipped a bootleg local brew out of old soft-drink bottles – a variety of *tuak* made of fermented sago palm and tinted pink by ripe mango skins. They smoked, drank, and waited patiently for Mama Fatima to emerge, entranced and transformed. This was a world the people of Noli hid from and denied out of respect for the great religions of the book which governed their lives in their waking hours; it was the world they surrendered to in times of personal despair or collective strife.

Assisting Mama Fatima, as usual, were the brothers, Kamal and Din. Dim but wily, Kamal and Din collected consultation fees; they also cooked, played the drums that set the trance in motion, and otherwise ministered to Mama Fatima's every need. The money had been good these past few days, with large sums handed over for the promise of protection from bullets, spears, and arrows. Fighting in the name of sublime religions of the book required protection from the profane world of spirits.

The great warrior queen of Ternate announced her presence from inside her hut with a deep, masculine clearing of the throat. Then she spat and farted loudly. The crowd hushed and necks strained to catch a glimpse of Mama Fatima's demeanour. A glance at her face indicated whether the spirit that possessed her was in a benign or malevolent mood. Near the foot of the stairs leading up to the house, Kamal heard requests with a nod of his shaven, almost conical, head. Meanwhile, Din struck up a dull rhythmic thud on his goatskin drum. Suddenly, Mama Fatima appeared on the threshold of her house. She crouched, frog-like, and stared with glazed and bloodshot eyes out into the middle distance, her bulky torso bulging voluptuously out of a bright red batik sarong. With one hand, she gripped a long ceremonial sword; in the other, she clutched a fisherman's net bag filled with her betel paraphernalia. On her head, she wore an elaborate feather headdress. Suddenly, she puffed out both cheeks and, without warning, emitted a stream of bright red betel juice, spraying the first, and highly-honoured, line of supplicants. Then she smiled, revealing a row of broken red-stained teeth. Her head shook violently, and from deep within her throat a string of sounds, more animal than human, pierced the night air. Many in the crowd nodded and winked to one another. They seemed reassured: the spirit was in a benign mood. The séance had begun.

From the back of the crowd, Father Xavier tried to keep a low profile. It was hard for the island's priest to find a disguise, so he acted as if he was just passing by. Nonchalance didn't become Father Xavier and people mostly assumed that, like them, he was seeking other forms of assurance.

"Isn't it wonderful, Father? Look, she's about to speak," said a passing parishioner with wonderment in his eyes. Father Xavier had been a priest long enough on Noli to know that no edict of either church or mosque could penetrate and dispel the island's parallel spiritual world. In fact, as her normal self, Mama Fatima was a good Muslim who prayed five times a day. The crowd was hushed now, expecting to hear the warrior queen's pearls of wisdom. A light breeze rustled the palm fronds that brushed her house. Above, a parting in the clouds revealed the imperfect circle of a waxing moon that cast a dim light on the beach and etched out freshly made footprints in the phosphorescent sand.

Somewhere in the crowd, Father Xavier hoped, was the man he wanted to see. By his calculation, as Cartesian as a Jesuit can be, the feud between the two communities, Christian and Muslim, would fester and linger so long as there was no resolution to the original slight. "It's clear that a moral transgression triggered the violence," he had reasoned with Ghani, who was sceptical. "Sure, but there were surely other forces stoking the fire," Ghani countered. "Go ahead and find the rapist, but what kind of justice can you deliver after so much unpardonable bloodshed? What would the punishment of one man achieve when so many more have blood on their hands?" Father Xavier thought for a while and fixed Ghani with a serious look. He wasn't ready to abandon all the pillars upon which the morality of the church was built, no matter how badly his own faith in them was shaken. "I can demonstrate for future generations to come that wrongs must be righted…justice must be served. You can't leave the younger generation with the notion that if your people are abused, you have licence to go on a rampage and kill everyone in sight." Ghani nodded in reluctant agreement. And so Father Xavier planned to persuade the man who had raped the Muslim trader's daughter that day he could not go out fishing to apologise and submit to punishment. Father Xavier hoped this would mean arrest and imprisonment on

Ambon. "Sounds logical enough, I suppose," said Ghani. "That's the problem, though. What happens when he confesses? He'll be lynched, of course. Who will oversee his arrest and deportation to Ambon? Perhaps you could summon Captain Widodo's ghost? Be realistic, Father. Let things be."

But part of him reasoned subconsciously that it may be no bad thing for the man to be killed – a single life sacrificed for the good of the community; a communal catharsis of sorts. The priest found refuge in the Scriptures. Had not the Lord Jesus been effectively lynched by the Hebrew rabble and given his own life to save mankind?

Now the crowd grew restless; apparently Mama Fatima's spirit was disturbed. Around the priest, men murmured and gave each other knowing looks, as if they already knew the gist of the impending message. The smile disappeared from Mama Fatima's face, which instead was darkened by shadows cast by her pouting cheeks and furrowed brow. It was uncanny how much like an angry old man she looked. "She says there are foreigners in our midst, foreign devils who must be expelled – or beheaded and their livers eaten," translated the excited parishioner. He wore a torn shirt that revealed a scrawny, scarred torso. Then Father Xavier noticed that he wore a headband soaked in something dark and familiar: it looked like dried blood. There was a dried and shrivelled cock's comb pinned to his shirt. Father Xavier turned away in horror. Next to him, another man waved a shirt soaked in blood. All things are cleansed with blood, the Bible taught – Christ's blood, replacing the blood of calves and goats in the ancient sacrifice. But here, apparently, was another form of redemption: the blood of your enemy. Once, long ago when the Europeans first came, the warriors of Noli smeared themselves with the blood of their enemies before going before their leaders to receive honour and reward. "Is there no escaping all this killing?" Father Xavier asked the man next to him. The man didn't seem to hear, he was gazing so intently at Mama Fatima. "What is it that whips us all into a violent frenzy at the sight of blood? Can't we find another way? Must we use violence?" "Hush, Father, Mama Fatima speaks," the man finally said in an irritated whisper.

Father Xavier stepped back into the shadows in a state of deep depression. What's the use? Even if he could identify the primary culprit, as he saw it, these people suffered no guilt or shame; there was no pause for feelings of remorse. The look in their eyes said: kill or be killed. It was a wild, animal instinct that seemed to draw them to the edge of Mama Fatima's grotto. They came to seek protection, not absolution. So much for his preaching and so much for the power of the church, Father Xavier reflected bitterly. Against all his instincts as a priest, he felt hope evaporate; he felt his belief in God shaken undone to the rhythmic beat of Mama Fatima's trance dance and the murderous murmurings of her supplicants. His faith was reduced to a mere illusion. What kind of salvation did the church offer but one attained after death – an illusory reward. Here and now, the island's sudden warriors, steeped in the blood of their neighbours, could find a tangible form of salvation in the endowment of magic powers to help them survive and wreak revenge. Before him, the crowd chanted and waved in a frenzied response to the soothsayer's crude message. It appalled him that in the end, after everything these people had suffered, they turned to a half-crazed drunken medium for answers. But who were these foreigners Mama Fatima spoke of?

～ ～

The answer came the very next day when a young soldier under Colonel Wahyu's command was found decapitated and his body horribly mutilated along the beach, not far from where Mama Fatima's little hut on stilts sat. The colonel's response was immediate and drastic.

188

"Father, Father, what will you do?" It was Matthew, the chief choir-boy, shaking the priest out of a long afternoon nap. Now that the army had arrived and the violence had died down, the situation was calm enough for Father Xavier to move out of the hotel and back into his little tin-roofed house along the shore. As much as he enjoyed Ghani's company and the warm seediness of Hotel Merdeka, he needed a break from the burdens of his traumatised flock, as well as a chance to loosen the bonds of Sonia Ling's illicit companionship.

"Do? Do what?" The priest sat up and rubbed the back of his neck, which was clammy and bathed in sweat. Sleep had etched lines on one side of his face. It was still hot and a deafening chorus of cicadas invaded his ears.

"They say that the colonel wants you arrested."

"Arrested? For what, exactly, son?"

The boy hesitated and stared at his feet, biting his lip. The priest swung his legs off the bed. He was still weak with exhaustion, emotional exhaustion.

"Come on now. Tell me what they say. Arrested for what?"

There was a note of irritation in Father Xavier's voice – he was accustomed to waking up alone and certainly not with threats of arrest.

"They say you incited the mob to kill that soldier. He was a Muslim."

Matthew was a bright lad with a cheerful, pockmarked face, the by-product of infant smallpox. Breathlessly, the boy related how the colonel had already rounded up dozens of Christians and someone had heard sounds of people in pain coming from a room on the first floor of Hotel Merdeka that was occupied by Colonel Wahyu. First a sanctuary, then a church, now a torture chamber; Father Xavier gagged at the thought.

"What will you do, Father? What will you do?" The boy was anxious because he looked up to the priest as a father and a guide to life. He was close to applying for a place at the seminary in Ambon. Father Xavier studied the boy's craggy face and saw written on it the same fear that he felt deep inside. This tangle with the army was something new for him. This was about politics and wider issues, not about Noli.

As he sat on the edge of the bed, adjusting to the news Matthew brought about the murdered soldier and his impending arrest, it occurred to Father Xavier that, in fact, the island was grappling with a new form of an old menace.

"Matthew, my son, do you know much of our island's history?"

"Only what you've taught me, Father."

Father Xavier sighed deeply and looked into the boy's large almond-shaped eyes.

Such innocence, he reflected, was the hallmark of Noli. Yet, innocence and the goodness of mankind, like ripe fruit, are vulnerable to the forces of nature.

"Five hundred years ago, these Moluccan islands were hotbeds of international intrigue. Dutch and Portuguese fought and killed one another as well as the Arab and Malay traders they called Moors. Our ancestors, the natives, gleefully took and changed sides as and if it suited them. They used the foreign intruders as proxies for their own internecine disputes largely centred on religious difference. Yes, that's right; we have fought over religion before. Why, do you think Muslims and Christians have ever really got along? It may seem that way, Matthew. Yes, we help build each other's places of worship, we respect each other's holy days, and we even attend marriages and funerals to honour our neighbours. But let me tell you: in this world of ours, man competes with man for scarce resources. Pluralism and tolerance, which we celebrate and honour, are hard virtues to sustain – it's more natural for us to fight over what we have." Father Xavier paused to let these words sink in. If young Matthew was serious about the priesthood, he needed a hefty dose of reality before the walls of the church closed in on his life – before he was trained to feel guilty about man's true state, sending him into denial.

"The decline of the spice trade returned these islands to a tranquil state of neglect. Isolation turned the people of Noli into a benign and trusting lot who buried their differences in the interests of survival. Rare visits by outsiders brought news and replenishment but little else."

"Yes, but Father, what's that got to do with anything?" Matthew asked.

"Well now, let's see. Up until Mama Fatima's revelation, Colonel Wahyu and his company of troops were welcomed with open arms in the absence of any form of law enforcement. Isn't that so? But now it's dawning on Nolians that these soldiers and their smooth-talking, arrogant commander aren't really looking out for our welfare. Indeed, they've started to behave much like the early European soldier-traders: they take things without asking and see every young girl as a potential sleeping partner. What, with religious passions already inflamed, it's not hard to imagine why that poor young soldier had his throat cut." For a while the two of them, Father Xavier and the young choirboy, contemplated the situation. Matthew shifted awkwardly from one foot to the other – he desperately wanted the priest to run and hide before the soldiers reached him. But Father Xavier was calm and made no move. He wasn't sure whether this was because, being who he was, he needed to face his accusers rather than run from them, or whether he was just too tired.

"Leave me, Matthew," Father Xavier said after a while. "Go home and stay home. You're not part of any gang, are you, son?" Matthew looked uncertain and stared at the foot of the bed, avoiding Father Xavier's gaze. Finally, he looked at the priest with tears in his eyes and said: "Father, I did some bad things the other night. It was just that we were attacked. We had to fight back, Father, honestly." Matthew wrung his hands while his eyes locked onto the priest in search of approval. "Didn't you tell us the other day that we should seek justice? Didn't you, Father? Well, for me it was more basic – we needed protection." Matthew paused again and lowered his head. His confession came in a barely audible whisper: "Father, I cut a man. I cut a man and he bled. There was a lot of blood. Father, he could have died, I'm not sure. Oh, Father, please help me…" As Matthew began to sob, Father Xavier rose from the bed and went over to the boy. He wasn't sure what to make of it; here was a boy, pure in faith and who sung Te Deums and Ave Marias beautifully. Yet this same boy had stabbed a man and watched him bleed. Father Xavier needed no better proof that God had taken His eye off Noli. They were on their own now in a soiled and sinful state, tossed on the waves the bigger storm affecting the whole nation. He held the boy's trembling shoulders and said: "I understand. Now go home and stay safe. Do not go out. The army will be looking for people like you."

Unused to being a fugitive, Father Xavier needed time to contemplate, so, after washing his face and swilling his mouth with a cup of cold tea, he took a stroll along the beach close to his home about half a kilometre from the hotel. His aim, eventually, was to go there and turn himself in to Colonel Wahyu – perhaps after evening prayers, or maybe in the morning. How does a man submit voluntarily to the abuse of authority? Nonetheless, he reasoned, it was unseemly for a priest to run from the law, even if the law was an ass in a uniform. There would be questions, perhaps even some physical abuse, as Matthew indicated. Since the army didn't trust civilians, how could they believe anything a citizen told them? Then there was the fact that he was a Christian, which, with this particular colonel, seemed to count against him too. He was prepared to endure physical pain, or so he told himself. But this resolve came from his training as a priest, not his true nature, which was that of a survivor. Sacrifice in the name of faith sounded like a nice ideal, but what would pain and injury count against or achieve? Would his death really bring the world rushing in to save Noli? Father Xavier often wondered about the serene expressions of composure and resignation the European masters gave early Christian martyrs in their paintings. Were they really so calm in the face of such a painful death? In his mind, the notion of surrender as the basis for a state of grace baffled him, truly it did.

It was late afternoon, his favourite time of day. Usually the fishing boats were beached and the catch landed, except that the fishermen were still too afraid to leave their families – and too ashamed to rub shoulders with boatmates from the other side of the religious divide. He removed his shoes and felt the warm sand between his toes, awakening his dulled physical senses. The sun was low, blinking at him sensually through a woolly bank of clouds low on the horizon; the dying rays threw up a delicate cloudscape mixed from a palette of bright blues, yellows, and reds, like a Fra Angelico fresco he once saw on a poster at the seminary. He stopped and turned to face the great orange orb, staring so hard that it began to wobble and he felt dizzy. Light-headedness allowed the doubts, which had been nibbling away at him for some days now, to seize bigger chunks of his consciousness. In addition, he longed to embrace Sonia again. As if the arms of a woman could rescue him, the way his mother used to scoop him up and press him against her warm and ample bosom when the playing got too rough. No wonder the church insisted on celibacy – how else could it count on its soldiers to stay in the fight? Above him, a sea gull wheeled and squawked, inbound with a gullet-full of krill. Beneath his feet, small crabs darted into holes with speed and precision. Nature made so few mistakes, Father Xavier noted; mankind walks into brick walls with alarming regularity.

The beach swept up towards a freshwater creek that Father Xavier knew well. It was the place where, as a child, he spied on the girls as they bathed with their mothers, their lithe brown bodies gleaming in the afternoon sun. An arbour of broad-leaved trees shaded the creek, and the water was always clear and cool. He and his friends could hear it was bathing time when the mothers started slapping soapy clothes on the worn pieces of basalt ballast that for years served as rudimentary washing machines. He thought he could hear the slap-slapping noise drifting his way, along with the sounds of laughter. But it was only his memory loosening, like the grains of sand between his bare feet. Imagination, once hemmed in by vows now fraying and coming undone, began directing his senses. And these aspects of his character, so deeply recessed, served as a conductor for all the pent-up frustrations of the past few weeks.

He turned towards the creek, and then stopped. The priest smiled, perhaps for the first time in a week or more. Something long forgotten in him stirred – something mischievous and adolescent. There, just behind a clump of coconut trees was the spot from where, as boys, they spied on the girls. He made a move towards the spot, then he stopped again; what on earth was he thinking? Wasn't it bad enough that he'd been tempted by a woman and lured into a passionate embrace not several metres away from here? Oh Noli, he sighed, how sensual and tempting your charms can be; how hard they are on a spirit harnessed to a higher calling than nature itself. He turned back to face the sea, feeling the warmth of the sun's dying rays tingling on his cheeks. As a boy, he used to sit on the beach and watch the sunset because it made the day just ending seem more important. His hand searched for the comb in his shirt pocket. He applied it roughly to his scalp. But this time, there was no relief.

In the distance, Father Xavier saw the hotel. The fading sunlight glinting off the seaward windows beckoned the priest, for it was time he usually set aside for a late afternoon libation with Ghani. But then he saw, riding at anchor just offshore, the ugly grey landing craft that had brought Colonel Wahyu and his soldiers. He stopped again, this time finding a perch on a fallen coconut trunk. I was good, he thought shamelessly; I was a good priest. "Damn this country and its leaders for the way they use religion as a tool of politics," Father Xavier cursed aloud. He looked down and noticed a button was missing from his shirt. Then, for no particular reason, he unbuttoned the rest and let the shirt fly open in the breeze. He sucked in a mouthful of air and longed for a drink, perhaps even a cigarette. He thought of Ghani and was deeply ashamed of his own suspicions towards the man. He'd turned out to be the hero of the hour, this corpulent rogue. And now Ghani was perhaps the only person who could protect the church and its representative on Noli from the army. The priest wondered what his superiors would have to say when they learnt that a Muslim trader of questionable morality had saved the Christian flock on Noli. Failure weighed heavily upon him. His eye fell on a beached boat nearby. According to ancient island custom in the Moluccan islands, there were two types of punishment meted out for serious crimes – death by decapitation, or expulsion to sea. Stories handed down through the generations told how most convicts preferred the certainty of sudden death to the unfathomable uncertainty of being cast off in a bare canoe with two oars and nothing else but the ocean beyond the reef.

As a child, Father Xavier was a strong swimmer who liked the thrill of night dips. There was adventure in the sea at night, when all you could see was the phosphorous surf and the odd luminous jellyfish. He and his siblings pretended they were beyond the reef hovering over the great black deepness of the ocean. Every so often, a small harmless shark would brush against their legs, its abrasive skin adding to the thrill. Then his father would call out from their modest house on the shoreline and they would all run shivering and naked into the house to hear stories from the old folk whilst they munched on sweet sago cakes. Even Sonia, who had not known Father Xavier very long, noticed how he reflected on his childhood when he wanted to summon up feelings of happiness.

When Father Xavier looked up again, it was already dark and the lights of the hotel danced like Christmas tinsel on the water. Above him, the stars were arrayed in the same haphazard way that once made him believe they were holes in the night canopy pulled over the sun. The warm lights and the clear sky disarmed the moment and dispelled his gloomy foreboding; the balming effect of Noli's bewitching beauty. Perhaps he could squeeze in a light meal and a beer with Ghani before the colonel started questioning him. Wouldn't it be nice also to take a dip? With his shirt already unbuttoned, the rest was easy and he was stripped down to his underwear without thinking too hard or for too long. Before he knew it, the waves were lapping at his ankles. The sea was warm and beckoning, and so forgetting everything, Father Xavier plunged into the inky swell and became a boy again.

꿈 꿈

The soldiers roused Father Xavier sometime after midnight.

"You're wanted by the colonel," the young Javanese informed him blankly from behind a flashlight. He spoke politely but firmly.

"Why?" he asked, dazed and blinking in the light.

"Orders," the boy replied blankly, motioning with his weapon to the door. The priest moved slowly. Every sinew and bone in his body strained to resist, yet he knew that would be pointless as well as inappropriate. He was not allowed to get fully dressed, pair of slacks and a shirt, no more, before being bundled into a minivan. The night air was chilly and he shivered, adding to his shame and embarrassment. When they come for you, he reflected, there's no longer any respect; the process of undermining your dignity has begun.

Colonel Wahyu was waiting for him in the room with a smile.

"Father, what a pleasure, and at such a…how do you say? Ungodly hour. So good of you to come." The colonel looked relaxed and, despite being the middle of the night, he wore his aviator sunglasses and, of all things, was chewing gum. There was a faint smell of aftershave mingled with mint in the room, which was hot and airless.

"What is it you want from me?" Father Xavier asked, desperately trying to bring his body under control and appear calm. The colonel wore the same smile except that now he was rubbing a large gold class ring and a bead of sweat had appeared on his smooth brow.

"Come now, Father, we can have a civilised dialogue, can't we?" Father Xavier turned towards the colonel and forced a smile through his trembling lips. The room was dimly lit; most of the furniture had been removed, leaving only a table and two chairs. Father Xavier sat on one, Colonel Wahyu on the other. Dibyo hovered in the background holding a green paper file stuffed with papers. Oddly, a camera was slung around his neck. Neither of the two soldiers carried any weapons and the colonel fiddled with his radio.

"I am happy to discuss things with you, Colonel. I take it that's why you called me in for this interview," said Father Xavier, as he fought to calm his nerves.

"Sure. We meet as friends," the colonel laughed and snapped his fingers at Dibyo who instantly handed over the green file.

"Let me see, now," the colonel said, leafing through the file. "Semarang, eh?"

"Jesuit seminary. That's where I trained as a priest."

"I see that. I served in the local command there. Two years. Of course, the military academy is nearby in Magelang, but you know that, right?"

"Have I met you before?" Father Xavier asked, blinking at the colonel. What did Ghani mean when he described the colonel as "political?" Ghani wasn't around when he'd been taken upstairs to the room on the first floor where the colonel had been questioning people all day and night.

"No, I doubt that. Doubt we ever met," said the colonel, stretching his neck muscles and suppressing a yawn. "I did know some of your superiors, though." Perhaps this won't be so bad, Father Xavier thought to himself. Maybe he just wants a friendly chat.

"Oh, yes. Father Sudiono? Did you know him?"

"I don't recall, I'm afraid. I know we arrested one of them as a communist a short while back. Troublemaker, he was, stirring up trouble on the campus at Salatiga – also in Gajah Mada. Older man, he spoke Dutch." Father Xavier's heart fell. Father Sudiono spoke Dutch. He knew enough about the army and its ways to know that any connection with the left was tantamount to being condemned. Is that why the colonel implied the past tense? It was hard to tell in the Indonesian language, where no specific tense exists except for the future. After struggling for years to master Dutch and a little English, Father Xavier came to understand how vague Indonesians kept even ordinary unevasive conversation. So much depends on context and the degree of understanding between both parties. Here, the specific reference to the left was menacing, implying his own past, a past that he was vague about himself because it brought on painful memories. The colonel ignored him for a while and studied the file. Where had all this information come from? Father Xavier wondered. What could they possibly dig up about a timid priest who did what he was ordered to at seminary and then came straight home to the island of his birth?

All of a sudden, the colonel slapped down his file and leant over the table. Gone was the jovial tone. His eyes flashed as he clutched the radio and stabbed the aerial in the priest's face.

"Your father was a traitor. You know that, don't you?"

"What? My father?" This reference to his family took him completely by surprise.

"Yes." The colonel's eyes looked down at the file, which was open and he read the name slowly and deliberately. "Pieter Lunas. That's him!"

"How…what…" Father Xavier was at a loss. He sat back in his chair with his mouth open in amazement. Why drag his poor drunk of a father into the picture? The colonel, meanwhile stood up with such force that the chair he was sitting on fell back and made a loud clattering noise. Perhaps Ghani was downstairs, would hear the commotion, and come up and speak with this lunatic, Father Xavier prayed. To stop his shaking hands, he grasped both thighs and tried to look outwardly calm. The colonel meanwhile did a little circle of the room allowing these words to sink in, and then came back to the table. He was so practiced in the art of intimidation that the steps came to him as easily as breathing.

"Traitor to the Republic. You ask how?" Here, the colonel paused for effect; this was often the point at which a look in the eyes of the accused gave him away. "Why? He supported the Republic of South Molucca. That's right; he was a partisan for the Dutch – your father, Pieter Lunas. What do you have to say?"

"Impossible," stuttered the priest, winded by this outrageous accusation. A recollection of his father's kindly face swam before his eyes. The leathery dark skin – a mark of someone who spent his days riding the waves in an open boat hauling in tuna lines. He wasn't the least bit interested in politics, as far as Father Xavier recalled. He was partial to drinking *tuak* after dark with his boatmates. In fact, Pieter Lunas was, as far as his son was concerned, the very image of island innocence – ignorant to a fault.

"Which makes you suspect, Father," the colonel continued. "We have long experience dealing with traitors and find that this kind of deviant, treacherous behaviour passes down through the generations; once a turncoat, always one; once a commie, always one; and so on. That's why we must always be vigilant – why our struggle never ends."

Father Xavier felt faint. His throat was parched and he desperately needed to drink. He looked around the room; there was no water in sight. His knees were weak and he longed to lie down. And yet he felt sure this was only the beginning of many hours of interrogation. The soldier who was killed was one of the colonel's favourites, a young lad from Surabaya. He'd wandered off for a smoke early in the evening, although some of the islanders had seen him smiling at some young girls in Merdeka Square. There was another pause before the colonel continued.

"And so that's why you're a prime suspect in our hunt for the murderer of that young soldier. Yes, you," Colonel Wahyu stabbed the air with his radio, just inches from the priest. "A traitor hiding behind the cloth," he sneered. With that, the colonel snatched the file from the desk and walked behind Father Xavier.

"You dare to deny all this?"

"Yes. Yes I do." The priest coughed nervously. He felt tears in his eyes.

"Liar!" screamed the colonel. "Liar!" he screamed again, this time bringing the file down hard against the priest's ear. Father Xavier closed his eyes and lowered his head. His ear burned and he could feel a trickle of blood making its way down his face. It had begun. "Oh, my Lord," he prayed, "make it quick."

When the priest opened his eyes again, the colonel was on the far side of the room studying his fingernails as if nothing had happened. His ear ached and he desperately wanted to touch it and make sure it wasn't bleeding. But he kept his hands firmly on his thighs in a stubborn attempt to show he was in control. He knew it was pointless to deny the tissue of lies the colonel had woven into the script for his interrogation. The colonel must have known that his father was long dead and so were most of his cronies. There had to be a point to all this, Father Xavier adduced, a larger agenda, but what?

Colonel Wahyu looked up and glared at the priest, then slowly walked behind him; Father Xavier winced expecting another blow. "There, let's get comfortable and then you can tell me all about your little Christian army…"

"What army? I…" Father Xavier leapt up from his chair and swung round on the colonel, who looked at him with that smile again.

"Yes, and the plans you had for this island. We know all about them," the colonel continued. He must have been a little nervous because Father Xavier noticed that his hand was trembling too.

"You have been misled, Colonel. I'm a priest, not a politician."

"Then explain this Christian militia that is harassing innocent Muslims with lethal weapons—and explain how my men get murdered in cold blood." The colonel screamed these words at the priest with such ferocity that even Dibyo hugged the wall of the room, trading his usual look of awe in the face of his boss for one of fear.

"Colonel, please. Don't forget the Muslim militia that came in and provoked the violence by burning the church and then going on a rampage…"

"Nonsense. There was a call for help answered by brave defenders of the faith. They came to protect Muslims from arrogant Christian rapists…"

"If you mean the incident on the beach, I can explain…"

Then, the colonel snapped.

"Damned priests, you're all the same. Dibyo, bring in the equipment."

CHAPTER EIGHT

The storm passed, leaving the young couple exhausted but alive in their little fishing boat. The mast and tattered sail did not survive the storm, and they were adrift in the ocean at the mercy of wind and currents. Alicia busied herself in the cramped cabin below, salvaging the rest of their food; Adam hung onto the tiller in a vain attempt to steer the boat and stay awake.

"If we're lucky, the winds will continue to push us southwest towards Timor," Adam mumbled through the dry crust of a compressed sago biscuit Alicia had brought up from below. His lips were swollen and caked with sea salt, as were hers. Skin peeled off their sunburned faces. And they suffered blinding headaches on account of hunger and anxiety. They were almost out of water because the storm had destroyed their rudimentary rainwater trap. They made do with rainwater they managed to collect from the bilge that was not too salty. All they could be thankful for was the sturdiness of the boat's timbers and quality of its tar caulking, for it had sprung no leaks. The sea was calm and oily now, and the sun shone like a blowtorch in a cloudless sky.

"Come," Alicia said weakly, "Let's go below. We'll die of sunstroke out here."

Reluctantly, Adam let go of the tiller. His shoulders were cramped and his hands raw and badly blistered after a night of vainly trying to hold on to the sheets of the flapping sail.

"All right, my love. Let's sleep and see what the next day brings."

In his dreams, Adam was back on Noli as if nothing had happened and the biggest problem he faced was not providing enough food for all the wedding guests. They came, armies of them; everyone wanted to eat a plate of rice and to kiss the beautiful bride, whose face he could not make out for some reason. The day was bright and happy, but there were too many people with false smiles and empty, grasping hands. And there was the priest and the mullah from the mosque, counting off their subjects on a clipboard. Too many Muslims; better bring in some Christian reinforcements, the priest was saying to

Alicia's father. The priest was Father Xavier, who wore a European suit of armour with a huge Red Cross emblazoned on it. In his hand, he carried a large double-edged sword. Meanwhile, his father and uncles were busy hauling more Muslim guests in from the mosque. They all wore white skullcaps and white flowing robes with prayer rugs slung over their shoulders. Now his father was arguing with Alicia's parents over their as yet unborn child – would he be circumcised? Would he be taught the Koran? Alicia's mother, dressed like the Virgin Mary in long flowing blue and white robes, was bleeding from her palms, at which point Adam awoke, bathed in sweat, without Alicia by his side.

Outside, it was a dark and starry night and the only noise was the gentle lapping of wavelets against the side of the boat, which was becalmed. Alicia was sitting upright staring at something over the bow.

"What is it?"

"Lights. A ship, I think. Very bright, look over there."

Adam clambered to the front of the boat and peered at the horizon. He had never seen so many lights on a ship before. The ship was so brightly lit it threw up a halo that glowed in the sky above. The whole effect was ghostly and Adam wondered if he was still dreaming. The ship was heading past them about a kilometre or so to their right. Then, Adam woke up and remembered the oars stowed below and dashed to retrieve them.

"Come on. Let's row. Row, Alicia; I think we're saved." Exhausted as he was, Adam dug his oar in deeply which turned the boat towards the oncoming ship.

"Are you sure? They could be pirates."

"No, my sweet. It's one of these expensive ships that foreigners use to see the world. It's our salvation, I'm telling you. Now row harder."

They rowed hard and grunted with all the effort. The little boat swung closer to the ship, which now loomed, a huge tower of lights over them. There was no way of telling whether they'd been seen. But once they got close, perhaps within two hundred metres and were bathed in the ship's lights, someone from the bridge shone a spotlight, which caught Adam full in the face. Next, a horn sounded and within minutes, one of the ship's boats was lowered, a great bulbous orange structure made entirely of plastic. Inside were some very rough-looking men with brown skins speaking a strange language. One of them spoke to Adam in Malay.

"Where are you from?"

"N-Noli," said Adam. His teeth were chattering and his hands were shaking. The last few minutes of rowing had sapped all of his strength.

"Where's that?"

Adam could not explain. If you hadn't heard of Noli, it was almost impossible to locate the island because it wasn't near anywhere.

"Over there," Adam said, pointing vaguely behind him.

"We ran away from the killings," Alicia added rather sensibly, for they had not given a reason for being in a tiny boat without food or water in the middle of the ocean.

⌣ ⌣

Once on board, it felt firm as if they were on land. They were taken to a sparsely furnished cabin with a bright light. The light disturbed Alicia and Adam, who weren't accustomed to such powerful artificial lighting back on the island. At home on Noli, there were two kinds of lighting; dim light bulbs and weak fluorescent tubes, the kind sold at Noli Superstore. They were shown the bathroom, which had a shower and toilet so clean and modern they gasped. The only ceramic sit-down toilets on Noli were at Hotel Merdeka. The man who spoke Malay smiled kindly and invited them to clean up and rest. He spoke about an interview later. The cabin was fitted with bunk beds, one on top of the other. After showering and changing into simple blue overalls provided by the rescue crew, they both lay on the bottom bed. The crisp white sheets smelled of mothballs, which reminded Alicia of the doctor's clinic. They were asleep in minutes, lulled by the hum and throb of the big ship's engines.

This time in his dream, Adam saw nothing but heads, the decapitated heads of all his friends. They lay around the village grounds, like fallen coconuts and Adam kept stumbling over them as he tried to go home. Standing at the threshold of their home, Adam's father carried a sword and wore two heads around his neck – they were Alicia's parents. His father waved the sword at Adam, demanding that he go out and kill Christians.

When they woke up, light was streaming through the porthole, which was the type that couldn't open. The cabin was air-conditioned and cool, which made Adam sneeze violently because he wasn't used to the change of temperature. The door was locked, so they lay on the bed and waited. It wasn't till much later that the door opened and the man who spoke Malay summoned them outside. The ship was from Singapore, he explained, but was full of foreigners from Australia and the United States. He was taking them now to see the security officer who would ask a few questions. Were they hungry? Breakfast could be arranged after the interview, he said with a kindly smile. Adam learnt that he was from the Philippines but had worked on Indonesian ships.

"We're safe now," Adam told Alicia as they waited outside an office in a bright corridor that smelt of engine oil. Sailors came and went, some of them wearing the same blue overalls; some wore orange ones. They seemed to be closer to the ship's engines, because the hum had become a louder clanking noise.

"This is a Western ship and the people here will protect us. Perhaps even take us to somewhere like Australia," Adam explained. "We can settle and forget about all the hatred. I read somewhere that if you run away from violence, Westerners take you in and give you a new life."

"So easily? Just like that?"

"It's their law, I think. They call it human rights."

"This applies to both Christians and Muslims?" Alicia asked. Adam blinked at her and hesitated before nodding his head vigorously.

"Of course, of course."

The interview, it turned out, was a medical examination.

"That's why we locked you in last night," the Filipino sailor explained. "We wanted to make sure you weren't carrying any disease. We have a lot of old people on this boat. They could easily catch something." He said nice things, Alicia thought, but his face looked worried — as though he was taking orders from somebody else. His eyes were always darting sideways, as if expecting somebody to contradict what he said. Adam had the sores on his hands dressed. Alicia was badly sunburnt, her fair skin a legacy of distant European ancestry, and her face and arms were dressed with lanolin cream. Otherwise, they seemed fine, the doctor told them through the Filipino sailor. Then they were taken back to the cabin and the door was locked again. The offer of food seemed to have been withdrawn.

"What's going on?" Alicia asked. She was suspicious.

"Perhaps they need to see if we're really sick. You heard the man talk about all those old people. They're being cautious."

"The doctor said we're okay."

"I don't know, then," Adam said irritably, kicking the side of the bunk.

Alicia was nervous because it was her idea to escape from Noli. She had expected to land on another island and find a more familiar refuge. In her mind, they would be like the refugees who had landed on the North Shore and were embraced by the community, though she was determined to bring a message of love, not hatred. Instead, here they were, saved from the angry sea, yet thrown at the mercy of strangers. All the same, Alicia was proud of Adam and how he'd handled the boat in the storm; her love for him had intensified and matured, as if they'd been married for years. In her dreams, she wove scenes of dull domestic tranquillity into long bouts of passionate love-making that resulted in her waking up gasping in a state of arousal.

It was some hours before the door was unlocked again. This time a white man wearing a clean white uniform with three gold stripes on his shoulders accompanied the Filipino sailor. The man wore a serious expression as he listened to the sailor tell what they thought must be the outline of their story. He did not ask them any questions and left after about five minutes. Once again, the sailor promised food and drink. "Just wait, for a while," he again said apologetically.

"Why do they treat us like this? Don't they know what we've been through?" Alicia asked. Adam had no answer, so he embraced her instead. He realised that they were prisoners.

"What are they and where do they come from?" the captain asked gruffly at the breakfast table. He hated unforeseen occurrences that interrupted his schedule and upset the passengers. There had been calls to the bridge wondering what had happened because the boat had stopped in the middle of the night.

"Not sure, sir," the first officer replied. "Said something about a place called Noli, or some such nonsense. Know where that is, sir?"

The captain shook his head. "You can't be too careful about who you pick up in these waters – infested with pirates. Were they checked for TB? Did they get an AIDS test?"

"Doctor checked them out – nothing immediately communicable, he says."

"That's no guarantee…."

"Sir, they seem harmless enough: boy and girl, scared and mal-nourished. Seems like they've experienced some sort of trauma," the first officer said.

"Alright, but we'd better put them ashore in Makassar."

Eventually, the food arrived. The Filipino sailor seemed friendly enough. He kept glancing with a leering eye at Alicia. Sailors, Adam thought. They're the same everywhere. He was proud to see Alicia by his side.

"We'd like to get some air," Alicia asked, wearing a sweet smile.

The sailor frowned and said something about it being against the rules and all that. Alicia then said she wasn't feeling too well, so the sailor said if that was the case, he didn't see why not. He took them up to the promenade deck. There, as expected, Alicia saw some passengers strolling or sitting in long chairs in the sun. They were all older people, she guessed them to be in their seventies. But it was hard to tell because they were very white and wrinkled. The skin on their arms hung off loosely and they had blotches and patches of red all over their bodies, rather like plucked chickens, she thought. Some wore hats and sunglasses. Their hair was grey and in some cases dyed a colour close to purple. Adam thought they might all be sick but the sailor affirmed they were all just old, retired, and very rich. "That's what they look like in the West. It's normal," he said. No one noticed the very dark young couple pass by in their blue overalls under the watchful gaze of one of the crew. It all seemed to Adam rather pointless to be fussing over them and keeping them under lock and key – but the sailor insisted they return to their cabin, mumbling something about procedure and orders. It wasn't clear at all to Adam whether they were saved, or still threatened in some way.

"Look," the sailor told them after the same ruddy-faced

Westerner with the stern look had been to visit them again. "You're not exactly under arrest, but, how can I say, you're under observation. Do you understand what that means?"

"This is ridiculous. We're refugees. A case of human rights abuse," Adam protested.

"All the same. I'm sorry. We have rules and the other passengers to think about." Alicia had an idea.

"I know, let's ask them what they think. I'm sure they'll agree that we're refugees and should be protected, taken in, even offered asylum – let them decide. After all, they're paying for all this, no?"

The sailor thought about it, rubbing his brow and wearing an expression that suggested he had neither the authority nor mental agility to decide these things.

"Okay, I'll ask," he said finally, managing a friendly grin.

"Sea gypsies, that's what they are." The gruff man with a bushy beard sat at the end of the captain's table with his arms folded. "Can I have some more of that prawn thingy, mate?" he asked a passing waiter in a deferential tone.

"Indeed, always on the lookout for a place to shelter and scavenge. I met lots of them during the war, you know. Over in Timor," said another man closer to the captain. Everyone called him Major. His face was very red from sitting in the sun.

"If we let them stay onboard, they'll only come back with us to Australia, won't they," said a woman with an equally ruddy complexion sitting at the captain's elbow. She was Major's wife.

"More damn black fellas to deal with." The gruff man at the end of the table added.

"They're putting them in camps, I see now," the captain ventured, not sure whether this was helpful or not.

"And a good thing too – otherwise we'd be swamped," Major said.

"What with all the religious troubles around here, just imagine how many of them would come," Major's wife chimed in.

"You see, their values are so different from ours."

"And of course they'd end up bringing their whole families in."

"Swamped, we'd be…"

"That's right, dear."

The captain noted the prevailing sentiment and changed the subject.

The next morning, the ship hove into the great port of Makassar. It was oppressively hot and the surface of the water was still and oily. Here the programme for the passengers was to spend a day touring the city and another travelling by bus to the quaint animistic community of Toraja-land, where the dead are shelved instead of buried, and buffalos are slaughtered for funerals. The programme also stated that there were good souvenirs, including silk and painted wooden objects, to be bought here – not forgetting the famous Toraja coffee. That morning, Adam and Alicia learned they were to be put off the ship here and handed over to the authorities.

"The passengers believed it was best," the sailor said sheepishly. He'd not been told much, just that the consensus was against keeping the couple on board.

"So much for asylum," Alicia said after the sailor had left to give them time to wash up before leaving. She felt humiliated – first by the suggestion that they were carrying disease, now by their rejection at the hands of these aged Westerners. And presumably Christians to boot! Weren't older people supposed to be wise and compassionate? She recalled the old wrinkled faces from the ship's promenade deck and imagined them in church belting out hymns and wearing stern pious faces. She saw them being asked to give to charity, and they gave generously, coins and notes filling up the collection basket. But when asked to care for a castaway boy and girl, they turned away with malice in their hearts and hurriedly left. Her mother had been wrong about Muslims being different; when it came to the basic fears that compel humanity to hatred and prejudice, there is no difference.

"Makassar! We'd have been better off staying on Noli," said Adam gloomily.

"Maybe," Alicia replied, staring out of the salt-stained porthole at the heat-drenched quayside. She guessed that things might be rough for them, a mixed couple in this fiercely Islamic town. The Makassar and Buginese people of these parts travelled widely in the islands and had a reputation for being intolerant and unscrupulous. "But then we wouldn't have learned a little more about the world, and where we truly belong," she added. "Come, let's go home."

CHAPTER NINE

The island that Adam and Alicia returned to was not the one they had left. For one thing, their parents now lived in different places. To end the violence, Colonel Wahyu, in his wisdom, divided Noli into two principal communities: Christians on the North Shore and Muslims in the south. It was the first time in the island's history that people of Muslim and Christian faith had lived apart and it decimated traditional ties between the North and South Shore settlements – bonds that were captured in the colloquial slogan, "one heart, one womb."

"You simply can't do this," Ghani pleaded with Colonel Wahyu at a heated meeting of the newly reconstituted island council, which the colonel presided over with Sultan Tarmizi by his side. "The island will whither and die. On my mother's grave, please, I beg you, don't do this."

"Nonsense, Ghani," the colonel replied. They had gathered in the grimy office that once belonged to the late Captain Widodo. The windows were shut for privacy and the heat was unbearable. "The sultan here has assured me that traditional customs will prevail and that this island has always been Muslim-led." Seated beside the colonel, his shoulders hunched, and wearing a pair of dark glasses, much like the colonel's shades covering his beady eyes, Sultan Tarmizi nodded vigorously.

"Tradition will survive. Tradition must prevail. That's the pledge my family has made, with ancestry going back to the great Arufa…." The sultan croaked. He wasn't feeling comfortable and had only come to the meeting at the colonel's insistence and on condition that it wasn't held at the hotel, which was Ghani's territory.

"Enough of this nonsense," Ghani shouted, leaping to his feet and pounding the table with his fist. There was passion in his voice. "How would the great Arufa have reacted to the way we've been killing each other these past few weeks? How are we supposed to put a community back together again if we're segregated? And now you've deprived the Christians of their sole leader by locking up Father Xavier. Meanwhile, your pet monkey walks free preaching jihad – you know who I mean." Ghani stabbed a pudgy finger in the colonel's direction. Normally, he would be reluctant to challenge the military so openly. Respect for authority came instinctively to a man whose business thrived off fortune and favour dispensed from above. But for the past few weeks, Ghani had not only fed and watered the colonel, but he'd also played host to his brutal interrogation sessions – one of which had almost killed his friend Father Xavier. Ghani's patience with the greasy colonel had worn paper-thin.

The colonel's face went blank, although from the violent grinding of cheek muscles beneath his baby-smooth skin, everyone around the table sensed a raging fury behind the mask of calm authority he preferred to wear. Seated next to him, on the colonel's left, the ever-hovering, always obedient Dibyo, whose expression rarely displayed anything other than total awe of the colonel, winced. The colonel calculated his next move carefully – for it was still hard for him to target the popular Ghani. Having the meddlesome priest under house arrest was, it seemed to him, the easy part. Taking Ghani down and installing his own cipher as the island's leader would be more challenging.

"Under the terms of this agreement, the villages must be segregated. It's the only way I can guarantee order and security," the colonel calmly intoned, indicating a green folder in front of him. In a flash, Dibyo opened the folder and, with a flourish of his wrist, handed the colonel a sheet of paper. The colonel cleared his throat and read aloud. "This being the draft version of the peace agreement assented to by the North and South Shore communities on Noli, signed on this day, and henceforth to be known as the Merdeka Agreement." He paused and surveyed the room. Corneilus Lahathula and Felix Ling, the two other members of the council, wore looks of sheepish submission. Ghani simply blinked in astonishment. It was the first he'd heard of any agreement.

> Article (1): To end the conflict and all kinds of violence.
> Article (2): To uphold supremacy of justice in a lawful, stringent, and honest way, impartially and supported by the whole population. Article (3): To counter and combat all sorts of separatist activities. Article (4): No organisations, denominations, or groups are allowed to be in possession of weaponry without permission. Either they must hand over their weapons, or the weapons will be confiscated whereupon they will be prosecuted according to the law. Article (5): A national independent tribunal will be established to investigate conclusively the events that led to the start of the conflict. Article (6): Refugees will be returned to their original homes, so long as the new demarcation of

religious communities is respected. Article (7): Stability and firmness of the Military and Police Forces, according to their respective functions, is categorically necessary in order to maintain discipline and security in the whole area. Article (8): In order to guarantee correct communication and harmony between the adherents of the various religious denominations, all forms of religious services and religious display will respect the local diversity and culture.

The colonel paused, long enough for Ghani to suck in his breath, before producing an expensive ballpoint pen and saying: "Gentlemen, shall we sign?"

Ghani exhaled loudly through pursed lips and stood up again. His face was red and he was perspiring furiously. He took a handkerchief from his pocket and wiped his brow, then, feeling composed, he again raised his finger and pointed at the colonel.

"No. I will not sign. This is an act of dictatorship. I refuse. Go ahead and arrest me if you like. I will not be a party to the segregation of Noli."

Colonel Wahyu's expression froze. The sultan sniffed and stared at the ceiling, while Cornelius and Felix Ling stared in astonishment as Ghani turned and stormed out of the room. As he left, Sultan Tarmizi turned to the colonel and whispered:

"You see, you see. I told you that man is dangerous – a communist, even."

Beside himself with anger, Ghani made straight for Father Xavier's house along the shore. Inside, the priest sat reading a dog-eared book, one of several that gathered mildew on a sloping shelf above his bed. He was still sore from the beating he'd received at the hands of Colonel Wahyu and his assistant (Dibyo had turned out to be the real sadist, despite the passive face of submission he wore around the colonel). Being alone and in intimate touch with his suffering had, ironically, helped the priest dampen his despair. He'd lost the urge to run away from everything. He smiled warmly when Ghani stumbled over the threshold, wiping his brow, his eyes bulging with anger.

"Calm yourself, my friend – have some mango juice, freshly squeezed." Father Xavier put down the book, rose stiffly from the bed and moved over to the table at the centre of his tiny room, where a pitcher and two glasses sat in readiness for any guest who chanced by. Being a prisoner did not mean that one abandoned simple island etiquette, he reasoned.

"Agh. I'm sick and tired of this tin pot colonel and his schemes." Ghani said, collapsing in the room's only easy chair.

"Ah yes, the little Caesar." Father Xavier poured a glass of juice from a pitcher and handed it to Ghani.

"Eh? What's that mean? Please don't speak in riddles," grumbled Ghani who, for all his father's erudition and learning, had hardly spent more than a few hours with a book in his life.

"What I mean is that here's a man who would sacrifice all notions of justice for the ends of power – it's not a new phenomenon," Father Xavier explained. Ghani squinted at the priest through a film of heat and sweat. There was a long pause, while Ghani gulped noisily at his mango juice and Father Xavier studied the palm of his hand, which, for the first time in weeks, wasn't trembling or bathed in sweat.

"You seem calm," Ghani said, observing the priest with a quizzical squint.

"I am. I am. Staying at home is good for the soul," he replied with a smile.

"Ah, but you're under arrest. Doesn't it hurt to be deprived of your freedom?"

"On one level, yes. But you see I've used this time to find liberty on another plane. I've had a chance to think and overcome my fears. I was stuck before, trapped in a morass of my own making – ashamed of my shortcomings as a priest, and of my own physical impulses. Then I realised…you know, a great man, I forget who, once said: as we are liberated from our own fears, our presence automatically liberates others. I think I've discovered myself. I feel stronger now."

They sat listening to the waves gently hitting the shore outside. It was hard not to be seduced by the metronomic rhythm of the ocean. After a while, Ghani felt calm enough to explain what had just happened at the island council meeting.

"Sign it," Father Xavier said, once Ghani had finished.

"But it's sheer madness."

"Yes, of course. Sign it all the same."

"But why, Father?"

"Listen to me. I have an idea we can harness this agreement to the island's advantage."

"I can't see how – it calls for segregation and gives the military supreme power. It turns that maniac Wahyu into a little sultan."

"Yes, but can't you see these are facts, anyhow? Once the Christians leave the hotel, you think they'll go back to their villages and face their Muslim neighbours? Do you see Colonel Wahyu leaving Noli anytime soon?"

Ghani blinked at Father Xavier, his mind drawing a complete blank on a course of action.

"So what's the way out of this, Father?"

"Our friend the jihadi. Umar," the priest said emphatically. Ghani noticed that there really was a new sense of purpose in the priest's voice, a calm tone of authority. He certainly was drawing strength from his predicament – quite why was beyond Ghani's comprehension.

"Umar?"

"Yes. He and his rabble will oppose this agreement. You'll see."

"And how does that suit us?

"Simple. We – that is, you and I acting in concert, Muslim and Christian leaders, we'll set the example for cooperation and harmony. It'll be hard for the colonel to argue with that – so long as we're alive."

Ghani wasn't sure how this might work, given the priest's own situation. "Well quite. He beat you to within an inch of your life, no?"

Father Xavier winced as he recalled the beating. He'd passed out some time after the colonel's assistant, Dibyo, had begun thrashing a thick rubber hose against his knees. When he woke up, his eyes were clamped shut and there was an intense burning sensation in his groin. He shivered at the recollection, then turned to Ghani and said:

"Now all we need is a project, something that will pull people together. You'll see, this will work."

Sure enough, Umar was furious with the agreement, and he used the Friday prayer gathering at the island's main mosque, his first appearance in some days, to make his feelings plain.

"Since the first slaughter of Muslims, we have been asked to consider reconciliation," he thundered from the floor of the mosque. "It's like somebody who has been beaten up, and, while still recovering from the beating, has to agree to terms of 'peace,' wrapped up in the word 'reconciliation.' Oh, but my brothers, don't be fooled. This reconciliation is just a camouflage. It hides the rotten intentions of these Christian revolutionists." At this the congregation stirred and from the back of the room came shouts of "Long live Umar!" from his followers. He waited for the murmuring of assent to die down before continuing. "My brothers in arms, to the Muslims of Noli, reconciliation means voluntarily giving up their lives. Surely, for Muslims, any reconciliation is hard. Anticipating any act of justice and truth while the slaughterers are still freely roaming about, the word 'peace' is hardly acceptable. Before the inflicted injuries have healed, treachery upon treachery is taking place…" Now the shouting grew louder and a few of his followers called out, "Death to all Christians!"

"How strange it is," Umar continued, "that all parties can effect reconciliation. As if by this reconciliation, everlasting peace will be accomplished. They lay the roof for protection, but are forgetting the foundation and pillars. As if everybody wants to close his eyes, not caring about the carnage on the North Shore. They don't care about the presence of the separatist movement seeking to break away from the Republic, covering up the rottenness of the church and those provocateurs that hide behind the 'Word of God.'"

Those gathered in the mosque, sitting cross-legged or with their legs tucked behind them on the carpeted floor, listened intently. Many in the congregation had hoped that the arrival of the military would bring justice as well as peace – they saw themselves as wronged. In fact, the soldiers roamed the island committing petty crimes and demanding material support. "Contributions" the soldiers called them; in fact, the fishing had been lean these past few weeks and the boats lay idle along the shore, bleached in the sun. For his part, Umar was angry at the way his backers appeared to have abandoned him and his men. He'd not been consulted about the agreement and was intent on burying it. "It is too early to talk about reconciliation whilst one community is still traumatised with this expression. The delegates who drew up this agreement are not sufficiently representative to talk in the name of the people. This reconciliation even turns upside down the Muslim ranks. One by one, those who used to be public figures have been caught associating with the Christians and now have become people that are good-for-nothing. Trash. Of course, if justice has to be done in Noli, the Muslims themselves must do it. In what way must they act? There is no other way than jihad! *Allahu'A'lam*."

॰ ॰

It was at this point that Adam and Alicia showed up on Noli. They were dropped off by a Buginese fishing boat, after prowling the docks in Makassar, pleading for passage to Noli – or at least to Ambon. The scene at the little jetty where the boat's cutter dropped them was desolate. People no longer lounged in the shade of the jetty's awning or dropped a desultory line or two to hook the fingerlings that swarmed in the vivid green water. Gone were the little boys who raced tethered crabs along the jetty's planks, sometimes falling laughing into the crystal-clear water close to the shore. A solitary fisherman, who lingered on the jetty smoking in the shade, nodded but otherwise ignored the young couple as they stepped gingerly ashore. A lot of people on Noli minded their own business these days – it was healthier to do so.

"Where is everybody?" Adam asked Alicia after thanking the brusque Bugis boatman and pushing the cutter off the jetty for him.

"Perhaps there's a meeting, or some kind of festival," said Alicia hopefully. Her hopes were pinned to the idea that the violence that forced them to flee had been a bad dream that passed, leaving their beloved island unscarred so they could resume their plans.

"I'd better see if my uncle's around – let's go to the hotel," Adam suggested. They carried only a small bag between them with a change of clothes they were given onboard the cruise liner. Adam wore an outsized white crewman's shirt over a pair of blue shorts, while Alicia had been presented with a yellow cotton dress discarded by a departing passenger on an earlier cruise. We must look like tourists, Adam thought.

Upon reaching the hotel, they found Ghani asleep, slumped over quite a few empty beer bottles, alone in the coffee shop. Once wakened, he was overjoyed to see his nephew and the beautiful Alicia still alive – he'd long feared them dead. Scattering bottles and a bowl full of stale prawn crackers, Ghani embraced Adam and planted a great wet kiss on Alicia's forehead.

"We all thought you were dead – you left no word of your escape. Where an earth did you two go – and how?"

It took a good half an hour for Adam and Alicia to relate their story — a precarious few days at sea in a storm-tossed boat, their rescue and disillusionment. Ghani's eyes lit up and wandered over Alicia's now hardened, weather-beaten features. There was a reddish tinge to her long hair and the first sign of wrinkles around her eyes. Adam, knowing his uncle's lascivious inclinations, felt compelled to gloss over the long, starlit nights on the boat. Conditions were so bad, it was a constant struggle to keep the boat afloat, he said. As for their sojourn on the cruise ship: they were kept like prisoners apart from the other passengers.

No sooner had they finished telling their story that Ghani reverted to the melancholic state in which they'd found him. "You can forget about the wedding," he said. "The whole thing has been called off."

The young couple sat while Ghani explained what had befallen the island in their absence. It had a strange effect on the young couple. They'd walked in holding hands, but by the end of Ghani's monologue on the state of affairs between the two communities, Muslim and Christian, their hands were unentwined and they could barely glance at each other.

"Have you seen my father?" asked Adam. He spoke in barely a whisper, his gaze fixed on the floor.

"I have, yes. He's always in the mosque praying. He's on the *ulama*'s council that has embraced Umar and his thugs. They talk about self-defence, but what they mean is revenge."

"And my parents? What news of them?" It was Alicia's turn to ask.

"Up on the North Shore. Shaken, but unharmed so far as I know. I haven't seen them in weeks. But your cousins, agh," Ghani paused and wiped a tear from his eye. Alicia's two teenage cousins, Jimmy and Johnny, had been the village tear-aways before the troubles hit. Big, strapping boys with curly hair and infectious laughs;

between them, they were always in some kind of trouble.

"What about them?" Alicia asked, with a tone of urgency in her voice.

"They've become animals. They joined a band of thugs calling themselves "Noli's Holy Warriors." They rode around in a pickup chopping heads like it was some kind of game…I…I really can't explain what's happened to people here…."

"What has happened here, Uncle? What really happened?" There was a serious edge to Adam's voice, one that demanded attention.

Ghani thought for a while, cradling his great jowls in the upturned palm of one meaty hand, while with the other, he spun an empty beer bottle. The joy and exhilaration of turning back the mob outside the hotel had subsided. His Christian charges had begun to disperse, under the terms of the agreement – along with the sense of close communal unity they shared. The reality he faced now was purely sectarian. Umar had lost the battle but won the war.

"We were provoked. What else can I say? Whether out of fear or driven mad by loss and grief, our people behaved irrationally. It was like some kind of magic spell. I swear you wouldn't believe it; one moment you're neighbours, the next, a band of brutal killers cutting each other to shreds. Gentle fishermen turned into killers who murder in the name of their faith. And the kids; God strike me down, they were the ringleaders. Older people looked up to them and believed that if they died they would gain rich rewards in the afterlife. That's what happened."

Ghani paused to wipe the sweat from his brow and studied the faces of the two young islanders sitting across the table from him. He seemed to read their thoughts. "What happened to all that love and respect for one another? Ha! Harmony was an illusion – all an illusion. It seems that we Nolians aren't really so neighbourly after all. Bound together like womb and heart, we said. What nonsense! More like mouth and arsehole – depending from whose perspective you're looking at things. I'm sorry, my dear…." He cast a watery eye towards Alicia and sighed. "Then there were the festivals, all that false respect for one another. Such an illusion!"

"No, Uncle Ghani. That's not true," Alicia's eyes flashed and her voice carried conviction. "This evil came into our lives and brought us into sin – it wasn't there before. The refugees, they carried it in by boat, like some foul cargo that contaminated us."

"I wish I could believe it was as simple as that." Ghani sighed again. His heart grew heavy when he reflected on what had happened. Lately, he'd suffered from blinding headaches, for which the only cure seemed to be long bouts of drinking. He wasn't sure whether the return of his young nephew and his fiancée was a good or a bad thing, and he feared for their safety. "Come," he said, managing to muster a weak smile, "you two must be starving. These Buginese, they live on nothing – just gnawing at the jib rope is a meal for them. I'll have the kitchen make some fish cakes and sago pudding. Gus the noodle seller now works for me and the cuisine has improved tremendously."

When Father Xavier heard of the couple's return, he smiled. He'd said a prayer for their safety almost daily – along with a host of others. It pleased him greatly that at least this one had been answered.

"Where are they?" he asked Ghani the next day.

"Safe for now – at the hotel. I found them rooms. Don't worry. Their rooms are at the opposite end of the hotel from the mad colonel."

"Good," said Father Xavier.

"Their parents, of course, now live at different ends of the island, and I doubt we can plan on a wedding now," said Ghani. Father Xavier nodded and stroked his chin deep in thought. There was something prescient about Adam and Alicia's return which lifted his spirits. This couple bridged the religious divide and fought against all the odds to survive, and they came home; their return was an omen.

It was a spark of hope. Of course! Wouldn't a wedding, if it could be arranged, help bring the communities together again? Wasn't this one ritual that might act as a healing agent?

"No, I disagree," the priest said emphatically. "In fact, we must make preparations for their wedding."

Ghani's jaw dropped. "Now? At a time like this?"

"And why not? Noli needs some good news, a distraction."

There was a gleam in the priest's eye. The news of the couple's return seemed to have energised him.

"But the matter of religion. These are still sensitive times, Father."

"Simple. Alicia will convert to Islam. Her willingness to enter the faith of her beloved, with my support, will help unite the community again." Father Xavier crossed his arms and beamed at Ghani. The hotel owner's astonishment gave way to admiration for the audacity of the priest's plan.

"Father," he said with a broad smile, "you may not be a saint, but you are a genius."

The wedding plans were made in secret. Colonel Wahyu enforced a strict corralling of the communities in their designated locations, ostensibly to prevent any further outbreak of violence, so it was difficult for members of each community to communicate. There were physical barriers as well as social constraints. Leaving the South Shore northward and along the coast, the road was blocked by a barricade of stone-filled oil drums manned by Umar's followers, armed with rifles that could only have been supplied by the army. As a small concession, Colonel Wahyu allowed Father Xavier to conduct mass every Sunday at an improvised chapel up on the North Shore. He was escorted under guard there and back – that's how he communicated with the Gordon family about the planned wedding. The Junaidis were more challenging, however.

"Your place is by my side, now. We must work together, pray together, and defend our faith together," Adam's father told his son after ritual homecoming prayers held in their new home along the southern shore. Adam sat on the floor of the new family home, which belonged to an evicted Christian family. But for the unfamiliar physical surroundings, everything appeared normal. He'd bathed and wore a fresh sarong, much as he would after a long day on the fishing boat. The smell of his mother's cooking wafted in from the back of the house – another of her simply mouthwatering fish curries. The air was cool and his body was refreshed, but inside he was burning. It was almost three days since he'd last seen Alicia, who had been reunited with her parents on the North Shore. There was no way for them to communicate, except through the priest – and Sunday was another day away.

"I'm happy to be home, father," Adam lied. It wasn't fair to his mother to betray his pangs of longing for Alicia – as well as the deep despair he felt about his father's sentiments. He'd not told them of Alicia's role in his escape – although they kept asking about her in a way that suggested they knew. Besides, now wasn't the time to engage his parents, which would spoil the homecoming celebrations. He decided to wait for the following day.

It made little difference. His father was furious and his mother wept when Adam announced his intentions the following day.

"How could you still want to marry that girl? After all we've been through – all the murder and treachery. Her family, you know, they've, they've…" Adam's father was so enraged that he lost the ability to speak. They were sitting cross-legged around a tray of sweet tea and cakes shortly before midday prayers. Adam had promised his father to join him at the mosque, although he was dreading the prospect. The main mosque of Noli resembled more a fortress than a place of worship. Umar had his headquarters in a building that formerly housed a small Koranic school in the mosque compound.

"Father, please try to understand," Adam pleaded. It was no use, though. He held back when his father, a scarlet prayer rug slung over one shoulder, brusquely left the house for prayers. From the small porch in front of their temporary home, Adam saw other men heading for the mosque. He recognised some of them as his former boatmates, and he wanted to call out to them. But he noticed that they wore sullen faces and hung their heads. No one laughed or joked as they used to. Some carried long knives and wore Arab-style *keffayas* wrapped around their shoulders. He wondered: why go to pray when there was no goodness in their hearts?

It started to rain. Large raindrops hit the dark earth beyond the porch and soon a large pool of water formed. The dark sky and pungent smell of damp earth momentarily restored Adam's sprits, as if nature could wash away all the blood. Perhaps his union with Alicia would help heal the deep wounds that afflicted this place. It was a nice thought to have as he prepared to leave his family.

≈ ≈

Father Xavier stirred his morning coffee, and with it, a jumble of thoughts. There was no question that he felt closer to his faith than at any time before. Privately, he'd always had trouble calibrating belief in God without reference to his doubts – it was something his superiors in Semarang recognised, which is why he failed to make the missionary order. As a child, he grew up believing that life was too perfect on Noli to require blind faith in a higher being. When he returned as the island's priest, he conducted the rituals of his office in the firm conviction that the church played an important social role. There was no need for miracles when the sun provided one each morning. Imagining God became easier once the imperfection and immorality of the people he lived among was exposed by the spate of violence. For this reason, he reckoned, good and evil cannot be entirely divorced. Certainly, the plan he was hatching involved a great deal of danger and deception in order to achieve what he hoped would be a constructive conclusion. It amused him also that the chosen vehicle for this revolt against Colonel Wahyu and his hired thugs, a simple wedding ceremony, was nothing extraordinary, merely a basic social convention.

"Gus, you're a saint. Truly, you are."

The garlic-laced aroma from the fried noodles filled Father Xavier's little room.

"Father, there's no need to go that far over a simple plate of noodles," Gus said bashfully. Under the terms of the priest's detention, he was brought all his meals, and the task usually fell to Gus to bring food from the hotel, where he now presided over Ghani's grimy kitchen. He usually stayed while the priest wolfed down the meal.

"You've heard about Felix, I suppose," said Gus.

"Hmm?" came the priest's reply between slurps. Gus took this as an invitation to continue.

"Well you know, his business collapsed. His marriage – you know about that. So, in any case, he's resolved to leave. He'll take the next boat out of here. Tells me he's thinking of going to Singapore – says Jakarta is too dangerous. Can't say that I blame him for thinking that way."

Father Xavier looked up from the plate, but could find no words, so plunged back into the noodles. This was dangerous territory given his relationship with Sonia, and he wasn't sure how much other people knew. It sounded like Gus was fishing for something.

"Sonia is staying," Gus said in a matter-of-fact way. Father Xavier felt his ears burn.

"Quite a lot of chilli in this one," he said, grinning sheepishly at the noodle seller. Gus smiled. "No more than usual, Father. No more than usual." Then they both started laughing because it seemed the best way out of this embarrassing cul-de-sac. They were still chuckling when a loud explosion shook the house. Gus almost fell off his chair. Father Xavier leapt to his feet and rushed to the window that faced the beach. "Oh my God," he said. "It's the hotel."

There was dust and debris everywhere. One side of the old wrought iron gate lay flat across the threshold. From inside the hotel came the sound of dripping water and breaking glass. It took Colonel Wahyu and his men some five minutes to race over from their new office in the old police station. A small crowd had already gathered at what was left of the hotel entrance. Everyone asked themselves one question: where's Ghani?

"Inside, men. Get inside," the colonel directed a squad of his soldiers who looked very reluctant to follow orders. They scratched their heads and peered in at the smoking black hole that once was the hotel lobby. There was a musty smell in the air, as if an old pile of books had been disturbed. "Looks like a bomb, sir," said one of them. "I know it's a bomb. I want you to go inside and see if there are any casualties, idiot." The soldier looked at the colonel, then back at the bombed out entrance, as if he wasn't sure which posed the greater threat. "Yes sir," he said finally, and marched inside holding an olive green rag over his mouth.

It wasn't the first time that Gus had witnessed a trauma, and he cringed on the edge of the crowd, fearing the worst. He'd hurried back from Father Xavier's house and fully expected to see Ghani's bloodied corpse brought out. He prepared himself to lament the loss of another friend and benefactor. This was the last straw, and he made silent plans to leave Noli. But just as he was pondering where he might go, the crowd erupted in cheers. Gus moved into the thick of the crowd, jostling his way to the front where he saw, to his relief, a shaken but still very much alive Ghani, dusting shards of glass off his sleeve.

"I'm okay. Okay. No injuries inside – just a lot of smoke and glass," he said to the group nearest him. Colonel Wahyu came over and shook his hand. "Don't worry, Ghani. I will look into this," he said, giving the dust-covered hotel owner what passed for an earnest look. Ghani threw him a cold stare.

This time, it was Sonia who brought the news to Father Xavier.

"Ghani is safe. There was a lot of smoke and noise, but thankfully very little real damage to the hotel," she said breathlessly. Sonia had run all the way from the hotel across the beach and they embraced briefly when she arrived, which made her flush.

"Thank God, he's alive," breathed Father Xavier. "But a bomb, of all things. Why the hotel – what madman would have risked killing the colonel as well? Has it come to this now? Haven't we suffered enough from terror?" The priest turned away, lost in thought and for a few moments it was as if Sonia wasn't there. When he turned again, she looked downcast and her shoulders heaved with sobs.

"Sonia?" Father Xavier asked gently.

"I couldn't stay away," she said softly. Father Xavier moved towards her, but stopped short of embracing her again and instead laid a hand on one shoulder. It was an awkward moment, but one he felt more in control of now. That night on the beach, he'd lost his way and found it again in the arms of a married woman. If this one act helped him back on the path, was that so bad? There was no need for another detour, he resolved. He retracted his hand, oddly feeling no pain or frustration. Things were different now, he felt closer to God and there was much to do.

Things weren't going according to plan for Umar and his band of holy warriors. Hemmed in on one side by islanders not fully trusting of their intentions, and on the other by a wily army colonel and his tricks, these were hardly the ideal circumstances for waging jihad. Umar's mission was simple: sow hatred and, if possible, kill Christians.

Well, he'd done a lot of that these past few weeks on Noli, but he saw little reward, neither from the Muslims nor their masters.

"It's hard enough to keep this going on so little money," Umar fretted with his henchmen one afternoon in their makeshift head-quarters, the former Koranic school adjacent to the mosque. "But now we have the colonel telling us what to do and what not to do. Agh, I'm confused, I tell you. One moment he's handing out guns and ordering me to set up barricades, the next he's selling me out to that priest and his lackey infidel-lover of a hotel owner." Umar spat on the ground and trod on his own saliva for good measure, grinding the very thought of Ghani – the man who had so embarrassingly de-feated Umar that day outside the hotel – into the earth.

"What does he want us to do, this colonel?" asked one of the henchmen dumbly. These simple folk, ruffians for the most part, fol-lowed Umar, as they had followed him when he was a petty street gang leader in Jakarta. To them it made no difference who he served, or what cause he fought for – their loyalty was to Umar, their *ustad* and paymaster.

"What the army always wants – to use us for their own ends. Nothing's changed since the time of my grandfather when the army used us against the communists at Madiun. Then there was the time of my father, when the army provided the guns and told him to go and slaughter communists again. And what do we get in the way of thanks? My grandfather jailed for supporting an Islamic state; my father beaten up for belonging to a Muslim party. And me? Look at us, walking into the same trap. We're just tools for the military; tools that can be discarded once the job is done."

"Should we go? Leave this place?" asked another follower, who sounded like he was itching to leave.

"Yes, *Ustad* Umar. The bomb didn't work – Ghani still lives and the colonel is on his side now." The dumb henchman had a point, and Umar knew it.

"No. Not yet," said Umar, irritated by the reminder of this failure. "I have a new plan that will make them all sit up and pay attention."

Their discussion was interrupted by the arrival of a messenger. He looked like a civilian, but in fact was a soldier dressed as one. It was Colonel Wahyu's crude way of disguising his links with these mercenaries. The messenger approached Umar and handed him an envelope. After reading it, Umar said: "I have to go to a meeting. I'll be back in a couple of hours."

⁀ ⁀

Father Xavier's plan had a big hole blown through it by the hotel bomb blast.

"There can be no wedding at the hotel," said Ghani emphatically. "My decision is final." The hotel owner's brush with death appeared to have weakened his resolve. He scowled at Father Xavier from one end of the priest's meagre room and stood his ground.

"For one thing, the awful colonel is watching the place day and night. He's set a guard on the door and I can't even leave for the fish landing without an armed escort."

"I'm touched by his concern, as I'm sure you are," said Father Xavier sarcastically.

"Fine for you to laugh – I could have died in there." Ghani shifted his weight on the chair, which was too small for him. In fact, Ghani was having lunch in the coffee shop when the blast occurred. Thankfully, no one was in the lobby where the bomb, consisting of two grenades and a detonator hidden in a box of mangos, had been left. Father Xavier searched the worried man's face. Was this the same Ghani who bravely faced down the Muslim mob and saved the island's Christians from wholesale murder?

"I know what you're thinking, Father," Ghani said, reading

the priest's mind. "But this is different. It's like being lynched in the street, taken from behind – you can't imagine the terror of being bombed. I have palpitations, I can't sleep."

"Yes but we must end this now – and I know how to end it. Believe me, it's the only way."

Father Xavier stood up and walked over to Ghani, who sat by the window facing the beach. He stared out at the shore, where some boys were playing with an old and perished rubber tyre, flotsam perhaps, from a passing boat. It would have been a normal scene, except these boys were Muslims forced to move down from the North Shore.

"See those boys out there? They're Noli's future. But they are growing up in the shade of trauma. The shade lengthens with each year of separation. They are exiles and even though they might never see violence on the scale we've witnessed these past few weeks, as exiles, they carry its memory like a genetic strain. One day they will be ready to kill more easily because of the burden of separation. You see how it goes on, how it is perpetuated? Unless, of course, we restore what we had."

"And just how does a wedding achieve this, this impossible dream?" Ghani looked up at the priest, who stood close to his chair, looking out of the window. There were no bars on the window, yet this was his jail.

Father Xavier turned away from the window and walked over to the bed. He reached up and pulled a book down from the shelf. It was old and dusty, its pages yellowed and stiff with mildew. Carefully, the priest peered over the top of the book, searching for something. Then he sneezed.

"Bless you, Father," said Ghani.

"Aha, here it is," said the priest, prising open the book at a page apparently marked by a tiny slip of paper poking out of the top. Slowly he ran a finger down one page and started reading: "They used to have neither law nor religion. They worshipped the celestial bodies, the sun, the moon, and the stars, and idols they made to the honour of their fathers and forefathers. And these were made of wood or stone with faces of men, dogs, cats, and other animals towards which they were more inclined. They had no knowledge at all of the first Creator, nor of the revolution of the heavens. Nor had they moral discipline, religion, or priests, except for a few who were said to have visited the other world. These performed ceremonies, spoke with the gods, and gave answers." Slowly he closed the book and walked over to Ghani, who wore a puzzled look, his head tilted on one side.

"*A Treatise on the Moluccas*. It was written some time in the mid-sixteenth century by the first European to govern these islands. He was Portuguese and his name was Antonio Galvao – he came before my great namesake, St. Francis Xavier."

"Forgive me, Father, what's your point?" Ghani showed no inclination to take the book. He didn't like books all that much.

"He writes of a time before the schism, before two great religions of the book clashed on our soil. It was to be sure a time of profanity and moral laxity, at least seen through European eyes. No doubt through Muslim eyes, too. But as the man says, the people of these islands back then had ways to find answers to everything they needed to know – there was a simple order to things. And it was rooted in the simple beauty of our surroundings."

Ghani blinked and stared at the priest, at a loss for words. He began to wonder if the recent experience at the hands of Colonel Wahyu might have damaged his friend's senses.

"I'm sure, Ghani, that you must think me a heretic." Father Xavier laughed and Ghani nodded slowly in affirmation, thinking that the priest had gone mad. Father Xavier strode back to the bedside shelf and lodged the book back in its place, then he turned and said: "Look, when I was in Semarang at the seminary, I learnt that the Javanese suppress religious conflict by reference to a common culture, much of it steeped in pre-Christian, pre-Islamic Hindu ritual. The sultan in those parts is the head of the Islamic religion, but balances the forces of nature by holding frequent meetings with the Goddess of the Southern Seas. Don't you see, our own traditions can play a healing role here. Why not?"

"I see that, Father, but what connection does this have with Adam and Alicia's wedding? Haven't we agreed they will marry as Muslims?"

"We have, and they will. But now that the hotel is out, and no Muslim *qadi* or Catholic priest can get involved. Instead, they will marry under the moon and stars with our island's ancestral spirits as witnesses."

"And, so?" Ghani was breathless and perplexed.

"So our people will gain strength for this affirmation of tradition – and who better but Mama Fatima to act as the go-between? Oh, Ghani, dear friend, don't you see? The church, the mosque; they are irrelevant. Umar and his thugs will have no power over the setting as outsiders. The union of Adam and Alicia will return Noli to us."

CHAPTER TEN

Mama Fatima kept irregular hours and Ghani found himself with an appointment to see the seer a little after one in the morning. "Better that way," said her guardian, Din. "Mama Fatima doesn't make much sense in daylight." Din sat husking a young coconut on the sharp edge of a very sharp knife. The noise made by the fibrous skin over the edge of the knife matched the consumptive rasp of Din's voice. "And what is it you're after? Any special charm?" he asked absentmindedly. Din had an air of authority about him that overcame his dishevelled appearance and missing front teeth. "I'd rather speak directly to Mama Fatima," mumbled Ghani, casting Mama Fatima's unsavoury gatekeeper a suspicious look. "Have it your way, then," said Din, continuing with his husking. At the appointed hour, Mama Fatima was nowhere to be seen and Ghani was fast asleep at the foot of the stairs leading up to Mama Fatima's shack. In fact, it was some two hours later when Din came and kicked Ghani's shins. "Wake up. It's your time," he rasped.

After Ghani had proposed the idea, Mama Fatima sat back and let out a shrieking laugh. "You want me to preside over a wedding? Ha! You want my protection? Oh my bones, my ancient bones." Her natural voice was cracked and throaty. A large bulge on one side of her mouth indicated the presence of a large wad of betel nut and lime.

"You can do it, then?" Ghani asked.

Mama Fatima didn't say anything. Instead, she sniffed and aimed a long stream of betel nut juice at a bowl by her side.

"I'll take that as a yes, then," said Ghani, heaving himself up from the floor.

Mama Fatima grinned at him, exposing an uneven row of red stained teeth. From behind, he heard Din clambering up the steps to Mama Fatima's lair. What on earth was he doing here? he wondered. How could this sordid old medium hold the key to Noli's future? There was, of course, no real alternative.

Word spread quickly, conducted across the island through tangled noli bushes, their tendrils performing perfumed synapses. There was to be an event, a spectacle. It was to be something important for all those who called themselves Nolians. Details were sparse, and deliberately so. People spoke about upholding tradition, a prayer for unity. Yet there was no mention of either religion – no suggestion of this being a Christian or a Muslim affair. There was instead an alluring anticipation of pagan renewal.

For Father Xavier, the prime mover of this event, there was an inner, secret sense of fulfilment associated with the ceremony. He'd asked for the erection of a fragrant arbour on the beach in front of Mama

Fatima's shack. There was to be bougainvillea laced through thorny noli branches and framed by young coconut fronds and held up by the lime green stalks of young banana trees. Two chairs decked in flowers were to be set under the arbour and strewn with fresh magnolia – and as many shells as could be gathered placed around the marital throne. This was the church altar he'd always dreamed of.

On the appointed day of the ceremony, the air was still and the sea was flat calm. It was one of those days when the heat drove people into the shade of their homes and the murmur of the Noli pigeon filled the air. Dusk fell, shrouding the island in a pink glow. Waves lapped gently at the shore in front of Mama Fatima's meagre shack. Just as the first stars appeared in the darkening sky, Din emerged with his goatskin drum and started beating a slow, summoning rhythm.

People arrived in ones and twos, for travelling in large groups these days drew attention and risked attack. They came and sat cross-legged on the packed sand in front of Mama Fatima's little house, beside which the freshly-made arbour stood covered in palm fronds. They made nervous small talk and lit up cigarettes and soon the area was covered with a pall of sweet-smelling kretek smoke. A bigger than usual crowd was anticipated, so Kamal and Din, the two accomplices, had planted a row of flaming bamboo torches as far back from the house as possible. Under cover of Din's slow drumbeats, the island gathered with great trepidation to hear the great warrior queen of Ternate speak.

From where he stood near the back, Father Xavier prayed that the bundle of cash he'd thrust into the eager hands of the young soldier guarding his door was sufficient to keep the young conscript from reporting his absence to Colonel Wahyu. He'd calculated that the colonel would stay away, along with Umar and his thugs, because these weekly gatherings had proven harmless enough – and besides, the Javanese were terrified of any kind of foreign mysticism. Just in case, he'd asked Felix to post himself at the hotel with a crate full of imported delicacies, among the last salvaged from the Noli Superstore.

"If the colonel makes a move, use all your charm to keep him in the hotel," the priest had instructed the timorous shopkeeper.

"You think I'm used to this kind of activity, don't you," grumbled Felix. He was ashamed of his racial stereotype; the idea of the Chinese shopkeeper's natural inclination to bribe the authorities, without thinking of alternatives.

"Let's just say that for once, your experience in dealing with higher authority is serving, shall we say, a higher purpose," Father Xavier replied.

When the drumming stopped, everyone turned to face the stairs. For it was the signal that Mama Fatima was ready to appear. A loud rustle of dried palm fronds and a deep gurgle announced her presence. Kamal appeared in the doorway first. He wore a black velvet *peci* tilted at a rakish angle and clutched a large dagger in one hand. He backed out of the narrow entrance making a swishing sound rather like someone shooing away flies. Din struck up a faster drumbeat and the crowd murmured a subdued greeting.

It was hard from the back of the crowd to discern the features of Mama Fatima's face, but the whites of her eyes shone like tiny points of light. Her mouth was smudged red with betel juice. She shook her head and flashed her eyes, grimaced and then burped; it was her usual prelude.

"The great Arufa asks the people of Noli to come together," she said at last. Her voice was guttural, masculine, and clearer than usual.

"Great people have come to teach us things and opened our eyes to truth and wonderment. But these same people have infected our hearts with hatred and taught us to regard each other differently, according to what we eat, or how we worship. The great Arufa is pained by what has become of us. We who grew from the same root and grew from the same branch. How can two fruits from the same tree taste so differently? Is there one noli nut more fragrant than the other?"

There was a murmur of assent from the audience.

"The great Arufa asks for purification. We who have divided and fallen upon one another – yes, you who would ask me for protection from your neighbour, or a potency to kill him. He asks that we come together and reassert our common tradition. He calls for a ritual union of our island's people."

Mama Fatima spat and the light from the torch nearby caught a long stream of red betel juice. It was a signal for Din to start beating his drum again. Meanwhile, Kamal started removing the lattice of palm fronds that screened the arbour. There was another audible gasp as it was revealed. Then, from behind Mama Fatima at the top of the rickety stairs, Adam and Alicia appeared. The crowd was stunned. There were audible gasps and short intakes of breath – a lot of finger pointing and mutterings. It was a delicate moment and one that Father Xavier was gambling on; would the couple be cheered or lynched? He watched them slowly and uneasily descending the rickety stairs. Adam wore a loose white cotton shirt over a red sarong of the finest Bugis silk. Alicia's hair was oiled and braided, old island style, with jasmine and magnolia flowers. She wore a simple Javanese lace *kebaya* over a blue sarong woven with gold thread. They both smiled to mask the deep fear in their hearts, for this was the gamble of their lives too. When they reached the bottom of the stairs, Kamal led them to the arbour. For a moment, the crowd sat in silence and the future of Noli hung in the balance.

"This is treachery, the work of the devil," rang out an anxious female voice from near the back. "Yes, stone them, they are betraying their faiths. Stone them!" shouted another. Father Xavier tensed. He felt sweat running down his back and a huge claw grip his insides. "Please, please dear God, don't let this happen," he muttered under his breath. The crowd shifted uneasily, their eyes on Mama Fatima, who seemed to be in a semi-conscious trance, lolling her head from side to side. "Where's the great Arufa now?" shouted a man from near where Father Xavier was standing. Just then, Ghani stepped forward. On one side of him was the old *ulama* from the mosque with a befuddled look on his face. Ghani's face was pale and drawn. In one hand he carried his father's copy of the Koran, the one that had served him so faithfully outside the hotel that fateful day a few weeks back when Umar and his thugs threatened the refugees. He raised the book high above his head and said: "It's alright. They will marry in the Muslim faith – just as tradition and the law prescribes." The crowd fell silent, taking this in. The Christians among them looked uneasy. Muslims nodded with tentative satisfaction. It was Mama Fatima who settled the matter: "The great Arufa ordains that this ceremony is pure – these young people are the new shoots that must be nurtured, for from their union, a new tree will grow and shade our island; it will bear fruit and provide us with sustenance. He commands that we all respect their wishes to marry." Again, the crowd fell silent. Ghani moved closer to the couple, accompanied by the *ulama*, his eyes were moist with tears. Then, from somewhere in the middle of the crowd, a man stood up and shouted: "Long live Adam and Alicia! Long live Noli!" Then another, and another – soon the whole crowd was on its feet.

Father Xavier felt a huge weight fall from his shoulders and tears well up in his eyes. He raised his head skyward and, for the first time in weeks, he cried without restraint. It was more a laugh, a cry of joy. For if there was ever a time when God had manifested Himself during this whole period, it was now, he thought. How foolish of him to believe that God worked through specific channels. How did he ever imagine that the church alone could contain God's spiritual presence?

This, he reflected, was a principal folly of man. We spend our lives looking for salvation by building fences and hiding behind them. Yet here, under the stars, in plain view of the heavens: here is the answer. He examined the awe that now lit up the faces on either side of him, their eyes full of hope, inspired by a broken-toothed spirit medium and her frog-voiced clown of an assistant.

The couple clasped hands under the arbour and wore wide smiles of relief. The *ulama* mumbled a few words from the Koran; sanctifying a union that was so natural it seemed hardly worth wasting time with words. Where was the heresy in that, wondered Father Xavier. This was God's work. With this certainty lifting his weary spirits, the priest turned to go. Suddenly, he felt very tired, and besides he wasn't keen on testing the strength of the bribe that kept his guard looking the other way. Just as he turned to leave, he felt a light tap on his shoulder. It was Ghani.

"Father, what's this? Not staying for the festivities?" Ghani asked with a broad smile. He tapped one of his pockets, which bulged. "I found something rather special, rummaging behind the bar, you know. Real Scotch." Father Xavier faced Ghani and embraced him warmly.

"How did you manage to pull it off?" the priest asked after they separated.

"Very simple. The power of Mama Fatima," Ghani replied with a wink. "Umar promised paradise in the world after this; Mama Fatima assured peace and prosperity in the world we live in now."

Father Xavier laughed and said: "That's a deal even I can't match."

PART THREE

It's late afternoon and the fishing boats are beached. The catch is in bins and the fishermen are hauling it up the shore, laughing and joking after a full day beyond the reef casting lines and murdering tuna. Ghani no longer presides at the fish landing, which now sports a fine corrugated tin roof and a new set of scales. There's a new cooperative and the members, who are the fishermen themselves, manage the work for which they receive a greater share of the profit. Watching all this, Ghani sits out on the verandah of Hotel Merdeka wearing a satisfied grin and a foam moustache from a newly-poured glass of beer.

"Look, Father, a good catch today."

Sitting across the table from Ghani, Father Xavier Lunas squints down at the tips of his fingers clasped just beneath his nose, as if in prayer. But Father Xavier isn't praying. He's deep in thought about mundane, earthly matters. The church-rebuilding programme is behind schedule. Materials are scarce and the island committee has declared that strict building standards must be adhered to. His instructions are that the new church should be no bigger than the old but it must be sturdy. How easily the old church burned, he argued. Surely, the new church needs a high wall for security. The wall was vetoed – it would look too much like a fortified structure and that would be provocative, the committee ruled. Father Xavier feels like arguing the case again, but instead turns to the chairman of the committee and says:

"Ah yes, the fish are always so obliging around Noli." If only the same could be said about this new island committee, he thinks resentfully. Ever since the island's troubles, people have been tiptoeing delicately around each other, like strangers embarking on a new acquaintance. "But we're not strangers," Father Xavier argued with Ghani shortly after the committee meeting. "We're brothers, sisters, neighbours and friends. For God's sake, why all the delicacy? Let's confront each other frankly about what happened and learn from it."

"Come now, Father. You'd have us wear all our sins like a collar. You can't ask people, after what happened, just to sit around a table and discuss it afterwards over a cup of coffee. People they know have killed people they know; everyone has lost friends and relatives. This is something beyond the pale of normal human comprehension. Why, the only parallel I can think of is sleepwalking. Imagine sitting down with you to have a rational discussion about what you did last night while you sleepwalked."

Father Xavier unclasps his hands and reaches behind his ear where there is still a raw patch, although it has been months since his beating. He winces slightly.

"The wound still bothering you, Father?" Ghani asks gently with genuine sympathy in his voice.

"A little. It's a good reminder."

Father Xavier fights to suppress a caustic remark about his treatment at the hands of Colonel Wahyu. It bothers him that he cannot recall how long he'd been held in one of the hotel's stuffy upstairs rooms. Just above the room where he is sitting now, in fact. Why was he singled out for this brutality? He still wondered: was it something somebody said? A betrayal?

"Perhaps if I'd listened that day to old Yaakob's confession. He tried to warn me about the fisherman who raped the Muslim girl. You know that. Maybe things would have turned out differently."

"Nonsense, my friend. That dismal incident was just a pretext. The forces sowing the seeds of chaos across these islands could easily have drummed up another like it. Don't you see? When the powers that be want to play their games, they choose remote corners of the country to stomp around in. That's how selfish our rulers are. They have no regard for this place; it might as well be a back alley used for tipping out garbage."

Not being schooled in the politics of the Republic, Father Xavier doesn't appreciate Ghani's cynical perspective. What worries him is that blood has been spilt and the urge to seek revenge could linger and erupt in the future.

"All the same, it could happen again," says Father Xavier, who has vowed to listen more carefully to what his parishioners tell him from now on. In his view, complacency was a major contributor to Noli's loss of innocence, and he felt as guilty as anyone. The fisherman who attacked the girl on the beach never came back to claim his outboard motor and disappeared without trace. Old Yaakob died a month back of a heart attack, taking to his grave a deep love and respect for the priest that Father Xavier felt was undeserved.

"So we'll be better prepared. We won't take things so much for granted. You priests and your obsession with guilt: let it be," Ghani says irritably.

The priest can't argue with this, so they fall silent and watch the finale to another perfect day in glorious Technicolor, accompanied by a cool refreshing beer. The edge of the sun's burning disk dips into the sea. Sea gulls hover over the golden surface, darting in every so often to pluck a morsel. Ghani's optimism is infectious, and is well-lubricated by the perfection nature imparts to the day's end, helping greatly to sustain man's hope and desire for the next one to come. Indeed, just at this moment, it's hard to imagine anything has happened, that any tragedy could have befallen a place of such bewitching beauty.

The bond between the two men is stronger but less equal. In the wake of the troubles, Ghani has become the unquestioned paramount leader of the community and therefore of all Muslims, which makes him also the church's protector. Father Xavier, following advice from the bishop, prudently accedes to Ghani's authority and steps back from his once prominent role in the community. Births, baptisms, weddings and funerals are now his principal duties – life's passages. He feels like a humble town photographer, recording the inexorable cycle of life. He no longer fishes for souls, as Ghani liked to put it. They agree that Muslims and Christians, whether newly born or close to death, must be allowed to follow their own conscience or the wishes of their family.

In this respect, Adam and Alicia set the perfect example. Alicia has been an exemplary convert to her husband's faith; she attends Friday prayers wearing a light scarf to cover her head and reads the Koran in the evenings. Adam's father mellowed as soon as there was news of the impending birth of a grandchild. The two families have since met over a dinner hosted by Ghani at the hotel. Father Xavier's hope that the couple would help begin the healing between the two religious communities has, in a small way, been realised.

Yet a lot has changed on the island. This year, there will be no procession for the Feast of the Virgin, no demonstrative breast-beating over faith and allegiance, which is what such processions are all about. Instead, both religious communities will hold a festival promoting communal harmony. Felix Ling, once a generous benefactor for any ritual occasion, now lives in Singapore – his former wife Sonia works for a Chinese Christian charity in North Jakarta and has arranged for generous donations for the church-building programme. Cornelius Lahatula, now retired from government service and a full-time business associate of his wife (who has taken over the Noli Superstore), is chairman of the island's festival committee. Not taking any chances, the island's social life has acquired nuance, a formal organisation, and even a bureaucracy. "It's not that anybody wants to control your lives," Cornelius explained to a meeting on the issue at the hotel. "But we must ask ourselves whether we can be trusted any longer to maintain our civility? Ask yourselves: could it happen again? Shouldn't we take precautions?"

People already are more cautious. They go out of their way to accommodate religious differences in a demonstrative, showy way. Christians aren't bothered on Sundays when their Muslim neighbours work, and they show respect for the observance of Friday prayers by taking half a day off as well. There is one sad spatial legacy: The North Shore village is mainly Christian now, while the Muslims are concentrated in the south. Another committee deals with thorny issues of land title and shared fishing tackle. Once a month, the island holds a community meeting where communal issues are raised and ironed out. Ghani presides when he isn't away in the capital attending to matters of national unity and political importance.

Despite all the conscious precaution taking, still no one speaks openly or directly about the tragedy that struck Noli. People instead refer vaguely to a period of "difficulty" as they would perhaps to the aftermath of a bad storm; there is never any intimation of life lost, of horrors witnessed. A visiting journalist left after a week scratching his head and wondering if all this talk about killings and burnings was exaggerated, a story concocted by a certain interest group as a political provocation perhaps. In interviews with islanders, the journalist heard that things were hard to get – yes, life was interrupted, to be sure. Whole weeks were wiped off the calendar. The charred remains of burnt houses stand as testament to what happened, although the island's vegetation is rapidly taking over: nature's way of covering for man's embarrassing lapses. Everyone lost loved ones, their homes, suffered terrible injuries and watched horrific brutality occur on their doorstep. Yet in casual conversation, the period of "difficulty" might as well have been little more than passing squall. It is over for them. Life goes on, as Ghani has suggested it should. It has to.

It isn't quite over, though. There remains the question of the official inquiry, which winds laboriously through the Republic's corrupt and creaky court system. Umar's grand plan went awry. After the bomb failed to make an impact, either on the hotel or Ghani's corpulent frame, the frustrated zealot decided to arrange an all-out invasion of the island, enlisting the rest of his army of martyrs in Central Java. They came, armed with crude weapons and a blind desire to die, in a rusting coastal steamer from Ambon, having flown in on a commercial flight from Semarang disguised as pilgrims. But the invading holy army didn't get much further than the reef before Colonel Wahyu's landing craft intercepted it. It seems that Wahyu had fresh orders; political priorities had shifted from making trouble at one end of the archipelago to the other. Rebels in the North Sumatran province of Aceh resumed their long war of independence, and for once, the army had a real rebellion to deal with. There was to be no more religious conflict in the Moluccan islands. Umar and the ringleaders were taken back to Jakarta where they went on trial in an effort to prove that the army was the true guardian of the nation's stability, a move that backfired.

"Can anything really be achieved at this inquiry?" the priest asks after a while, his tone suggesting that he already had an answer.

"The military is resisting, you know. Wahyu was one of theirs, even if he was crooked. The colonel was up to no good, that's for sure. I told you he was political. Smelt it on him from the start."

Ghani goes on to describe what has emerged so far from the official inquiry that has dragged on for the past month and which he attended for a week in his capacity as the newly-appointed representative to the People's National Assembly – in a fit of guilt, the government felt it was time the little island participated in the life of the nation.

"At the tribunal, it emerged that Colonel Wahyu was the chief mover behind the Front for the Protection of Islam," Ghani explains. "Specialist officers loyal to Wahyu recruited members among the poor and dispossessed from slums around the capital and trained them in Special Forces camps. They were told about a jihad; they were taught how to kill and maim. For legitimacy, they were shown doctored news footage of Muslim militias at work in the Balkans and Afghanistan. This whipped them into a religious frenzy. Ignorant people from the dregs of society, these kids were paid next to nothing and fed badly, but promised a place in paradise if they killed Christians. For most of them, it was an offer hard to refuse. Think of another way out of unceasing misery."

"I see," said the priest, tapping his knee impatiently. "They put religion out of bounds in the popular realm of debate, but then abuse it in the scramble for power. No wonder it's so easy to raise an army of fanatics. Tell me, have they managed to round them all up?" It's the first time he's hearing details of the tribunal, which isn't covered widely in the media.

"I'm not entirely sure. They managed to produce a teenager who confessed to being recruited. He was a university student from Central Java, in computer science, of all things. He called himself a "volunteer." Normal looking fellow, a little plump, myopic, and wearing a white haj cap – he could have been the boy next door, I swear. A military prosecutor asked him why he had gone off to fight Christians. Strangely, the fellow simply said: "I was on holiday from college and had nothing to do.""

"Is that the only reason he gave?"

"Well, no. And here it gets a little complicated because don't forget that Colonel Wahyu is sitting there, glaring at him. So he mumbles something about national duty as well. I remember he said that everyone knows that the Christians want independence from Indonesia. They want to break up the state. So the prosecutor asks him who told him this, but the boy gets a glare from the colonel and shuts up."

The game's up anyway. Wahyu has confessed to everything. The militia, the violence, it was all the colonel's doing. "I am proud of what I have done as a solider and servant of the nation," he told the tribunal, wearing the same smirk that Ghani recalled from his lunch at the hotel – the same expression he wore when Father Xavier first entered the hotel room that night. It was an expression of supreme arrogance common among high officials of the old regime, confident that higher powers are protecting them whatever they may do.

"There's no shame," says Ghani. "Money came from the old regime that was trying to discredit and bring down the government – to show that it could not govern under democratic rules and keep the country together. The idea was to sow discord between religious communities across the nation. Can you imagine it? All this tragic bloodshed was part of a strategy to seize power, a game played by the elite. A game they played and lost at our expense."

Father Xavier allows some moments to pass during which he tries to remember at least some of the faces of those who perished. One recurring image is the boy he caught stealing jewellery from corpses and the look of confusion he wore: everything is crazy, he'd said. Someone was culpable, but not that boy. Then Father Xavier quietly asks:

"Will the colonel be punished?"

"Yes and no. He's been dismissed from the army, honourably mind you. No jail sentence, though."

"After what he did, no conviction? No jail?"

"Nothing. He's agreed to leave the country for a while and live in Europe. It's their way; clear up the problem but avoid retribution. Retribution begets bitterness and allows old sores to fester. It's bad for unity."

"That's not how I see it. People were killed; there was a

massacre." There is now real anger in the priest's tone, and an edge to his voice that Ghani has never heard before. The passion in this priest overcomes and brushes aside the discipline and rigour of church dogma. In his anger, Father Xavier's wounds flare up and he can feel the blood throb in his head. Now he remembers the colonel's dumb but obedient assistant wearing a maniacal smile as he applied the two greasy leads from a car battery to his raw scrotum. He had passed out with the pain, refusing to sign a "confession" that stated he, Father Xavier, had incited the mob; that he was the architect of Noli's troubles. Ghani seems to read his mind again.

"And you were thrashed and tortured to within an inch of your life."

"Forget about me. What about the families who lost brothers, sisters, mothers, fathers? What about...what about justice?"

"Father, please calm yourself."

"I will not be calm, Ghani. This is totally absurd. We must protest and seek redress. This man, this animal, he should..." Father Xavier wants to say die, but thinks better of it. He is very much aware that Ghani is the one who seems more inclined towards compassion, and yet he is no priest. Perhaps he would make a better one. He pauses and sucks in his breath, letting it out in short, impatient bursts. Then he says quietly: "He should rot in jail for the rest of his life."

They fall silent again. Ghani is a little shocked and Father Xavier feels a little ashamed about this outburst. He has revealed a weakness for freethinking, a lack of self-control. What would he most likely do if Colonel Wahyu were brought before him now? He isn't sure that he could prevent himself from aiming a kick at his genitalia. It wasn't even the physical abuse: what really hurt was the colonel's contempt for him as a Christian and how this prejudice, like one drop of potent venom, poisoned the whole island and destroyed a civilised society. It is Ghani who remains calm; that's why he's the island's natural leader. If all that has happened affects him, it doesn't show at all. He has grown a hard carapace that shields his emotions, a shield as tough as the hairy land crabs that scuttle beneath the coconut trees along the shoreline. Father Xavier read something once about how the crab is one of evolution's oldest creations: so too Ghani is the epitome of man's good nature, the reason why the species survives, in spite of itself. To this day, Ghani cannot explain why or how he faced down the Muslim mob outside the hotel and saved the island from further bloodshed. He usually shrugs his shoulders and says:

"Somebody had to do it. I had the gun."

The night enfolds them suddenly and the lights come on in a frantic buzzing of voltage converters and flickering neon. Silently and unbidden, Sarah the waitress brings fresh beers. She smiles and, it seems to Father Xavier, throws a knowing look at Ghani; life in the hotel is back to normal at least. From the kitchen wafts the smell of frying garlic, the signature of Gus the noodle maker, who has given up his greasy kitchen beside the police station and is now the hotel's full-time chef. Father Xavier smiles and lights a cigarette. Taking them up since his arrest was one way to dull the pain.

"And what about us?" he asks.

"Us, Father?"

"Yes. Us – the people of Noli. What about our own behaviour? We did the killing, even if we were driven to it. Does that go unpunished too?"

Ghani looks out to sea and stares for a long while at the dying shafts of sunlight on the ebbing horizon. Soon the little square will fill up and the people of Noli will move another inch or so back towards normality. The wounds are still visible though: the Javanese food sellers have segregated pork from beef in a new respect for Muslim sensibilities. People meet each other with averted gaze and keep discreet distances from one another.

"Noli has suffered enough. As you say, we were driven to it."

"We had it in us, though."

"Nobody's perfect, my friend."

"Yes, but we thought we had created perfection here."

Another silence envelops them. The realisation of this misconception is too awful to contemplate further. Even though it technically isn't important to him, the doctors have told Father Xavier the damage to his testicles is temporary. Physically, the island hasn't changed much otherwise, the teeming schools of fish and the neglected pungent noli trees, the aura of solitude about the place – all is the same as before. If anything, people are better off since the establishment of the fish cooperative and a scheme, dreamed up by the irrepressibly entrepreneurial Ghani, to revive the tuna market for Noli. But, for Father Xavier, nothing is the same. He will always fear the worst when a car horn sounds on the street or a boy cries out over a game of football in the dusty little square. He lives with the memory of the mob. He has learnt that paradise cannot be taken for granted; which is why he doesn't miss a single afternoon by the shore, sitting on the verandah of Hotel Merdeka, watching the fishermen land their catch and waiting for the sun to sink below the crimson-fringed horizon. Just to make sure it isn't an illusion.

༄ ༄